Argos and the Argolid

States and Cities
of Ancient Greece

Edited by
R. F. WILLETTS

Argos and the Argolid

From the End of the Bronze Age
to the Roman Occupation

R. A. Tomlinson

Cornell University Press
Ithaca, New York

First published 1972 by Cornell University Press

This edition is not for sale in the United Kingdom
and British Commonwealth

International Standard Book Number 0–8014–0713–3
Library of Congress Catalog Card Number 78–38286

Printed in Great Britain

Library of Congress Cataloging in Publication Data
(For library cataloging purposes only)

Tomlinson, Richard Allan.
Argos and the Argolid.

(States and cities of ancient Greece)

Bibliography: p.
1. Argos, Greece-History. I. Title.
DF261.A67T64   913.3'8'8   78-38286
ISBN 0-8014-0713-3

FOR HEATHER

Contents

PREFACE   page xiii

INTRODUCTION   I

PART ONE   THE LAND

I   THE ARGOLID   7

2   THE TOWNS   15

PART TWO   THE HISTORY OF ARGOS

3   THE CREATION OF DORIAN ARGOS   51

4   THE RETURN OF THE HERAKLEIDAI AND THE LOT
    OF TEMENOS   58

5   THE DORIAN SETTLEMENT   64

6   ARGOS IN THE NINTH AND EIGHTH CENTURIES   67

7   PHEIDON OF ARGOS   79

8   ARGOS FROM THE END OF THE SEVENTH CENTURY TO
    THE PERSIAN WARS   87

9   479–461   101

10 461–451   110

11 451–404   116

12 404–370   126

13 370–336   142

14 ARGOS IN HELLENISTIC TIMES   147

Contents

15 THE INTERVENTION OF ROME   164

16 EPILOGUE   172

PART THREE
THE ARGIVE STATE AND ITS ACHIEVEMENT

17 MILITARY ORGANIZATION   175

18 POLITICAL DEVELOPMENT TO THE FIFTH CENTURY 187

19 THE ARGIVE DEMOCRACY   192

20 RELIGIOUS CULTS OF THE ARGOLID   200

21 THE ARTS IN THE ARGOLID   221

    ABBREVIATIONS   262

    NOTES   263

    SELECT BIBLIOGRAPHY   277

    INDEX   279

Plates

Between pages 18–19

1 Doves at the Argive Heraion
2 The plain and the Charadros, from the Larisa
3 Corn and olives near Mycenae
4 Argos: the Larisa and the flanks of the Aspis, from the north
5 The theatre of Argos
6 The Aspis, from the Larisa
7 The altar of Apollo Pythaieus
8 Mycenae: Hellenistic rebuilding at the centre, Bronze Age (Cyclopaean) to the right

Between pages 34–5

9 The pyramid of Kenchreiai (Hellinikon)
10 The citadel of Hysiai and its valley
11 Hellenistic tower at Asine
12 The citadel on the Larisa—Classical and medieval
13 The Argive Heraion: the terrace wall of the old temple
14 The Argive Heraion: early Doric capital
15 The Argive Heraion: the foundations of the new temple
16 The Argive Heraion: decorated blocks from the altar

Figures

1   Map of the Argolid   *page* 9
2   Plan of Argos   16
3   Early Geometric amphora   225
4   Middle Geometric amphora   225
5   Middle Geometric amphora   225
6   Late Geometric amphora   225
7   Wrestlers under the handle of the Argos krater   226
8   Man leading a horse, from another late Geometric krater   226
9   Plan of the Argive Heraion   231
10 Plan of the sanctuary of Apollo Pythaieus at Argos   247

Preface

This book is an indirect result of three seasons spent excavating at Perachora, which comes under the Argolid division of the Greek Archaeological Service, and of visits paid then to members of the service; I should like here particularly to record my tribute to the late S. Charitonides, then Ephor of Antiquities. The book is also a reaction against the all-consuming attention which the Bronze Age in the Argolid has received and it therefore makes no attempt to present yet another account of that age, though the fact of its existence is of necessity the starting-off point for my argument. The difficulties involved in the attempt to present a coherent account of a region whose history and achievements were inadequately recorded in antiquity are considerable; inevitably gaps and inconsistencies result. The Argolid was not so prominent in the first millennium B.C. as it would seem to have been in the second, and I have not tried to exaggerate its importance. Nevertheless, when the history of mainland Greece in the Classical Age is so readily concerned with the affairs of Sparta and Athens, the cities which undoubtedly dominated it, the investigation of a state of lesser rank is not without its value. Not all the cities of mainland Greece were supporters of one or other of the two leaders, and in the history of Argos it is easier to appreciate their point of view.

I am deeply indebted to Professor R. F. Willetts, who urged me to write this book and has given me every encouragement. I am grateful to the University of Birmingham for giving me a research grant which enabled me to write the section on the topography of the Argolid from first-hand knowledge and to take the photographs. I should like also to thank my assistants in the Department of Ancient History and Archaeology at Birmingham, Mrs Brenda Timmins who made the map and the other drawings and Mrs Gillian Davies who patiently translated my almost illegible scrawl into a typescript.

Preface

It is usual to explain in the preface the principles on which Greek words have been transliterated into English. It will soon be apparent that I am inconsistent in my approach to this problem, for I find forms such as Krete and Korinth pedantic, and others, such as Polyclitus, ugly. To those readers whom my lack of method offends, I tender my sincere apologies.

Introduction

Argos has been unfortunate in her history. In the Heroic time of the Late Bronze Age, before history was written and great events and great names were recorded only in traditions handed down by word of mouth, the region round Argos—the 'Argolid'—was about the most important in all Greece. It contained the city ruled by Agamemnon, whom Homer regarded as overlord of all the Greeks, even though modern scholars may disagree with him; the name of that city, Mycenae, is often used to describe the entire Late Bronze Age of Greece. In the Argolid the remains of that Mycenaean age, at Mycenae, at Tiryns and elsewhere are the most spectacular antiquities that survive, their walls piled high with such massive boulders[1] that later Greeks thought they must be the work of superhuman beings, the Cyclopes. The Argolid is the scene for many of the Greek legends which betray, even if they do not record, the lost history of the Bronze Age, and though Argos was of lesser significance than other cities in the region at that time, its name is used by Homer as a synonym for Greece.[2]

By contrast, in historic times Classical Argos is a neglected area. It was no longer a region of first importance, and the lead in Greek affairs passed to other states—to Corinth, to Sparta and to Athens. Increasingly Argos was involved in a struggle to maintain her independence, and in a history that inevitably reflects the Spartan or Athenian point of view, her struggles often involve her in action that appears to condemn her as a traitor to Hellenism, in her readiness to make friends with the enemies of that other Greek world of Sparta and Athens, firstly with the King of Persia, and then, more successfully, with the kings of Macedon. Little of Argive history is recorded, and inevitably that occurs chiefly when she is involved with other Greek states. Argos produced no great historian, no Herodotus or Thucydides, whose writings were preserved during

I

the merciless rejection of the less relevant or readable in Late Roman or Byzantine times. Argos produced no great statesmen in the Classical Age, and no citizen that emerges in recorded history as a recognizable individual, in the way that the great Athenians still live for us. Her chief political figures are a king whose achievements belong to the remote days that saw the original formation of the classical city state (and whose date is a matter of some dispute), and a series of autocratic despots who governed her in the third century B.C. and who are known ultimately from the writings of men who were their bitter enemies. Argos has for us no literature, no poetry, no drama. At the present day the Argolid contains no striking archaeological remains other than those of the Bronze Age to attract the attention of the traveller. The chief classical sanctuary, the Heraion, now comprises only blank terrace walls and bare foundations. The most spectacular ruins in Argos itself belong to the Roman period.

Nevertheless, Argos is not negligible, and her history is important. Her long-drawn-out feud with Sparta, which is its main theme, was of profound significance in the restricted world of the Peloponnese and, ultimately, for the rest of Greece. Without Argos the whole of the Peloponnese must inevitably have fallen under Spartan control. Sparta's grip on Greek affairs would have been that much the stronger, the position of Athens in the fifth century that much the weaker in consequence. In Hellenistic times her relations with Macedon were cordial. The family of Philip and Alexander the Great claimed descent from the kings of Argos, and though the Hellenistic rulers of Macedon belonged to another dynasty[3] the close relations they maintained with Argos, almost unchallenged from within the city for over a century, demonstrate that Macedonian supremacy was not universally hated by the once-free cities of Greece. The apparent lack of great statesmen and politicians, of individuals comparable with the great names of other cities such as Athens or Sparta, though unfortunate for the historian who traces the successes and failures of states through the achievements of such men, does not imply that Argos was poorly or ineffectively governed. It is unfortunate that the most spectacular features of Argive political history, those that made the greatest impression on outside observers, were massacres, one of which is described as the most bloody in Greek history (though in all probability far fewer were killed than the number of those put to death more discreetly by the

2

oligarchs in Athens in 403 B.C.). Yet these are in reality most infrequent; on the whole Argos appears politically to have formed a stable community with a system of government suited to its particular conditions, which effectively preserved the identity of the state when it might have succumbed to external pressures. Nor was Argos a city without art. If the sanctuary of Hera preserves little for the modern tourist, before its decay it ranked as one of the major religious sites in Greece; moreover, it had developed monumentally at an early period, in the seventh and sixth centuries B.C. The section which has been excavated of the agora at Argos shows that it was already provided in the fifth century B.C. with sheltering colonnades of advanced form. The Argive school of sculpture was important, again from an early date, and one of the greatest classical sculptors, Polykleitos, belonged to the Argive school.

Thus the neglect of Argos has been unfortunate. To us, Classical Argos is overshadowed in her own region by the remains and legends of an earlier millennium. It has suffered, disastrously, from the chances of later times which have destroyed, not only the monuments, but so much of the record of what it achieved. This book is an attempt to gather the fragments together.

Part One   The Land

I   The Argolid

The heart of the Argolid is the plain.[1] At its edge are, and were, the chief towns. Here is the best land, which needs only water to bring it into abundance, and it was this part that made the Argolid important. The plain looks southwards, to the sun and the sea, to the gulf of Argos and the sea routes that lead to Crete, to Anatolia, and the wealth of Egypt and the Levant. This trade has now gone, for the only harbour with any pretensions to quays and the other essential works, Nauplia, belongs to the nineteenth century, and is far too small and shallow for modern shipping; that now goes perforce to the Piraeus. But in antiquity, and particularly in the remoter Bronze Age of the second millennium B.C., trading ships often preferred a long, gentle but sheltered sandy beach, and such is the coast of the Argive plain. These conditions were ideal for the ancient promotion of trade, and the Bronze Age communities of the Argolid became wealthy; later, in Classical times, their possession of gold had become legendary, and enough has been recovered by the archaeologist from the tombs of their kings to show us the reality of the legend.

Agriculture was the basis of trade, and abundant enough to support specialist craftsmen; but the Argive plain was important in other ways, and these also concern its history. The chief towns and regions of Classical as well as Bronze Age Greece are mostly on the eastern side of the peninsula, looking to the Aegean and the Near East from which their civilization ultimately derives. The overland lines of communication that linked those communities were therefore of considerable importance, in their trade, their diplomacy, their quarrels and their wars. The most crucial link was the isthmus that connected southern Greece, the Peloponnese, with the more northerly regions, and control of this gave Corinth her importance; but almost as important were the routes that led from southern and

7

central Peloponnese to the isthmus, and of these the most direct, and the easiest, went through the Argive plain. At the present day both railway and main road lead to Argos, and both, with unimportant modifications to suit the needs of mechanical transport, follow the line of the ancient roads. These routes, inevitably, are controlled by Argos, and dominated by its citadel, as they have been since the Bronze Age. The citadel, as we shall see, is now a splendid medieval castle at the top of a steep, almost conical hill, but its walls follow the line of the classical walls, and, indeed, incorporate considerable sections of them; its present medieval form serves only to emphasize the essential continuity from antiquity to the present day. Argos, at times, fell from its premier position in the history of Greece, but it was never completely deserted, or completely unimportant. Its position was sufficient reason for that.

The Argive plain, then, is triangular in shape. It is fourteen kilometres wide at its base, that is, the coast, and some twenty-one kilometres long, from the coast to its apex at the pass over to Corinth. This is quite large, compared with the other coastal plains of Greece. It is hemmed in by mountains, higher to the west than the east, Megalovouni, Bachriami, Megavouni, between which extend long, steep-sided valleys which reach to the still higher mountains that form the boundary between Argos and Arcadia; Parthenios, Ktenias, Artemision, Lyrkeion, Pharmacas.[2] Through these lead the roads to the Arcadian cities, Mantinea and Tegea. The eastern mountains isolate the plain from the rest of the promontory, Akte. This can be regarded as part of the Argolid, but its cities, Epidauros, Troizen, Hermione have a long history of independence as separate states; so to the east, as well as to the west, the mountains define a political boundary.

The land of the plain rises slowly and almost imperceptibly from the coast, more noticeably as it comes closer to the mountains. Here and there are isolated hills, some rocky, steep-sided and useful only as the potential sites of cities or citadels, others rounded, earth covered, capable of being ploughed and planted. Provided it is well watered the plain is productive land. The chief rivers of the Argolid descend from the western mountains; the Inachos, which rises on the western slopes of Artemision and runs northwards at first, before turning to the east, between Bachriami and Megalovouni to enter the Argive plain; and the Charadros (now called Xerias) which runs directly eastwards from Artemision and Ktenias, through

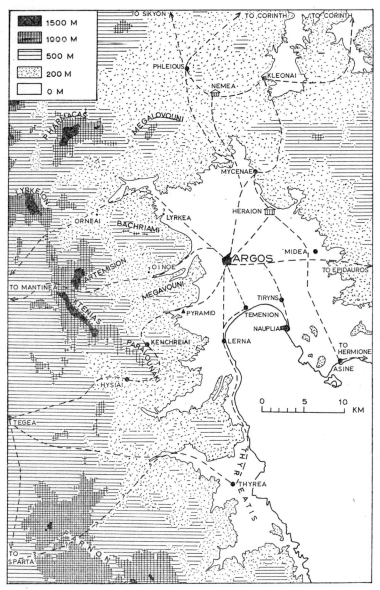

Figure 1 Map of the Argolid

a narrow valley, to enter the Argive plain by way of a gorge it has carved for itself between Bachriami and Megavouni. These rivers unite to the north of Argos town, and then turn southwards to the gulf. But these are not rivers in the usual sense, and for most of the year they do not flow. They are torrent beds, taking the sudden bursts of rainwater that result from winter storms as quickly as possible to the sea; and in practical terms they contribute nothing to the watering of the Argive plain. The same is true of the smaller torrents on the eastern side of the Argolid, but these do not have the strength to reach the sea; instead, they lose themselves in the thirsty lands of the plain. The only river that flows constantly is the Erasinos, south of Argos, which emerges as a full-grown stream from springs at Kephalarion, at the western foot of Megavouni, fed by unseen, underground reservoirs under the mountains.[3]

In the Argive plain, there are abundant resources of water stored naturally underground. To bring the land into full production, there is need for artificial irrigation on an extensive scale. At present this is achieved by means of wells, with powerful pumps that bring up a considerable flow from the underground resources. These pumps are driven by electric or internal combustion motors, and have replaced an older generation of machines, endless chains of buckets turned by animal power. The situation in antiquity is less certain. The natural unwatered state of the Argolid was proverbial— an adjective used by Homer to describe Argos means 'very thirsty'— but it was also known that this had been overcome, traditionally by Danaos, who came to Argos from Egypt, the land where the art of irrigation was so highly developed.[4] How Danaos achieved this must remain something of a mystery. He was reputed to have invented the digging of wells, so presumably the water was raised from the resources under the Argive plain. Whether simple devices or complex machinery were used to raise the water is uncertain; but machines were used by the Greeks in later times,[5] and the scale of the works undertaken by the Bronze Age kings of Orchomenos in Boiotia to reclaim arable land from the Copaic lake[6] suggests that the even more powerful kings of the Argolid need not have been restricted to minor works. There is better indication of what was achieved in Classical times. As we shall see, Argos town possessed a maze of open water conduits, and though these are known only to have served the city, similar channels could have been constructed to take water into the fields. The source of the water is less certain, but there were springs at Argos, and these may well have been improved, or the supply increased, by artificial means. Traces of artificial waterworks have also been found near the Argive Heraion.[7] Of the wells that presumably existed then, as now, in the central parts of the plain, none has been found, nor are there any traces of the lifting apparatus used.

At present, the best land in the Argolid is devoted to citrus orchards (and, to a lesser extent, other fruits such as apricots). This development is recent. Photographs of the Argolid, of the ancient sites and the excavations, taken in the nineteenth century show that the plain was then comparatively treeless. Nevertheless, it is significant that the citrus growing is restricted to a distinct part of the plain, originally round the villages between Argos and Nauplia, and to the south of Argos, though an increasing area of comparable land is being devoted to this form of agriculture. Citrus trees are not planted on the hillier land, or in the valleys between the mountains. They need good soil, the water pumped to them from underground and full exposure to the sun. The northern part of the plain remains more open, and is used for corn and other annual crops; melons, tomatoes, artichokes and so forth. The corn, as always in Greece, is planted in winter, grows while the soil is still moist from the winter rains, and is harvested in May or June. Even if the Argolid is thirsty, it could have grown corn in antiquity without too much need of artificial irrigation. On the other hand the summer crops, the tomatoes and the melons, do require irrigation. The hillier country at the edges of the plain and in the western valleys carries a fair number of olive trees, some in extensive groves, others more scattered. Where the trees are planted in open fashion, the land between them is ploughed and used for corn and other annual crops. There are no vines—a single vineyard by the road that leads from Mycenae to the Heraion is an exception.

It is difficult to reconstruct the ancient agricultural pattern from that of the present day. New crops have been introduced, and are still being introduced, that are completely foreign to classical antiquity. The scale of artificial irrigation is likely to be far vaster than that of past centuries. Even though the Argolid must have been irrigated in antiquity, this would not have served precisely the same agricultural purpose as present-day irrigation. Other adjectives used to describe the Argolid mean 'rich in corn' and 'nourisher of horses',[8] implying that open corn land and pasture were prominent features of the region. One feature most noticeable at present is the high degree of agricultural specialization in the Argolid, particularly the production of citrus fruit, and the way in which this works to exclude completely the cultivation of the vine. Specialization to this extent is made possible by the more complex economic organization of modern Greece, for the citrus fruit is now grown primarily not for consumption in the Argolid itself, but for sale to different areas of Greece, including, of course, the unclassical urban agglomeration at Athens; the classical ideal, that each area of Greece, each city state should be as far as possible self-sufficient, producing all it needs in its own territory, does not make economic sense in present-day society, in which it is easier and cheaper to obtain certain produce from regions particularly suited to their cultivation than to make the attempt to grow them in unsuitable localities.[9] The classical system makes it unlikely that such a degree of specialization was practised by Classical Argos. Yet a certain amount of specialization is possible, even desirable, and the need for this may help to explain certain aspects of Greek history, and Argive history in particular. The absence of vines in the Argolid at the present day is explained by the existence immediately to the north of an area devoted, and, presumably, more suited to the specialized production of grapes and wine. This is the district of Nemea, which includes the region belonging in antiquity to the city state of Phleious as well as classical Nemea. Though Phleious maintained a precarious independence, with the aid of a Spartan alliance, Nemea and the sanctuary where the Nemean games were celebrated was for a long time under Argive domination. Agricultural specialization had been a feature of the Athenian economy, though Athens' territory is greater in extent, and more varied in character than that of the average city state, from the sixth century B.C.—the time of Solon—onwards, when the production of olives and wine for export was encouraged, and the corn that did not grow so well imported from other regions. It could well be that the Argolid also was unable to grow in abundance all the different forms of agricultural produce needed, and that Argos had to seek means to remedy this, by taking possession of territory outside her natural, geographical boundaries.

Besides the Argive plain, there were other areas of land belonging to the ancient city. The western valleys have been mentioned already. In addition to the valleys of the Inachos and Charadros there are two others, one between Megavouni and the western extensions of Ktenias, the other the valley of Akhladokampos (the modern name) beginning between Ktenias and Parthenios, and reaching the coastal plain between the modern villages of Myloi and Kiveri. Agriculturally, these western valleys are less important. They contain areas of good land—the valley of the Inachos, particularly, before it passes through the narrowing lines of hills to enter the Argive plain—which at present grow corn or other annual crops; but for the most part their land is of second quality, corresponding to the hillier parts of the plain, growing olives, with annual underplanting. They extend the area available to Argos appreciably, but they hardly confer any other particular economic gain. Their inclusion in the Argolid is natural, but their importance depends chiefly on their strategic value, and the fact that they carry the routes from the Argolid to the central and southern Peloponnese.

On the eastern side of the plain there are two extensions. The more northerly, around the modern village of Berbati (now given the classical name of Prosymna) is the bed of a former lake, which eventually drained itself, in geological time, when the river that flowed from it to the Argive plain cut a gorge through the intervening hills. The gorge (which, like those on the western side of the plain, now contains only a normally dry torrent bed) is the only easy link between the district of Berbati and the rest of the Argolid. Otherwise the region is completely surrounded by mountains, through which there are high passes, to Mycenae, to the Corinthia to the north, and to the east. It is approximately seven kilometres from east to west, by four from north to south. Like the western valleys, it is second-rate rather than first-rate land, and at present contains only two villages.[10] Its strategical importance derives from the way in which it provides a short direct route to Corinth (the 'kontoporeia' route of antiquity), though there is a scanty record of this being used. The second eastern extension is formed by the district of Asine, the Asinaia. This lies on the coast, east of the hills that rise up behind Nauplia. An almost level route—certainly not a 'pass' in the conventional sense, but a gentle rise and an equally gentle decline—leads round from the Argive plain, passing to the north of the Nauplia hills. Nevertheless the Asinaia is a distinct region, with its own tradition. It is an Argive plain in miniature; good agricultural land, surrounded by hills. It is again roughly triangular in shape, four kilometres across at the base, which is at the sea, and four kilometres in depth. At present it is covered chiefly with citrus orchards. This was desirable land, and it contributed to the Argive economy. It supported a population large enough to resist, for a while, Argive attempts to incorporate it into her territory; when it finally became Argive, it yielded only to superior force, and the inhabitants were given a place of refuge by the Spartans in the southern Peloponnese.[11]

Geographically the region described represents the natural limits of the Argive state, the plain and the adjoining regions. Already, with the Asinaia, we have come to a region that wanted independence. But Argos, from time to time, also controlled regions that lay outside the natural boundaries. These are described more fully with the towns they contained in the following chapter. They included the district of Kleonai to the north, with which came the valley of Nemea and presidency of the Nemean games; and the isolated pockets of plain land, some larger, some smaller, that lie on the west side of the gulf of Argos, under the steep mountains that reach down to the gulf from Mount Parnon. Of these regions, Kleonai has at present a mixed agriculture, olives, vines and annual crops, while the wine of Nemea has been mentioned already. Though the Argives may have been attracted to this region because of its agricultural produce, this was most certainly not the prime cause of their occupation, as we shall see. The principal area on the west side of the gulf, the district of Thyrea, is at present mostly olive country; here again, there is an interesting variation from the modern agricultural specialization of the Argolid, and in this case we know that the district was an olive-growing region in antiquity[12] so that possession of it was a distinct economic gain. Further south, Argive possessions, or, rather, claims, for they were normally occupied by Sparta, included the coastal communities beyond the Thyreatis, the region of Kynouria, and extended as far as the island of Kythera, off the southern coast of Lakonia; but Argive possession, or even the title to this region was so dubious, that it is perhaps best to leave them out of this reckoning, and to see them rather in the context of Argive history.

2 The towns

In classical times, Argos was by far the largest and most populous town in the Argolid, and an account of the towns must naturally begin with it. This was not true of the Bronze Age, when no single community dominated in size the Argive plain and the adjacent regions. On the other hand, after Greece had lost its independence to the Roman conquerors, the predominance of Argos increased still further, as the other small towns were abandoned and totally depopulated.

Our knowledge of the towns comes from descriptions given by ancient authors, particularly Pausanias, whose account of the towns and sanctuaries of Greece was written in the second century A.D., when many of the Argive towns had been abandoned; other authors include Strabo, who wrote his geography in the first century B.C., while incidental information is to be found in the historians from Herodotus onwards. This is not sufficient for a full understanding. Archaeological investigation of the material remains helps, but this is beset with problems, such as the destructive effects of continuous post-classical occupation at Argos, and the desire of archaeologists to recover information from the earlier periods at sites which were important in the Bronze Age.

Argos

Argos has always been the only sizeable town on the western side of the plain which it dominates. It became important for three reasons: the presence of adequate water supplies, its position on the chief routes from the Argolid to south and west and its possession of a magnificently defendable acropolis, the Larisa.

The present town lies to the east of the Larisa and the lower

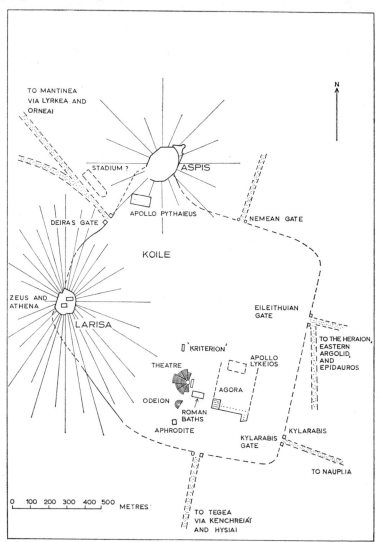

Figure 2 Plan of Argos

fortified hill on its northern side called in antiquity Aspis, 'the shield'.[1] It covers the ancient city so completely that the elucidation of the former topography is a matter of extreme difficulty. Since the beginning of this century systematic excavation of the ancient

16

town has been carried out by the French School of Archaeology in Athens, but of necessity this has been limited to the smaller areas not covered by modern buildings, or to private gardens and development sites when these became available. There is not a great deal of the ancient city visible at the present day. The town is dominated by the medieval castle on the Larisa, which corresponds to the fortification of the classical acropolis. In places, substantial parts of the ancient walls are still visible, incorporated in the medieval structure. A curtain wall encircled the whole of the city.[2] From the Larisa it extended north-eastwards to the pass between the higher hill and the Aspis, probably crossing a little beyond the summit of the pass, as one comes from Argos; parts of it are still visible on this section. Through here comes the road to Lyrkea, a village in one of the deep valleys to the west of the Argive plain, and to Mantinea, beyond the mountains in Arcadia. The road divided shortly after leaving Argos. One of the chief city gates was therefore situated where the walls cross this road; and this can certainly be identified as the Deiras gate, which is mentioned by Pausanias as the starting point of the road to Lyrkea and Mantinea. This is, therefore, one of the fixed points in the ancient topography of Argos; the name Deiras should belong to the ridge and the col between the Larisa and the Aspis. Nothing is now visible of the gate itself, though large blocks of stone which probably belonged to it were seen by visitors in the nineteenth century.[3]

From the col the city wall climbed the slopes of the Aspis. This still carries the remains of its own circuit, for classical and Hellenistic Argos was exceptional in its possession of two citadels.[4] The original circuit wall on the Aspis was constructed in the Bronze Age. In classical times it was rebuilt, and given additional bastions and towers. The city wall reaches this circuit on its western side, and leaves it on the south-east; thus the greater part of the Aspis, except at the summit, lay outside the city. Even more surprisingly the city wall appears to have turned due south, after the section that joins the Aspis fortifications, and thus excluded much of what is now in the modern town. A further turn to the east at the foot of the Aspis slopes is virtually certain, but from this point no real traces of the walls survive until, having completed the circuit of the lower town, we find them once more on the slopes of the Larisa.

For the rest, the topography of ancient Argos depends on the few visible remains of buildings within the former limits of the city, and the description given by Pausanias in his second book.[5] In addition, there are various structures discovered in excavation but no longer visible, together with a large number of tombs. It would appear that the buildings of the town were situated on the flatter ground at the foot of the hills, and in the valley between the Larisa and the Aspis. Except at the lower slopes, the Larisa is too steep, and there are no obvious traces of building on it. Thus the area available for houses is only a part of the total area enclosed by the fortifications; no precise estimate is possible, but the area available is likely to have been in the region of two hundred acres—eighty hectares—(allowing for public open spaces and so on). At a density of fifty persons to the acre—a hundred and twenty-five to the hectare—a population of ten thousand men, women and children, citizens and slaves lived in Argos town; and though this is little better than a guess, it serves to indicate that the majority of Argives lived outside the town, in the suburbs and in the other towns and villages.[6]

The most impressive remains of ancient Argos are those of a large brick and concrete built structure, situated between the Tripolis road and the southern parts of the Larisa. These belong to an imposing bath building, once lavishly decorated with sculpture and other works of art, but this was constructed long after the Roman occupation of Greece; it is not mentioned by Pausanias. In the open area round the bath building, and on the same side of the Tripolis road, extensive and meticulous excavations have been carried out by the French school; but although these have demonstrated how complex is the history of Argos, revealing traces of occupation from the Middle Bronze Age to the Turkish era, they have not thrown much light on the classical city, the remains of which seem largely to have been swept away by later occupation. Presumably there were few substantial classical buildings in this region, for, as we shall see, where such buildings did once exist, on the other side of the Tripolis road, they have left enough to be recognized and interpreted by the archaeologist.

Behind the bath building, on the slopes of the Larisa itself, is the second impressive structure that survives of ancient Argos, the theatre. The built parts of this have been destroyed, for the most part, but much of the seating was cut into the rock of the Larisa, and this survives. The theatre was partly cleared in the nineteenth century; it has recently been most thoroughly excavated and studied

1 Doves at the Argive Heraion

2 The plain and the Charadros, from the Larisa

3   Corn and olives near Mycenae

4   Argos: the Larisa and the flanks of the Aspis, from the north

5   The theatre of Argos

6   The Aspis, from the Larisa

7　The altar of Apollo Pythaieus

8　Mycenae: Hellenistic rebuilding at the centre, Bronze Age (Cyclopaean) to the right

by French archaeologists.[7] There were originally eighty-one rows of seats, rock cut at the centre; the first sixty of these once continued in stone over an earth fill to either side, so that in plan the seats extended beyond the semicircle, as was customary in Greek theatres. It would seem that only about half the total number of rows of seats extended for the full 200°. When complete, there were probably seats for twenty thousand spectators, making this one of the larger theatres of ancient Greece. The seats were divided into an upper, middle and lower section, and into eight blocks from side to side, separated by flights of steps reaching from the bottom to the top. The positioning of the steps does not conform to any regular plan, and the blocks are consequently of varying sizes. At the top of the auditorium a high wall once prevented unauthorized entry. In front of the auditorium was the conventional dancing floor (orchestra), circular in plan, being partly cut into the hillside, and beyond that the stage building, the earliest Greek version of which has been completely overlaid, in the usual way, with a more complex Roman construction. From the evidence discovered by the French archaeologists in the earth fill underlying the built extensions of the auditorium, it would appear that the developed theatre belongs to the last part of the fourth century B.C., to the time when substantial permanent theatres with stone seating were being constructed in other parts of Greece: for example, at Athens and, nearer to Argos, at Epidauros. Presumably the theatre existed in simple form before that date, and may well have served as a meeting place for the full citizen assembly of Argos from the time that the city was governed by a democratic constitution. In the Hellenistic age the dramatic performances in the theatre were the work of the local gathering of the 'craftsmen of Dionysus', the international guild of actors.[8]

A short distance to the south of the theatre, on the lower rocky slopes of the Larisa is another, but much smaller theatre-like structure, conventionally called the Odeion, or music-hall. Its real function is less certain but its small size suggests that it was the meeting place of a restricted gathering. This could be an indication of political, or perhaps religious, exclusiveness. Two main phases are discernible, the earlier with tiered banks arranged in straight lines, the later with the banks arranged in a semicircle, after the fashion of the theatre, together with a stage. The second phase belongs to Roman times. This structure is not mentioned by Pausanias.

Pausanias does mention two features of Argive topography in relation to the theatre. The theatre, he says, is 'not far from' a spot called the 'judgment place' or Kriterion, 'because they say Hypermnestra was here brought to judgment by Danaos', while beyond (or above—the Greek can have both meanings), the theatre is a sanctuary of Aphrodite. The 'judgment place' has been identified with a platform supported by a long terrace wall just over 100m north-east of the theatre, although Pausanias hardly implies such a massive structure, or indeed, anything other than a sacred locality, probably with no structure at all. This platform was investigated by the Dutch scholar W. Vollgraff, excavating in Argos as a member of the French school. It was originally 35m wide and 21m from back to front. The supporting walls were built in a polygonal style, found elsewhere in the Argolid and very difficult to date. Vollgraff suggested the third quarter of the seventh century, but it need not be as old as this; the late fifth or fourth centuries are more likely. There were no real traces of early structures on the platform, but in Roman times it was turned into an elaborate fountain, supplied by an artificial conduit. On the east polygonal wall were reliefs, depicting triads of divinities named as the Epitelides.[9] Vollgraff identified them with the Furies who in Athens (as the Eumenides) had a sanctuary by the court of the Areopagus. He suggested therefore that the Kriterion was a meeting place for a similar court at Argos, and to be identified with this platform. The sanctuary of Aphrodite was once supposed to be on the site of the chapel of St George, on a small platform on the rocky side of the Larisa, above the theatre. This identification serves to illustrate the difficulties of relating Pausanias' description with what is at present visible, for the French excavations have discovered the temple and sanctuary of Aphrodite, not under the chapel of St George, but in an open space immediately to the south of the Odeion. Pausanias' Greek therefore must mean that the sanctuary is beyond, not above the theatre; and that he is referring to its locality as seen from the judgment place, which was indeed somewhere to the north of the theatre.

With these few fixed or approximate points in the ancient city, it is easier to follow Pausanias' description, and this in turn helps with the identification of certain other structures that have been excavated. Pausanias begins from the most important and prominent temple within the walls of the ancient city, the temple of Apollo Lykeios, Wolf-Apollo. Though he does not himself make this clear, references to the temple in other ancient authors shows that it was in, or, more precisely perhaps, on one side of the agora, the main square or market place of the city.[10] Pausanias goes on to describe monuments in the temple and its sanctuary, and the other neighbouring monuments, ending with the judgment place. From here, as we have seen, he goes to the theatre and the sanctuary of Aphrodite, after which he 'descends and turns again towards the agora', though this is in fact the first time he has mentioned it. Whether this is due to an oversight in the writing of the description, or a subsequent omission that occurred at some stage in the transmission of the manuscript text (we shall see, later, a definite instance of this) must be uncertain; but the logic of Pausanias' account means that in this section he begins and ends with the agora, that the majority of the monuments (up to the judgment place) that he here mentions are in the agora; and that the agora itself is 'below'—that is, east of— the theatre and the sanctuary of Aphrodite.

In the years before the First World War W. Vollgraff uncovered the foundations and footings of substantial buildings to the east of the Tripolis road, opposite the Roman bath building. One of them was a long colonnade, or stoa, facing north towards what was presumably an open space. This is in agreement with the indications given by Pausanias for the location of the agora, and there is little reason to doubt that this colonnade marks its southern limits. If so, it is conveniently situated on flat ground, and could well have been at the centre of the series of roads radiating from Argos to the rest of the Argolid and beyond. It was probably nearer to the south than the centre of the ancient city (and at present is on the southern fringes of the modern town) but it is by no means abnormal for the agora not to be in the precise centre of a Greek city, particularly if that city was of ancient origin and slow development, like Argos, not the result of a deliberate and planned foundation.

The stoa is of unusual type, and a fuller excavation of its environs is needed before its peculiarities can be properly explained. The main central section, over 83 metres in length, faced north on to the agora. On its north side was a line of Doric columns, but with some, at least, of the spaces between them closed by barriers; these were subsequently removed. This section was only 5·6m wide, and its roof was supported only by the north colonnade and the continuous wall on the south side; there was no need for any internal colonnade, and the stoa had the form of a long narrow gallery, well lit from the north but with restricted access. At the eastern end there was a return, not, as one might expect, towards the agora courtyard but in the opposite direction, towards the south. This southern extension was 23·35m in length, and almost double the width of the main section, at 10·46m. It was open to the east, with eleven columns forming its façade. The roof was supported as well by a row of four columns inside the wing. The southern end was not at right angles to the colonnade. This wing therefore seems to define an enclosed space to the west; there was probably a similar projecting wing at the western end of the stoa, but this is less certain and its form, as yet, unrecovered. Such a space cannot have been part of the agora, but may well have been public; its function cannot yet be understood. The colonnade appears to date to the first half of the fifth century B.C.[11]

On the west side of the agora, near the south stoa are the remains of a square building with sides 32·6m in length, a distance which possibly represents a hundred 'Doric Argive' feet of 0·326m. It faced east, on to the agora square; on that side it would seem to have had a row either of columns or square piers, some, at least, of the intervening spaces again being closed, this time by grilles. The other sides were formed by walls, of which occasionally the lowest section is preserved. Inside, the roof was supported by four rows each of four columns; these were Ionic of a type found chiefly in the Peloponnesian cities. Again, the date appears to be the first half of the fifth century B.C.

The purpose of these buildings and the reasons for their construction in the first part of the fifth century B.C. remain uncertain. Pausanias' description of the area consists of a list of sanctuaries and other monuments or statues, which we have assumed were in the agora, but nowhere does he discuss the other buildings there, including the colonnade and the square hall. Possibly they had been destroyed by his time;[12] otherwise he disregards them because they did not serve a religious function. Similar halls have been discovered in or near the agoras of other Greek cities, for example at Sikyon. They would seem to be meeting places of the city council (bouleuteria) and it is not unlikely that the hall at Argos filled a similar function. This remains no more than a possibility; but it is interesting to note that at the time this building was put up there were important developments in the constitution of Argos. Otherwise, little else is known of the agora, and even the location of the temple of Apollo is uncertain.

In the area of the agora and the sanctuary of Apollo Lykeios there were numerous other sanctuaries described by Pausanias (though again, none of them has been certainly identified): the sanctuary of Nemean Zeus, the temple of Fortune, the sanctuary of Zeus the saviour, of Asklepios, of Artemis, of Athena, of Latona, of Flowery Hera. Quite clearly this area formed the religious as well as the political centre of classical Argos. Vollgraff thought that the remains of a large Christian basilica to the north of the agora 'not far from the theatre' marked the position of the temple of Apollo. This is only speculation, but a site somewhere on the northern side of the agora, which would be virtually in the centre of the ancient city, is not unlikely. Architectural fragments of fifth century date, re-used in a much later building that was put up in the ruins of the square hall, appear to come from the altar of the temple. This was decorated in the manner of the frieze of a Doric temple, with alternating panels (metopes) and carved blocks (triglyphs). Such altars are a particular feature of the Argolid and adjacent regions.[13] Of the temple itself we know nothing, since Pausanias does not describe its architectural form. He tells us the cult statue was made by Attalos, an Athenian sculptor who is otherwise unknown. It is strange that Argos, the home of one of the most important schools of sculptors in Greece should employ an unknown Athenian artist to make the cult statue in her chief temple, but without a secure indication of the date it is impossible to guess the reasons for this. Pausanias supposes that the temple was founded by the hero Danaos; but his evidence for this is derived only from an interpretation of the myth; it was usual to attribute the foundation of important temples to the Heroic Age.

The chief Late Bronze Age settlement in Argos seems to have been within the fortifications on the Aspis, with a burial place on the Deiras ridge, where numerous graves have been excavated. In Classical times there was another cluster of religious sites here[14] and although they have all suffered severe devastation, they are more readily recognized than those of the agora area, since this region does not appear to have been built on since antiquity. These include the sanctuary of Hera Akraia, another sanctuary of Apollo—Apollo Deiradotes, that is, Apollo of the Deiras—and the sanctuary of Athena. The sanctuary of Apollo has been excavated (Fig. 10); the god was worshipped as Apollo Pythaieus, Deiradotes being a nickname derived from the situation of the temple.[15] Near it, says

23

Pausanias, was the stadium where the Nemean games were celebrated—at least, in Pausanias' own times, after they had been
transferred to Argos from Nemea itself. The position of the stadium
has been identified tentatively near the pass over the Deiras ridge.[16]

There are other sanctuaries, as one would expect, on the higher
acropolis of the Larisa, dedicated to Zeus and to Athena. The badly
weathered foundations belonging to one of these are still visible
amongst the later medieval structures in the inner part of the castle.
Apart from these Pausanias gathers the sanctuaries of Argos into
two main groups, by the agora and on the Aspis, the more important
being those by the agora. It would seem that Argos is a double city,
the older, Bronze Age settlement on the Aspis, and the Classical
city centred on the agora. That there was a distinct settlement in
this lower region by at the latest the ninth century B.C. seems borne
out by the discoveries made by the French archaeologists, and others,
of innumerable tombs containing pottery of this period, more or
less surrounding the agora area on south, east and north. Since such
burials invariably took place outside the town or village, their
position clearly marks out its limits. The significance of this dual
origin for the early history of Argos is discussed below.

As we have seen, the fortified area of the Classical city included
both parts; the city had been extended, and many of the long forgotten early graves were in later times within the city limits. Where
these limits were is less certain but to the south the line is reasonably
defined by the existence of later, Classical cemeteries, in a region
recently developed as a suburb of the modern town.[17] These suggest
that the city walls, having descended from the summit of the
Larisa crossed in a west-east direction, some two or three hundred
metres south of the south stoa in the agora before turning to the
north. The circuit of wall was broken at certain points by the city
gates. One of these, the *Deiras gate* on the col between the Larisa
and the Aspis has already been mentioned; even though nothing of
it is now visible, its position on the road to Mantinea and its branch
to Lyrkea is assured. In addition, we know of four other named
gates. The *Eileithuian gate* got its name from the nearby sanctuary
of Eileithuia and it was through this gate that Pausanias, coming
along the road from Mycenae, entered the city. It has been identified
with the *Nemean gate*, presumably the gate situated where a road
led to Nemea; such a road must also have provided a reasonably
direct route to Mycenae, and would have left the city on the more

northerly side. However, recent excavations in the eastern area of Argos[18] have led to the suggestion that the sanctuary of Eileithuia was in that region and that therefore the Eileithuian gate was distinct from the Nemean gate. The road from Mycenae, if it approached in this direction presumably kept to the eastern side of the Inachos river, turning to cross it at a convenient point to the east rather than the north of the city. There should also be a road leaving Argos on this side and making directly for the chief Argive sanctuary, the Heraion:[19] but although Pausanias had visited the Heraion before coming to Argos, he probably returned to Mycenae before setting out for Argos. That there were several possible routes from Mycenae to Argos across the Argive plain can hardly be doubted.

The other two gates known are those called *Kylarabis* and *Diamperes*. The Kylarabis gate got its name from the chief gymnasium of Argos which lay outside the city. Pausanias reached Kylarabis along a straight street from the sanctuary of Eileithuia; but as he also mentions a gate adjoining the gymnasium it is clear that the Kylarabis gate is distinct from the Eileithuian. Both the Kylarabis and Diamperes gates were involved in an attempt to capture Argos by surprise in 272 B.C. when Pyrrhus, king of Epirus, tried to enter the city by night.[20] Again the names have been identified as in fact referring to one and the same gate, but it is more likely that they were distinct. Pyrrhus attempted first to enter the city by way of the Diamperes gate, which had been opened for him; but in the confusion caused by trying to take his war elephants through an opening that was too small for them the advantage of surprise was lost. Pyrrhus himself, Plutarch tells us, now entered the city by way of Kylarabis, and it seems better to suppose that this marks a second attempt, through a different gate.

The position of these gates is uncertain. Kylarabis and its gymnasium lay outside the city, at a distance of less than three hundred paces. Since a straight street led to it from the sanctuary of Eileithuia, it must have been on the eastern side, though south of the Eileithuian gate. Vollgraff, reporting the early excavations[21] and researches in Argos and following a suggestion made by E. Cirtius, tells of slab paving and mosaics, associated with an inscription in honour of Marcus Aurelius in the vicinity of the church of St Constantine. He considers that a saying quoted by Lucian,[22] a wish that 'famine may never seize hold of Argos to such an extent that the Argives have to try to sow Kylarabis', would make most sense if the gymnasium was in fact paved with stone slabs he discovered. It may be that the remains he discovered (perhaps all of them of Roman date) do mark the site of Kylarabis, but the saying is best explained as a reference to the sacred character of the gymnasium, which presumably put a strong taboo on its cultivation and the identity of the slabbed area and the gymnasium cannot be accepted as certain.

When Pyrrhus attacked Argos, his objective was the agora. Both the Diamperes and the Kylarabis gates should give the easiest access to it, and should be sought in the south-eastern part of the city. The Kylarabis gate also led to the district called 'the hollow' (Koile) which may represent the lower region between the Larisa and the Aspis; this suggests, along with the fact that there was direct access to it from the Eileithuian gate, that it was to the north of Diamperes.

Pyrrhus had advanced to Argos from Sparta, and the obvious point of attack was therefore from the road to the south; but as he was forced to desist from an immediate attack, he went instead to Nauplia, where he pitched his camp. His attack on Argos was therefore mounted along the Nauplia road. On the other hand, it is possible that the arrangement to open a gate was made before the king was forced to cross over to Nauplia, and when he anticipated a direct approach from the south; in this case the Diamperes gate could be that which most certainly existed (though otherwise unnamed) at the road running south from the agora, towards Tegea.

Though much uncertainty remains, it is obvious that the wall round Argos was provided with gates only at the main approaches from the Argolid. These were between the Larisa and the Aspis, on the road to Mantinea and Lyrkea, the *Deiras gate*; to the east of the Aspis, on the road to Nemea, and Mycenae, the *Nemean gate*; on the east side of the city, the *Eileithuian gate*, on the direct road to Mycenae, and probably also the Heraion; the *Kylarabis gate*, on the road leading directly to the eastern Argolid. Finally, the *Diamperes gate*, perhaps on the road to Temenion, and perhaps another the '*southern*' gate, on the road to Tegea and Tripolis, if these two are not to be regarded as one and the same, with the road to Temenion and Tegea dividing outside the city.

Within the city, in all probability all these gates were directly connected to the agora; this is proved in the case of the Diamperes,

Kylarabis and Eileithuian gates, certain by its position for the southern gate, and probable for the others. It is equally obvious from this, as one would expect of so old a town, that Argos was completely unplanned, with streets following the natural lines of communication within the walls. Pausanias describes only the public monuments, or, more specifically, those of religious significance. These were concentrated in the area of the agora, and on the hills, but there were other religious sanctuaries scattered throughout the city area, and others immediately outside the walls. The rest of the city was occupied with private housing, none of which of the classical period is well enough preserved to warrant description.

One of the reasons why Argos developed as an important city was the good water supplies it possessed. When Pyrrhus entered the city in the confusion of a moonless night, one of the difficulties he encountered was the existence, along the main streets, of open water channels. Such channels, and others more conveniently enclosed in pipe conduits, have been discovered by the French archaeologists, but they seem mostly to belong to the Roman or late periods. Since the development of Argos is early there must have been good springs,[23] though they did not achieve the fame of those, for examples, at Athens and Corinth. From the position of the Classical town, it is to be presumed that the springs issued from the slopes of the Larisa. At the same time, probably before Pyrrhus' adventure, and therefore, not unconnected with the existence of the water channels in the streets, the supply of water had to be increased artificially. A tunnel was cut into the Larisa to facilitate this. No trace of this now remains. It is referred to by Vollgraff,[24] who quotes, as a probable exaggeration, a description recorded in Dodwell's *A Classical and Topographical Tour through Greece*: 'Fourmont describes a subterranean inlet, which he says penetrated 3,000 paces in the Larisa rock, being cut through a dark coloured stone full of petrified shells; he says that the passage is perfectly straight, but has recesses in each side, not opposite to each other.' There seems no reason to suppose that this description is in fact exaggerated. There is a similar tunnel at Perachora in the Corinthia,[25] which also passes through strata of fossilized shells, and which is provided with recesses on each side alternatively; these would seem to have been intended for lamps, needed when the tunnel was inspected or cleaned out. The Perachora system is connected with a fountain house and water storage tanks. It seems that from practical experience the Greeks knew that it was possible to tunnel into hillsides to tap underground water supplies; there are other examples in the Argolid (at the Heraion) and in Corinthia.[26] The date of these works at Argos is uncertain.

The other towns of the Argolid

The towns of the Argolid are described in the order followed by Pausanias.[27]

In the second century A.D. when Pausanias visited the Argolid, the pattern of settlement would appear to have been different from that of earlier times. Argos itself was still a flourishing centre; the surviving Roman remains, the impressive bath building, the existence of numerous substantial houses in and around the city with mosaic floor decoration, the presence of paved streets as well as a number of inscriptions show that it was still a prosperous place.[28] In the Argolid, the other towns do not present such a prosperous picture. Though Pausanias notes and records their positions, and perhaps the continuing existence of a sanctuary, many of the smaller towns appear to have been abandoned. At Mycenae, Pausanias visited only ruins. Tiryns also consisted of ruins, depopulated by the Argives. Even more surprisingly Nauplia 'is now depopulated'. This is to be explained only in part by the undoubted drop in the population of Greece following the Roman occupation. More important is the change in the social pattern. The landowners (whose estates had increased in size, as their numbers had declined) were now concentrated in the single urban centre, with its developing amenities. The land was cultivated as a series of farms or estates. The smaller towns no longer served any useful purpose, and in consequence were abandoned. In earlier times, the fields were more often cultivated by people living in the smaller towns, particularly those on the eastern side of the Argolid, though obviously the land round Argos itself was farmed from that city. Several of the smaller towns in the earlier period, though subject to Argos, maintained a strong memory of former independence. As we have seen, in Classical times the majority of the population in the Argolid lived outside Argos town.

Pausanias approached the Argolid from *Kleonai*. Geographically, this town belongs rather to Corinthia; it is to the north of the watershed that divides the valleys reaching down to the Corinthian and Saronic gulf from those running into the gulf of Argos. However, for much of the classical period it belonged to Argos, or at least was in some way attached to Argos. In the sixth century B.C. it was for a time the place of residence of the Argive royal family, exiled from Argos itself; later it seems to have been more directly part of the Argive state, though not fully incorporated into the Argive system, for it frequently appears as the ally of Argos.[29]

Kleonai is situated in a broad basin of land drained by the river Longopotamos which flows northwards to the Gulf of Corinth, leaving the territory of Kleonai by way of the distinct gorge it has carved for itself in the soft rock. The main approach from Corinth, in antiquity as at the present day, was not by way of the gorge, but rather via the low hills to the east. These are hardly a barrier, but they form an obvious line of demarcation separating territory belonging to Corinth (the region of Tenea) from that of Kleonai. The town was on the western side, on a hill that projects out into the plain from the higher hills that define the territory of Kleonai on that side. It is a commanding position, though perhaps weaker from the point of view of defence; it needed strong fortification. From it can be seen the chief approaches from Corinth, and clearly visible over an intervening line of hills, the citadel of Corinth, the Acrocorinth. The pass through the southern mountains, the Tretos, leading to Argos is not visible.

Of the city itself, though the position is obvious enough, little remains visible. The line of its once strong walls is clear, as it follows the contours of the hill to give the greatest difficulty of approach, but most of the superstructure has been robbed away, and the parts that are left, forming the boundaries of fields or the footing for the modern track that leads past the city, have banked up the earth behind them, so that they resemble little more than a superior field terrace. At one point on the south side of the acropolis, where the line strikes up the hill against the natural contour the foundations of square towers are clearly visible. Earlier travellers described the walls as being built of polygonal masonry. Nothing that definitely merits that description is now visible. Parts of the wall, it is true, employ roughly shaped stones, but these appear to belong to the inner fill, and were originally behind an outer facing of squared

29

stone, now mostly robbed away (though enough of these ashlar blocks remain to indicate the character of the construction to which they belonged). It is possible that more than one phase of construction was represented in the walls—a point which can easily be settled by excavation—but the ashlar work suggests that in their final form, at least, the walls belong to the fifth or fourth century B.C., or even later.

Within the circuit, no certain foundation lines of buildings are now visible, though various travellers have noticed remains which perhaps belonged to temples. It is unlikely that the entire area (defined chiefly for defensive purposes) was occupied by buildings. A dense scatter of broken tile and other fragments on the south-eastern slopes of the hill (those overlooking the plain) suggest that this was where most of the houses were to be found.

The relationship between Kleonai and Argos is explained by its geography. The city possessed sufficient territory to make it independent and self-supporting, the Greek ideal. On the lower floor of the plain, corn grows readily, while the valley country that surrounds it is covered with olives. More corn, and other plants can be grown beneath the more widely spaced trees, and on the higher hills there is room to pasture flocks of animals. No doubt Kleonai would have preferred to live in rural, though isolated independence, but her territory was too desirable to others for this to be possible. The castle on the Acrocorinth, hovering over the northern hills indicates where the threat lay; at the moment of Corinthian expansionism Kleonai doubtless preferred to throw in her lot with Argos.

The easier of the two ancient routes from Kleonai into the Argolid proper was through the defile called the Tretos, which is now followed by the modern road and railway from Corinth to Argos. Another ancient road, in part massively engineered in the Late Bronze Age, led by a more direct pass to the east directly to Mycenae itself. Near the head of the Tretos defile a modern road climbs, on the western side, over the low ridge separating the Tretos from the district of *Nemea*. The ancient roads to Nemea, both from Kleonai and Argos, were in all probability more direct.

The Nemea, though smaller than the district of Kleonai, is similar in character: a region of flat land totally enclosed by hills, and drained by a river that flows north through a gorge down to the gulf of Corinth. At present it contains one small village (Heraklion), with others lower down, in the area about the gorge that goes rather with the region of the gulf of Corinth. The small population of modern times indicates that this is likely to have been the case in antiquity also. The Nemea is more celebrated for its sanctuary of Zeus and the athletic contests celebrated there than as a city. It was hardly in a position to assert its independence, even as a sanctuary; it had to go either with Kleonai on its eastern side, to Argos, or join with Phleious to the west. It went with Kleonai, and for a long time the Argives claimed the presidency of the Nemean games. At present, the Nemea is cultivated almost exclusively for its grapes, but the name means 'pastures', and it may rather have been used for this purpose in antiquity.

From the foot of the Tretos pass, the modern road and railway make directly for the Argos. The road followed by Pausanias instead turned eastwards, along the foot of the mountain to Mycenae, at present approached only by a side road from Phychtia (though the citadel itself can be seen among the hills over on the eastern side from the modern road).

Little remains of Classical and Hellenistic *Mycenae*.[30] The later inhabitants made use of the Bronze Age citadel for their much reduced town; in the Bronze Age, of course, many houses were constructed outside the walls. They built a temple of Athena, near the site of the earlier palace; since this development finds a parallel on other Bronze Age sites (at Tiryns, for example) it is presumably not by accident, but shows that some memory at least was preserved of the significance this spot had had in earlier times. Apart from the temple, the later town consisted of simple houses, constructed perhaps from the rubble that covered the site. None of these is of any intrinsic interest, and where excavations have been carried out, the later houses have normally been removed, to facilitate access to the earlier levels. Indeed, it is only with the development of more careful archaeological techniques that the later remains have been properly recorded.

Mycenae was destroyed by Argos probably in 468 B.C., after a brief return of local independence. The site was then abandoned, and buildings which covered the little citadel fell into decay, with the probable exception of the temple. Thus there are no buildings at Mycenae belonging to the great age of Classical architecture, and certainly nothing comparable with the fifth-century development of the agora at Argos. It is impossible to use these smaller towns to fill in the serious gaps in our knowledge of Argos, since their character and history are so different.

Mycenae was abandoned until the Hellenistic age, when it was once more inhabited, and, in a simple way, prospered. The walls of the citadel were extensively rebuilt, on the old foundations, and a further area enclosed in new walls to the west and south-west of the citadel. At one stage in this period it received support from a king of Sparta, Nabis, who sought in it a counterpoise to the hostility of the Argives; but this period was brief, and cannot account wholly for the Hellenistic revival which had begun well before the time of Nabis. In the end, Mycenae probably suffered rather than gained from Nabis' interest. The Hellenistic development is there more likely to reflect the general prosperity of the Argolid in the third century. Little remains of this, the final phase of Mycenaean history, since once again, the buildings have got in the way of archaeologists more concerned with the prehistoric levels, and have been ruthlessly swept away. There was a small theatre situated over the Bronze Age 'tomb of Clytemnestra'. It had one row of stone seats, the lowest row and therefore the seats of honour; but the rest, above this must have been of wood, and have left no trace. The stone seats are still preserved, except where they crossed the entrance passage to the tomb. Apart from this, nothing of great interest survives. Pausanias was shown the remains of the Bronze Age, which to him was a historical period. It is not surprising that he was more interested in the still visible remains of Mycenae's greatness than the shabbier ruins of its later decline. It is instructive to compare the insignificance of Classical and Hellenistic Mycenae, cut off from the sea by Argive territory, with its greatness and wealth in the Late Bronze Age.

During the flourishing days of Classical Argos, Mycenae was merely a dependence of the more powerful city and the question of the boundaries between their respective territory was unimportant. It would be interesting to know what happened during the brief period of independence. Presumably the people of Mycenae had previously retained the use of their land, paying part of their produce as tribute or a tithe either to individual Argive landlords, who took the tithe to the land when Mycenae became part of Argos, or to the state. Though the Bronze Age fortress—and therefore the later town—is tucked away in the hills of the north-east Argolid, it overlooks a not inconsiderable area of valley country, now mainly devoted to the cultivation of olives. A little further away is the flat land of the Argive plain, basically corn land, but now increasingly being planted with orange and lemon trees. It is difficult to suppose that all this land was resumed by the Mycenaeans when they became independent. The recovery of Argos was delayed, and the loss of territory may have contributed to this. Even so, compared with Argos Mycenae in this period of independence was a remarkably small place. Argive weakness had been caused by the loss of six thousand dead, killed by the Spartans at the battle of Sepeia; the figure may well be exaggerated, yet it illustrates the size of army that Argos could then put in the field. Independent Mycenae contributed eighty hoplites to the Greek army sent to fight the Persians at Thermopylai. Mycenae and Tiryns together sent four hundred to Plataia in the following year, and though some may have been left behind to defend the towns against the possibility of Argive attack, the chances are that half this figure gives a good idea of the total manpower in Mycenae of normal military age. Mycenae would not have needed much of the land she overlooks to support a population of this size, and it is possible that in fact she possessed none of it. Mycenae citadel is placed at the opening of a dale between two bare hills. This dale contains at present some cornland and olives, mostly close to the citadel. Beyond, much of the land has been allowed to go to waste (though with machines to clear the bushes and rough plough, an attempt is being made to put it back into cultivation), and it is not impossible that this, and this alone was the region, unwanted by the Argives, that supported the meagre population of Classical Mycenae.

From Mycenae Pausanias went next to the *Argive Heraion*.[31] The route he followed was presumably the old Bronze Age chariot road, that extended past the principal Bronze Age sites of the eastern Argolid. At the time of his visit the Heraion was still an important sanctuary, and a much more obvious attraction to a visitor approaching the Argolid from the north—Mycenae had been visited first, not for what it was, but for what it had been.

As with Nemea, the Heraion was not the site of a town, but of a religious sanctuary. It had been a place of habitation in the Bronze Age, and there must have been people living in the vicinity in later times, again as at Nemea, but it was not a town in the sense that Mycenae was. It is not clear when the cult of Hera was established on this spot, but the possibility of continuity from the Bronze Age cannot be ruled out. If so the cult—like most Greek cults—has essentially local origins, and should be significantly older than the earliest attested remains.

Behind the Heraion is the plain of *Berbati*, shut off by a ring of hills and mountains, and approached most easily through a defile at its south-east corner. Pausanias does not mention this region, presumably because there was nothing to take him into it. The modern village has been renamed Prosymna, the Classical name of a region which Pausanias associates with the Heraion, and not near the village, except in the sense that the Heraion is the nearest place to Berbati of the sites in the main Argive plain. Prosymna is more likely to be the name of the prehistoric settlement at the site of the Heraion. We do not know who farmed the plain of Berbati in Classical times, for it is land of fair quality, and extensive (at present covered with olives and fields principally of corn) and it is unlikely that it was completely abandoned. If there is no place name associated with it, presumably it was divided up into individual estates assigned to Argive citizens, rather than worked from dependent village communities; it may have belonged to Mycenae.

After visiting the Heraion, Pausanias made for Argos, probably returning first to Mycenae. On the way he passed a sanctuary of Demeter, at a place called Mysia, and near the 'tomb of Thyestes' called 'the Rams'. An inscription with a spiral band of relief decoration ending in a ram's head was discovered built into the wall of a church near Phychtia, a village on the modern main road to Argos, near Mycenae. The inscription appears to be a formal curse, and the vicinity of a shrine to Demeter, Persephone and Hades would be an appropriate place for it.[32] If the stone was found near the church into which it was built, it would seem that the tomb (and Mysia) were also near Phychtia. But this seems to have been a very small place—the general impression is that the centre of the Argive plain was largely given up to agriculture, the important towns and villages being situated in the less valuable land of the hillsides.

Pausanias seems to have stayed in Argos, and to have made a series of tours along the roads that radiated from the city. First, he followed the road to the south, that led to Tegea. Here he came to *Kenchreiai*. His route must have taken him more or less along the line of the modern road to Tripolis, probably a little closer to the hills, for he passes the copious springs of the Erasinos,[33] the first

9 The pyramid of Kenchreiai (Hellinikon)

10 The citadel of Hysiai and its valley

11   Hellenistic tower at Asine

12   The citadel on the Larisa—Classical and medieval

13 The Argive Heraion: the terrace wall of the old temple

14 The Argive Heraion: early Doric capital

15 The Argive Heraion: the foundations of the new temple

16 The Argive Heraion: decorated blocks from the altar

of a series of outlets where the rain collects in the plateau and western mountains of Arcadia and seeping underground finds its way to the surface; the modern road passes a few kilometres to the east of these springs. Beyond this point, the mountains recede, and a valley leads into them. The modern main road and railway to Tripolis (the present-day equivalent of Tegea) keep to the coastal plain, past the hills that form the southern boundary of this valley, and past the site of the ancient *Lerna*. Here there is a second plain, that of Kiveri. This is formed by the junction of the river valleys, that of the Xerias to the north (not to be confused with the Xerias that is the ancient Charadros, north-west of Argos) and the Xabrio to the south. The modern road turns into the Xerias valley, but soon starts to climb the hills that divide it from the Xabrio, sweeping up in a series of hairpin bends. The railway follows the Xabrio valley. The ancient road did neither. It needed to follow a route as direct as possible so that the line followed by the railway (which is designed to gain height as gently as possible, even at the expense of a considerable detour) was out of the question. The modern road is as direct as possible in this hilly country, but has to climb by a series of hairpin bends, a form of road construction not employed in antiquity. The ancient road therefore turned into the first of our valleys, that immediately to the south of the Erasinos springs, and climbed steadily towards the ancient Kenchreiai. The land in the valley is similar to that of the hilly parts round the Argive plain, used today for olives, corn and other various vegetables, rather than for citrus fruit.

One of the most intriguing antiquities of the Argolid is situated in this valley, on a low hill that projects from the northern side.[34] On the top of this, in a position that gives excellent views down to the coastal plain and across the gulf to Nauplia, are the ruins of what appears to have been a hollow pyramid. It stands on a vertical base, which in part incorporates the outcrop of rock at the top of the hill. Above this, the sides of the superstructure are steeply inclined, though it is clear that it cannot have formed a conventional pyramid. In the first place, its plan is rectangular, not square, and secondly, the south-western corner is recessed, to give access to a narrow passageway. At the end of the passageway is a door into a central room, with vertical sides. Though the side walls are nowhere preserved to their full original height, the vertical line of the inside and the sloping line of the outside would have met long before the pyramid could have reached an apex. The walls are built from blocks of stone of varying size and shape. In places the effect is of crazy-paving 'polygonal' walling, but elsewhere the blocks are more regular (trapezoidal). It has been identified as a tomb, for Pausanias mentions that at Kenchreiai was the burial place of the Argives who defeated the Spartans at the battle of Hysiai, though it is difficult to see why the burial place should be so far from the battlefield. However, the latest investigations of it have led to the conclusion that it is military in purpose, a blockhouse protecting the junction of the main routes from the south into the Argolid. Fragments of pottery found in the excavations suggested that it was built in the fourth century B.C. There are the remains of a similar pyramid blockhouse on the eastern side of the Argolid, by the road to Epidauros.

At the head of the valley, the ancient road (whose line is not certain here) appears to have swung round to the south-west to reach the pass that separates it from the head waters of the Xerias. At this point (called τὰ νερά, the waters) there are two copious springs, and a curious modern church that has recently replaced an older building. In this area are scattered fragments of tile, and by the church stands a white-washed column, probably of Roman origin. From this point there is an excellent view of the Xerias valley, which begins as a steep-sided gorge. Below the springs and overlooking the gorge is a rounded hill, covered to a considerable extent with tile fragments (far more than at the springs) and a great quantity of nondescript, but probably late, pottery. This seems the most likely site for Kenchreiai itself: high in the hills, with access to agricultural land (there is ploughland here, in some quantity) with an excellent water supply, and serving as a block post on a strategically crucial road leading to the heart of the Argolid, from the direction of Tegea and the supreme enemy Sparta. There is no obvious sign now of fortification walls, but the lie of the land, the way the earth is banked up on the hill clearly suggests that they once existed, and that their footings, at least, still lie concealed beneath the mound. The probable line for them indicates that only the acropolis was fortified and that the town (at least at a later period, when strategic considerations had lost their importance) extended outside them. At present there is a very small and very primitive chapel on the side of the hill; this contains squared blocks of masonry, and more fragments of columns, presumably fetched from the site by the springs, not white-washed, and so showing that they are of green veined stone. Pausanias put Kenchreiai 'on the right of what is called Trochos' ('the wheel'). The identity of 'the wheel' is uncertain. If it is a natural feature (and Pausanias' phraseology suggests that it is) it should have survived. The ancient site just described is on the right-hand side of the gorge, the most spectacular natural feature in the vicinity; though it is difficult to see how, and why, it should have been called 'the wheel'.[35]

From this point the road runs south-west, round the slopes of Mount Paravounaki that separates the Xerias and the Xabrio, until it reaches the modern main road, high above the Xabrio valley. The line of the two roads must now coincide, and before they reach the modern village of Akhladokampos, they pass the site of the ancient *Hysiai*. Hysiai is right by the side of the main road: the site is again marked by a church and a spring. It is an acropolis site, on a hill to the left of the road (as one descends towards Akhladokampos, coming from Argos). In this direction, part of the fortification wall is clearly visible. Apart from the neck of land that joins it to the higher hill to the north (and the main road) the acropolis is steep-sided, and in parts clearly needed no artificial fortification. From it one looks down to the valley floor (and the railway line, here climbing up from the coast) some distance away. The fortified site has marked similarities to that assumed to be Kenchreiai; chosen partly for strategic purposes, partly because of the presence of a spring, but not situated in the heart of the best agricultural land.

The walls are built in a mixture of polygonal and trapezoidal masonry, the transitional form that occurs elsewhere in the Argolid, and which is so difficult to date; though the site was presumably fortified at least from the great development of hostility between Argos and Sparta in the later part of the sixth century B.C. Besides the curtain wall there are the foundations, barely noticeable now, but perhaps clearer in the nineteenth century when they were first reported, of massive semicircular towers or bastions. The town was captured by the Spartans in 416 B.C., and destroyed, but was subsequently rebuilt; possibly the walls date from this reconstruction.

From Hysiai there is an excellent view of the valley, now called that of Akhladokampos; the best land, on the valley floor, grows olives, corn and annual vegetables, and undoubtedly formed a useful adjunct to Argive territory. But, more significantly, Hysiai keeps a watchful eye on the passes at the head of the valley to Arcadia. Any hostile movement could be seen, long before it reached Hysiai itself, and reported back by the road to Argos. Here, and at Kench-reiai, the impression of defence, of the fortified frontier post is paramount.

The second tour took Pausanias by way of the Deiras gate along the road to Mantinea. Here, he travelled as far as *Oinoe*; beyond were Mount Artemision and the pass into Arcadia. This valley is approached through a spectacular gap in the hills west of Argos, where the Charadros river has forced its way out to the plain through a gorge. Unlike the Berbati gorge, the valley behind does not open out into such a wide plain. High hills close it in to north and south, while a lower spine of hills running between (to the south of the Charadros, and isolating a tributary torrent) restricts the usable land still further. At present this is a remote backwater, containing only a few villages. It can hardly have been more densely populated in antiquity since there is not enough land available (even though the valley does broaden out somewhat at its western end, where a lower pass leads to the next northerly valley, that of Lyrkea). The chief difference is that then it provided a line of communication to Mantinea, the Arcadian city with whom the Argives were mostly on friendly terms. The importance of the Oinoe valley was political rather than economic. The site of Oinoe itself is uncertain.

Pausanias then returned to the Deiras gate, and took the more northerly road from it to *Lyrkea* and *Orneai*. The river Inachos descends to the Argive plain from the western mountains. It flows—or rather, its course leads, for it is rarely more than a dried torrent bed—through a western extension of the Argive plain itself, equally fertile, and in its lower parts today covered with citrus plantations; the upper parts are corn-growing land. At a distance of seven or eight kilometres from the point where today the local road leaves the main Argos-Corinth road, the hills close in, and though this in no way approaches the form of a gorge or defile, the narrowing is appreciable, and forms a distinct boundary. Beyond, and hidden from the Argive plain by the hills, the valley opens out again, to reveal a considerable area of good agricultural land, surrounded by hills and, to the north and west particularly, high mountains. Such an area clearly means the existence of a distinct community; the large modern village there, formerly Kato Belesi, has been renamed Lyrkea. Though there is an ancient site nearby, the distance from Argos, eighteen kilometres, does not correspond to Pausanias' figure for the distance from Argos to ancient Lyrkea, sixty stades, which is only twelve kilometres. Ancient Lyrkea, therefore, must have been situated before the narrowing of the valley, probably on the hills at the edge of the plain, and perhaps near the modern village of Schinochori. It follows that the inner part of the valley, round the modern Lyrkea was more likely to have been the territory of Orneai, though if the distance given by Pausanias from Lyrkea to Orneai—sixty stades again—is correct, Orneai should be further up the valley, nearer the mountains, than the modern village. It does not seem that Pausanias actually went to Orneai, and his figure for the distance need mean no more than 'approximately the same distance as that of Lyrkea from Argos'.

Lyrkea was not a very important place. It is mentioned in an inscription as the place of origin of an individual Argive citizen, but has no part in the recorded history of Argos. From that point of view Orneai is more important. It was not so completely integrated into the Argive state. At the battle of Mantinea in 418 Thucydides records the number of Argive dead 'with the men of Orneai and Kleonai'. In 416 pro-Spartan Argive dissidents were established at Orneai, stiffened by a garrison of Spartan soldiers. There they were attacked by the Argives, with their full army and some Athenian help. The Spartans withdrew, the dissident Argives slipped away, Orneai was captured and destroyed. It suffered destruction again in 352, when it was attacked by a Spartan army that had advanced from Mantinea. The contrast between the history of Lyrkea and that of Orneai illustrates the dangers and exposure suffered by what was obviously a frontier community. Just as Argos had established herself beyond her natural borders at Kleonai, at the expense of Corinth, so the Spartans hoped to establish a friendly community within the borders of the Argolid.

This history supports the view that Orneai was in the upper valley of the Inachos, not far from Kato Belesi/modern Lyrkea, accessible by a direct pass between the high western mountains from the territory of Mantinea. Perhaps a position at the head of the valley, corresponding more closely with the distance from Lyrkea given by Pausanias, is more likely than a site at Kato Belesi itself, though it is unfortunate that no suitable site has been found, for it would appear that Orneai was fortified, at least at the end of the fifth century.

An alternative site has been sought to the north of the Inachos valley. A little before Kato Belesi, at the point where the hills close in on the valley, a minor road leads off to the north. Passing through a gap in the line of hills caused by a torrent, it approaches a small enclosed valley, up which a track goes to the village of Tsiristra (other villages, higher up the valley, including the chief one, Kephalo-bryson, are approached by a different road, beginning closer to Lyrkea). Our original road avoids the Tsiristra valley, and instead climbs steeply and sharply up the sides of the hills by a series of hairpin bends, tending in a northerly direction. This steep ascent brings the road to flatter, more open ground at the summit of the pass; it then descends, far less steeply than in its ascent. There are two villages here: first Gymnon, and then Leontion, which occupy what is again a distinct valley with a fair area of agricultural land. To the north, the hills close in slightly to shut the valley off visually at least; but there is no barrier, and the road descends steadily to the more substantial plain around St George, the territory of the ancient city of Phleious, friend of Sparta and enemy of Argos. Both Gymnon and Leontion have been identified with Orneai, but both seem too remote from Argive territory to fulfil the role of that town. Both seem too close, and too easily accessible from Argos' enemy Phleious to have remained in Argive possession, even if Orneai had a special status akin to that of Kleonai. The contrast is, that Kleonai was closer to Argos, and approached much more easily from the Argolid, and in addition was by itself a much larger, more substantial and heavily populated region than any community in the remote plain round Leontion and Gymnon can have been. In addition Orneai needs to be easily and directly accessible from Mantinea, and this is not the case with Leontion.

The next excursion was a longer one, and took Pausanias away from the Argive plain to the more easterly cities of Akte. The road is that from Argos to Epidauros. The ancient road lay to the north of the modern main road from Argos to Nauplia (which has caused the diversion to the south) and Epidauros. Its exact line is uncertain, but is passed through the heart of what is now the rich citrus-growing region, probably more or less in accordance with the line of the modern secondary road that links Argos with the villages of Pyrgella, Laloukas and Merbakas (Ayia Trias, whose splendid Byzantine church is decorated with reliefs and inscriptions of Roman date, and carved stone from earlier Greek buildings). Pausanias therefore had to make a diversion to the south in order to visit the ruins of Tiryns, turning off the direct Epidauros road, perhaps at Merbakas.

Like Mycenae, *Tiryns* never recovered the glories of the Late Bronze Age. It is situated on a low rocky hill, isolated from the hills that border the eastern side of the Argive plain, and immediately adjacent to the arable land. At present, it is a little over a kilometre distant from the sea, which may have been closer in antiquity. The later town was protected by the massive Late Bronze Age fortifications of the citadel. (In Geometric times, at least, there was a cemetery to the south of the citadel, in the area now occupied by a prison.) The chief temple there was dedicated to Hera, and an inscription, dating perhaps to the last brief period of independence at the beginning of the fifth century B.C., records a priest of Athena. There are no imposing monuments of these last years of Tiryns.

From Tiryns Pausanias returned to the Argos-Epidauros road, which he then followed out of Argive territory. He soon passed (on the left) another of the Bronze Age sites of the Argolid, *Midea*. Midea is today remarkable for the substantial late Bronze Age fortifications that surround (where the sheer cliff is insufficient) an area at the top of a steep-sided hill. Until the modern reconstruction of the walls at Tiryns and Mycenae, these were among the most imposing of their date in Greece. The site—like the Larisa at Argos —is impossibly inconvenient and can hardly have been more than a place of refuge in the troubled times of the thirteenth century for people living on the lower ground (below the citadel, as one begins to climb the easiest approach, from the north-west, there is a good spring). The Bronze Age tombs of Dendra, which undoubtedly go with the citadel, are further from it than are, for example, the tombs at Mycenae from the citadel there. The citadel dominates the road to Epidauros, which lies at its southern foot; its siting is military in purpose. The history of Midea appears to have been essentially similar to that of Mycenae and Tiryns. By Pausanias' time there was 'nothing left except the foundations'. It had suffered the inevitable eclipse at the end of the Bronze Age, though occupation continued for a time. It was inhabited in the classical period—at least fragments of pottery of classical date have been found there. It was probably mentioned in a list of places laid waste by Argos because of disobedience, which includes Tiryns, Asine and Nauplia; a fourth town was included, but the name has been lost.[36] Geographically Midea is closest to the others. The date of this destruction is uncertain, but may be early, since Asine is known to have been destroyed at the end of the eighth century B.C.

Beyond Midea Pausanias came to *Lessa*, which, he says, is at the frontier between Argos and Epidauros. It has been suggested that the small, archaic temple underneath the chapel of the Profitis Ilias near the modern village of Ayios Adrianos may be connected with this village.[37] On the slopes of the hill on which the temple and chapel are situated are terraces, which may indicate the position of the village itself. On the other hand, the boundary of Argos should be further to the east, while the Ayios Adrianos site is hardly on the direct line of the road from Midea to Epidauros, which is more likely to have passed further to the north, under the slopes of Mount Arachnaion. If so, both the name of the Ayios Adrianos site, and the precise position of Lessa must rest uncertain. There is also a small hilltop fortress, with trapezoidal masonry and a double enclosure, near Ayios Adrianos.[38] Otherwise, Lessa is a totally unimportant place; Pausanias mentions the temple of Athena, which still contained an archaic wooden cult-statue 'like that on the Larisa' at Argos. Unlike the other places Pausanias had visited in the eastern Argolid Lessa was apparently still inhabited in the second century A.D.

After Lessa Pausanias entered Epidaurian territory and the account he gives of the places he visited in his tour round Akte does not concern us. He visited first the northern side of the peninsula and then returned along the south coast, so that he enters Argive territory again in the district 'once called Asinaia, where there were still to be seen the ruins of Asine, by the sea'.

Asine was essentially another Bronze Age site. It continued to be occupied at the end of the Bronze Age, and was finally incorporated into Argive territory at the end of the eighth century. The site has yielded archaeological evidence of continued occupation after this period; the ruined and abandoned state in which Pausanias found it probably resulted not so much from this remote period of Argive aggression as from the general depopulation of the outlying towns in the Argolid in Roman times, which has already been mentioned. Certainly, as we shall see, citizens of Argos were identified as coming from Asine in classical times, but the Swedish excavators of Asine[39] report that the site was abandoned from the end of the eighth century to the end of the fourth; so the Argive citizens of Asine lived in the surrounding territory, not the town. It was reinhabited about 300 B.C., and evidently prospered in the second century B.C. The remains of Roman buildings suggest that its subsequent abandonment was not so complete as Pausanias implies. Pausanias mentions that the Argives left untouched the sanctuary of Apollo Pythaieus; this has been identified by the excavators with a temple on the top of a hill a short distance to the north-west of the town.[40] In the town itself nothing remains of architectural significance, apart from substantial sections of the circuit walls. It was re-used as a fortress in the third century; the excavators believe that the walls belong mostly to the Hellenistic age, or even later, but the form of the entrance to the 'town', not dissimilar to that of the Lion Gate at Mycenae, suggests that the original arrangement was that of the Late Bronze Age.

The situation of Asine is a matter of some importance. Though there is no substantial barrier, Asine forms a separate region of its own, distinct from the open plain of Argos. In itself, it constitutes— like Kleonai—a complete, though small, city state unit. It has its own citadel (Asine itself), an excellent beach, more important in early antiquity, when ships were usually run up to the beach, than an enclosed port; and it is backed by a sufficient area of arable land of excellent quality with wooded hills to either side. In isolation, Asine could have existed as an independent state. Like Kleonai, and Nemea, which similarly form recognizable units of territory its independence was merged with its more powerful neighbour Argos; but this time the merger was clearly against the will of the people of Asine, who had no nearer and more powerful neighbour to fear, as did Kleonai.

From Asine Pausanias made his way back to the Epidauros road, and thence directly to Argos again. He omitted, rather strangely, to visit Nauplia, leaving that for his final excursion. In this excursion he once more used the southern road from Argos, but instead of turning westwards into the hills and Kenchreiai towards Tegea, this time he continued along the coastal plain to *Lerna*. Here there is another important prehistoric site, of remote antiquity;[41] but Pausanias mentions no town here, only religious sanctuaries. This region is more likely to have been occupied as a series of farms, well watered from the springs at the foot of the hills, and controlled from Argos, even before the Roman period.

From Lerna Pausanias moved southwards, towards Lakonia, but first he introduced a strange digression. He turned first towards the north-east, along the coast to *Temenion*. This formed the only village or small town in this region, but politically it was a place of no significance. It was situated among the coastal marshes, its probable site being now marked by the modern refugee village of Nea Kios. Foundations at this spot may indicate a place of habitation, not merely a sanctuary, and there are traces of an artificially improved harbour. The place gets its name from Temenos, the descendant of Herakles and founder of the Temenid dynasty of kings of Argos, who was supposedly buried there. With such a close connection with the early history of Argos, it can hardly have been an independent town. Pausanias believed that this was the original base of the Dorian settlers in the Argolid, but though this is possible, it is only an inference. Besides the tomb of Temenos, Temenion possessed a sanctuary of Poseidon and another of Aphrodite.

It is from Temenion that Pausanias at last reached *Nauplia*. Presumably he travelled by boat—a pleasant excursion. Again, it was only to record a formerly flourishing site which by his time was uninhabited. Nauplia marks the eastern end of the Argive beach, where the hills at last reach the sea. Here the beach is sheltered from the onshore winds, while behind is the steep hill that has acted as a citadel, almost without ceasing, from prehistoric times; at present it is covered with a substantial Venetian/Turkish castle. Below this are the modern quays, now almost deserted, with an equally unused narrow-gauge railway. Between quay and castle, and now spilling over into the Argive plain is modern Nauplia. Here the continuity and density of occupation has more or less precluded archaeological research, except in the outlying areas beyond the ancient city, where parts of the cemeteries have been found.

Significantly, Nauplia as well as Argos was a flourishing town even before the Greek war of independence. It seems natural, and normal for the Argolid to possess an eastern centre, such as Tiryns or Nauplia as well as a western one at Argos itself. That there were several important citadels in Bronze Age Argolid is hardly surprising, even if we cannot recover their relations with each other; what is more strange is the way in which Argos alone was able to dominate the whole area in classical times. Even so, Nauplia continued to exist, and possibly to flourish despite the punishment which, as Strabo records, was meted out to her for her disloyalty. Then her main function seems to have been to act as the harbour of Argos; but beyond the fact of this essentially secondary role, little is known about the town. It is surprising that Pausanias found Nauplia deserted; it may well be that this had been caused not so much by the general pattern of depopulation that we have already noticed, as by the development of Temenion, nearer and more accessible, as the chief harbour of Roman Argos.

Of Classical Nauplia, Pausanias noticed only the circuit wall of fortifications, the harbours, a sacred spring and the sanctuary of Poseidon. After this excursion he returned direct to Temenion and thence again to Lerna.

At Lerna the hills come closer to the sea, marking a possible southern boundary to the Argolid. Beyond this comes a series of valleys, and plains, running down to the sea, each distinct and potentially self-contained, and all of them too small to resist the expansion of a major city like Argos. They were essentially disputed territory, fought over particularly in the long series of wars between Argos and Sparta.

The first valley leads inland up to Hysiai, which Pausanias had already visited by the direct road over the hills by way of Kenchreiai. This time he continued along the coast, by a place called *Genesion* with a sanctuary of Poseidon and, a little further, a beach which he was shown as the place where Danaos and his daughters first landed in the Argolid. The Hysiai valley and its coastal strip had been in the Argive possession so long and so firmly that its identification as part of the Argolid was straightforward.

Further south still a rough and difficult path took Pausanias through a region called Anigraia, which constitutes yet another natural boundary, and obviously one that was more real than that near Lerna. The next valley forms the district of Thyreatis which changed hands more than once in the contest between Argos and Sparta. At the present moment, the Thyreatis (under the title of Eparchia of Kynouria) belongs to the nome (prefecture) of Arcadia. Its direct links by land both with the Argolid and Arcadia are difficult. A good road has been constructed along the coast from Lerna, by way of Kiveri and Xiropigadi. This gives excellent views of the gulf, but also demonstrates the original separateness of the Thyreatis. Even more recently a road has been opened from Arcadia by way of the Tanaos valley; to travel along this again emphasizes the considerable difficulties of the route, and the extensive area of agriculturally insignificant mountain that lies between the two cultivated regions. So long as Argos dominated the gulf, she controlled the only reasonable approach to the Thyreatis, which is obviously by sea. The extension of Argive influence into that region was natural. The Thyreatis is large enough to support a small independent city, but not a large one; its occupation by the Argives, as we shall see, was regarded as belonging to a remote antiquity. The loss of Thyreatis to Spartan aggression hurt Argive pride; though the region lies between Argos and Sparta, the difficulties of overland communication would suggest that the Spartans had no real business to be there. Thyreatis has good land; at present (and for some time past, to judge from the trees themselves) largely given over to olives. Certainly, olives here predominate in a way found nowhere else in the Argolid, and it is interesting that Pausanias, when he comes to describe the Thyreatis particularly remarks that olives thrive there. Its loss may have caused a real hardship to the Argive economy, and the political hurt, with the affront to Argive pride counted for much. The recovery of Thyreatis was a cornerstone of Argive policy in the fifth and fourth centuries B.C. The district takes its name from the chief town, *Thyrea*; surprisingly, Pausanias does not mention the town in this part of his description of Greece, though references to it in other sections of his book[42] prove that he was well aware of its existence. Its omission at this point may be the accidental result of damage to the text handed down to us in the manuscripts. Besides Thyrea, Pausanias knows of three other towns or villages, and the site of a famous battle between Argos and Sparta, the 'battle of the three hundred champions'. The other places are called *Athene*,[43] *Neris* and *Eva*. The precise identification of them has caused some difficulty. Pausanias says that he turned inland to visit the site of the battle. He then mentions the three villages, starting with Athene, which he describes as an Aiginetan settlement, then Neris, and finally Eva, the largest of them all. Behind all three rises Mount Parnon, the mountain that divides the Thyreatis from Lakonia, the region of Sparta, and the Arcadian city of Tegea. Luckily, we have other accounts of the region. When Athens expelled the inhabitants of the island of Aigina in 431 B.C., the Spartans placed them at Athene in the Thyreatis, and Thucydides,[44] describing the attack made on them by the Athenians in 424 B.C., mentions that Thyrea was at a distance of 10 stades (2km) from the sea.

The Thyreatis consists of two distinct sections, the Tanaos valley to the north, and another valley to the south, separated by the ridge of Sarantapsycho, a north-eastern outlier of Mount Parnon. Mount Parnon itself rises behind the southern valley: and since Pausanias mentions that Parnon is behind the three villages he describes, it seems likely that all of them belong to the southern valley. It then follows that what is missing is the description of the northern section. This in turn indicates that Thyrea was in the northern section and being about 2km from the sea, is likely to have been on the site now occupied by the chief modern town of the district, Astros.

Part Two   The History of Argos

3   The creation of Dorian Argos

The power and wealth of the Argolid in the Late Bronze Age is amply proved by the surviving monuments, and the riches deposited in the graves of their kings. Even the more ordinary tombs investigated by archaeologists have produced grave goods in some abundance;[1] not, perhaps the dazzling quantities of gold that were found from the royal shaft graves, but still articles which indicate a high general level of prosperity. Even if the organization of the Bronze Age people centred round the king and his palace, it is clear the wealth this created was not wholly devoted to his benefit. From the Bronze Age we have not only the remains of the palaces and the splendidly built tombs, but bridges, causeways, roads constructed on a scale never again seen in the Argolid. It is not surprising that today interest in the ancient Argolid more often than not is concerned with the brilliant prehistoric communities.

In the thirteenth century B.C. this brilliant world became less sure of itself. Massive fortifications were developed round the principal communities, at Mycenae and Tiryns, for example. The remoter hilltop at Midea, less easy to attack, was nevertheless given comparable walls. There are indications that an attempt was made to construct a wall across the isthmus of Corinth, the certain sign of unsettled times, and the expectation of an enemy who would come from the north. It is probably from this century that the later Greek tradition recalled wars and raids, sieges and the plundering of cities. The situation would appear akin to that in the later years of the Roman empire, when a civilization which had achieved great heights of power and material wealth found itself under pressure from tribes of dislodged barbarians, and neighbours who envied the imperial wealth, and desired a share in it for themselves. At that time, too, cities were given new fortifications, and, significantly, a wall constructed across the isthmus of Corinth.

As in Late Roman times, the precautions were in vain. Not all the communities were attacked at once. Those north of the isthmus were more vulnerable, and Thebes seems to have succumbed quite early on in the thirteenth century (though Athens, with her acropolis already fortified, may have managed to resist the attacks). The climax came towards the end of the century. The isthmus was passed, and all the principal Bronze Age centres in the Peloponnese, so far as we can tell, were ruthlessly pillaged and destroyed.

This collapse of the Late Bronze Age civilization poses many problems, which, in the absence of written historical records cannot finally be solved.[2] Even in the more fully documented Late Roman period the reasons for the weakness of the Roman Empire in the face of barbarian pressure cannot be straightforwardly elucidated to the satisfaction of every scholar, and with the prehistoric society of Late Bronze Age Greece, the problem is even more acute. One thing is certain. The disruptive influences were not felt in Greece alone, but all over the east Mediterranean regions, just as in Late Roman times the barbarians attacked in several directions. This implies that the destruction was not caused solely by internal quarrels and disputes between the communities of Bronze Age Greece, though this is not to deny that such disputes may have occurred, nor that, if they did, they failed to make the situation even worse. Thus it seems that the chief pressure came from outside Bronze Age Greece, from the movement of peoples further to the north, and from the general envy of neighbours who knew the wealth of the Bronze Age communities, but themselves had no share in it.

The first raiders came to destroy and plunder, not to settle. Whether they then returned home (wherever that was) or passed on out of Greece to attack the still rich communities of the Levant (an attack attested by the archaeological evidence of destruction, and the Egyptian documents) must remain uncertain. Nor is it necessary, as is sometimes supposed or tacitly accepted, to postulate only one major wave of destruction, for there may well have been several, and the result cumulative. Nevertheless, it does seem that at this time, the end of the thirteenth century or the beginning of the twelfth, there was no new influx of permanent population into southern Greece or the Argolid. That there was widespread disruption is certain, and that there were massive movements of population within the Bronze Age communities seems amply attested by the archaeological record; but this was more in the nature of an evacuation of the

more vulnerable or devasted regions, in favour of remoter, un-
damaged areas. Thus the Argolid, which experienced the full fury
of the onslaught was severely depopulated; but at this moment,
there were no newcomers to replace the refugees.

The destruction of the palaces proved particularly disruptive.
No attempt was made that we can discern in Greece to recreate the
organization they controlled. The art of writing was lost. The
gathering of produce and manufactured articles in the palace store-
rooms ceased and, probably as a result, overseas trade dwindled.
Only small communities survived, huddled for protection behind
the great walls of the citadels. The outlying and unfortified villages
appear to have been deserted. Even the survival society that existed
at Mycenae after the great wave of destruction was itself the target
for a further destructive raid in the twelfth century. After this, the
standard of living dropped, to such an extent that it is often difficult
to attest the presence of inhabitants, though it is to be presumed
that despite death, disease and dispersal, there were still enough
survivors to maintain a local memory, at least, of what had previously
existed, the days of greatness, the names of the kings, the holy places
and the names of the gods.

Thus the Argolid, underpopulated, undercultivated and poor,
became the target for a different type of movement. It no longer
provided the opportunity for plunder, but it did possess excellent
land available for settlement, or at least with a population so feeble
that little serious resistance could be offered to an invader claiming
the fertile region of the Argive plain. So the Dorians moved down
from their mountain homes in northern Greece to occupy much not
only of the Argolid, but other regions of the Peloponnese. It is not
unlikely that they had been involved in the earlier plundering raids,
perhaps not alone, anxious to obtain the possessions and riches
they could not produce for themselves. Now, when the wealth of
southern Greece, and of the Argolid in particular was gone, and
there was vacant land available for the taking, they moved in.

If this new movement differed in purpose, it seems also to have
differed in form from the earlier invasion. When the citadels of
Mycenae and Tiryns were stormed and plundered, the invaders
had been attacking civilized states, with extensive resources and
organization. True, there are signs that this strength had been
eroded (or perhaps dissipated in overseas adventures) during the
later part of the thirteenth century B.C., but nevertheless the

invaders must have been numerous to achieve the success they did, and in the military sense at least, they must have formed a cohesive force. The history of the late Roman Empire is studded with the names of individuals who momentarily wield their barbaric peoples into armies capable of sweeping aside the organization of Imperial Rome, men such as Alaric, Gaiseric, Attila the Hun, and there is no reason to suppose that the same situation could not have existed in the thirteenth century B.C. Equally, the history of the barbarian attacks on Rome suggests that the armies created by such leaders were ephemeral, and the force that swept into Greece at the end of the thirteenth century B.C. probably was not maintained after that success. Thus the plundering raids and the settlement movement can have taken very different forms, even assuming they both involved people from one and the same region.

This new movement was by no means restricted to the Argolid. Dorian settlers also entered Lakonia, to form the Dorian state of Sparta which was to become the bitter rival of Argos; and they also settled in Messenia, in the south-west Peloponnese. They are found in Crete, which they dominate, and other islands of the Aegean, including Rhodes. Such a dispersal could be the consequence of the fragmentation resulting when an ephemeral barbaric Empire (like that of Attila) disintegrated at the death of the man who had created it. It could also be the result of a gradual and protracted movement carried out by small groups of settlers dislodged sporadically from the areas they previously inhabited.

There is evidence for the former unity of the Dorians who settled in southern Greece. Whatever region they came finally to inhabit, they all belonged to one or other of three tribal groups, the Hylleis, the Dymanes, or the Pamphyloi. How far back in time this grouping originated is difficult to say; that it existed before the move southwards is evident from the way in which the three tribes are found in all Dorian areas. Such groupings are akin to the tribal organization existing, for example, among the Germans at the time that the Romans first came into contact with them; and it is interesting to compare the name of the third Dorian group, the Pamphyloi, which means 'all tribes', with the German Allemanni—'all men'. The German tribe certainly, the Dorian probably, refers to the amalgamation of various smaller tribes. We might even take the comparison further, for the Allemanni came together when the Germans were beginning to exert pressure on the Roman Empire;

so perhaps the Pamphyloi were formed when the Dorians became involved in the movements against Late Bronze Age Greece.

The political significance of the tribal groups is less certain. They must at one time—but when?—have formed independent political units, each ruled by its own chieftain. If this had been the situation immediately prior to the descent on southern Greece, we would expect to find the various regions occupied by people from a single tribe, not, universally, from all three tribes. So the identity of the tribes had already merged before the Dorians moved south, and the tribe, as such, was not therefore the principal political division. This, in turn, implies that the three tribes had become inextricably intermingled in a larger political unit—perhaps our hypothetical barbarian 'empire', growing up on the fringes of Late Bronze Age Greece. Such a unit might have existed at the time of the plundering raids, at the end of the thirteenth century. It is difficult to see it lasting much beyond that time.[3]

There is some evidence for a protracted movement into southern Greece, rather than a single incursion of a people forming a barbaric kingdom which subsequently disintegrated. The movement of refugees away from the Peloponnese is attested archaeologically in the areas in which they settled. The evidence points quite clearly to two separate movements, the first, to Cyprus in particular, at the time of the destructive plundering raids at the end of the thirteenth century, and apparently occupying only a brief moment in time; the second, to the western coasts of Turkey, beginning in the eleventh century, and continued over an appreciable period of time.[4] The nature of this second movement is also demonstrated by the archaeological evidence. Small, easily defended sites were occupied, large enough to hold two or three hundred settlers only. In Greece itself the archaeological evidence is less certain. The refugees who moved across the Aegean retained some of the civilized skills passed down from the Bronze Age, the art of epic poetry, as well as the more mundane craft of pot-making, so essential to the archaeologist because the residue of pottery is virtually indestructible. The Dorians who moved into the Peloponnese knew no such skills, and relied instead on the abilities of the people living in the survivor communities. It is thus comparatively difficult to recognize a Dorian settlement site; the evidence of burial practices helps, and the goods deposited in graves,[5] but the results are less than conclusive. Nevertheless, the sporadic movement of Ionian and other

55

settlers in small groups across the Aegean suggests that they were dislodged by a comparably sporadic movement of small Dorian groups into the Peloponnese. This is also borne out by the extremely slow redevelopment of Greece, which shows few real signs of revival for close on three hundred years. Some (but not all) of the memories that later Greeks retained of these years also suggest the sporadic infiltration of small groups. The more spectacular legends—those concerned with the return of the 'children of Herakles', who are either associated or identified with the Dorians—recall the movements of armies and battles, and the division of the Peloponnese into three kingdoms, each ruled over by a king descended from Herakles himself. But other traditions recalled gradual and piecemeal advances made by the Dorians, their arrival at Argos, the movement of a separate group to Phleious, of another to Corinth and so on.[6] In this apparent contradiction, we may again see the two distinct phases of the downfall of the Bronze Age Greeks; the plundering incursions of the large but ephemeral kingdom, and the later sporadic infiltration of Dorian settlers into the devastated lands.

The social organization of Dorian Argos seems to support the distinction between the organized plundering incursions and the later settlement. The Dorian Argives retained, as did the Dorians elsewhere, the division of their citizens among the three Dorian tribes. The earliest documents that survive from Classical Argos, in the form of inscriptions on stone, where they record the name of the citizen, normally also record that of the tribe to which he belonged.[7] Membership of a Dorian tribe was an essential qualification for citizenship, and it is probable that positions of importance were allotted (perhaps in rotation, perhaps in threes) to the particular tribe. Such organization reflects the period of Dorian Unity, when the three tribes, not yet scattered in the innumerable Dorian states of Classical Greece, formed a real political unity. Another social division recorded with the names of individual Argives is that of the 'phratry' or 'brotherhood'. Whatever its precise significance the 'phratry' is a normal feature of Greek social organization; and it is by no means restricted to the Dorian cities. The political significance of its use at Argos will be discussed later; but the fact that it first appears on inscriptions only from the middle of the fifth century onwards cannot be used as proof that it was first instituted at about that time, which in other respects, was clearly one of political development in Argos. Earlier inscriptions from Argos are, in fact, extremely rare. They are generally simple, and the omission of details such as phratry names is not of great significance; it does not mean that the phratry as an institution did not exist. We know the names of some thirty or so of the phratries, recorded on inscriptions. Some occur more than once, but, judging from the way in which newly discovered inscriptions can reveal previously unrecorded phratry names, it is unlikely that we have anything like a complete list.[8] The total number of phratries is unknown; but it is considerably larger than that of the tribes, and therefore in origin the phratry is a much smaller unit than the tribe. The names of the phratries that we know can be divided into various categories. Names such as Doriadai tell us little, except that, presumably, the members of that phratry claimed Dorian descent. Others indicate connections with a particular part of the Argolid—Naupliadai, for example—and prove that the phratry was organized within the Argolid. Some are connected with the worship of a particular god—Heraies—which might (but far less certainly) indicate a local Argive connection, with the particular cult at the Argive Heraion. But others are more puzzling: Moklai, Olisseidai, Smireidai, Sphyredai. Are these named after heroes or cults or places? That we cannot tell is due, of course, to our lack of knowledge, to the absence of information. Yet it would be strange, if these referred to cult or place names within the Argolid, that we have lost all other record of them, that no antiquarian scholar tells us about them. So it is possible, perhaps even likely, that these names were given outside the context of the Argolid, and so, possibly, before the Dorians began to move southwards.

Unlike the Dorian tribe names, the phratry names belong, at Argos and elsewhere, to particular states. Each group, as a unit, either came into being within the territory of the city state where it is later found, or moved into that territory as a unit from outside. Either way, the comparatively small size of the phratry suggests the movement of small groups at the time the Dorians arrived in the Peloponnese, in the same way that the archaeological evidence for the settlement of the Ionians on the other side of the Aegean at the same time also suggests small groups of people moving to new homes. We seem to be dealing not with hordes of thousands (which may have occurred during the late thirteenth century upheavals) but isolated bands numbering perhaps a hundred or two, migrating sporadically over a period that may have lasted two centuries.

4 The return of the Herakleidai and the lot of Temenos

Thucydides,[1] speaking of the events that followed the Trojan war, mentions how the Dorians, with the 'children of Herakles' (the Herakleidai) made themselves masters of the Peloponnese eighty years after the war. It is this event that is often called by modern authors 'the Dorian invasion', though Thucydides' phraseology suggests something more complex, that, perhaps, two separate movements, the plundering raids and the later settlement, have been merged into a single event, or series of events.

The tradition centred round the 'return of the children of Herakles' is interesting in itself, and of some importance for later Argos, since it formed the basis of Argive territorial claims in the long-drawn-out dispute with Sparta. How it was composed, and how it was handed down are questions that raise even greater problems than those that occur with the traditions of the people the Dorians displaced, the people of Bronze Age Greece, and the epic poems of Homer. The fullest version we possess is contained in a compendium of Greek tradition and mythology, the *Bibliotheca* compiled probably in the first century A.D., by Apollodorus.[2] An even fuller version was written in the previous century by the historian Diodorus,[3] but this unfortunately has not survived complete; from it we have the activities of the children of Herakles before the outbreak of the Trojan war. There is no doubt that the tradition was established long before these comparatively late authors were writing. In the fifth century B.C., both Thucydides and Herodotus refer to it, Herodotus in some detail;[4] and though he is concerned only with one particular part of the tradition, comparison with the later versions of Apollodorus and Diodorus show that Herodotus had heard essentially the same story (there is one minor difference, affecting the supposed chronology of events). Thus it seems that the essential parts of the tradition, at least, were common knowledge even outside the region to which they properly belonged by the mid-fifth century B.C. at the very latest; and there is a strong presumption that they had been in circulation for some time prior to that, though in a form distinct from the epic tradition of Homer.

This is the story as we have it. After the death of Herakles, Eurystheus, king of Tiryns (who had been responsible for assigning him his twelve labours) banished his sons. They took refuge with Keüx, king of Trachis, in central Greece, but Eurystheus subsequently ordered that they should be driven from Greece altogether. In vain they appealed to other Greek cities to harbour them, and it was not until they came to Athens that they were accepted. There they were settled at the town of Trikorythos, in the district of Marathon.

When they had grown up Eurystheus decided to take action against the Athenians, but, with their aid, the Athenians were able to defeat him. Eurystheus himself was slain by Hyllos (whose name has obvious connections with that of the Dorian tribe, the Hylleis), and Eurystheus' sons also perished. The children of Herakles were thus emboldened to attack the Peloponnese. This attack was successful, and they captured all the cities, but this success was followed by a great plague which so alarmed them that they withdrew, returning to Marathon. Three years later, misled by an oracle of Apollo, Hyllos led the Herakleidai back to the isthmus of Corinth, to threaten a second invasion of the Peloponnese. He was opposed there by Atreus, king of Mycenae (who seems to have succeeded to the role of Eurystheus of Tiryns), in command of a Peloponnesian army. This army was made up of the Achaeans and Ionians who then possessed the Peloponnese, and included a contingent from Tegea in Arcadia, under their king Echemos. Hyllos proposed that the dispute should be settled by single combat: Hyllos, if victor, would be allowed to return to his fatherland; if defeated the Herakleidai would keep away for a hundred years (so Herodotus: Diodorus says fifty). Echemos was chosen as champion of the Peloponnesians and was successful. The Herakleidai kept the promise made by Hyllos, and withdrew once more to Marathon. In the meantime another of the sons of Herakles, Tlepolemos, was admitted to Argos apart from the other Herakleidai. There he killed Likymnios, and was therefore forced into exile. He went to Rhodes, where he founded the three cities of Lindos, Ialysos and Kameiros; from Rhodes he joined Agamemnon at Troy.

When the years of the promise, however many there were, had passed, Tisamenos son of Orestes (and great grandson of Atreus, so the three generations explain Herodotus' hundred years, but not Diodorus' fifty) was king of Mycenae, and Aristomachos the leader of the Herakleidai. Now that the Herakleidai were entitled to resume the conflict, Aristomachos led an attack against the Peloponnese. But he was unsuccessful, and died in battle, leaving three sons, Aristodemos, Temenos and Kresphontes. Temenos consulted the oracle of Apollo, complaining that previously the Herakleidai had been misled. The oracle therefore explained the correct interpretation of its predictions and, encouraged by this, the Herakleidai prepared yet another invasion of the Peloponnese, this time by sea. Their expedition was made ready at Naupaktos, on the gulf of Corinth (in Greek the name recalls the building of the boats). In the meantime, Aristodemos was killed by a thunderbolt, leaving two sons, Prokles and Eurysthenes, who succeeded him. Though there were some mishaps, this invasion proved successful. Tisamenos was killed and the Herakleidai gained possession of the Peloponnese. This they divided into three: the Argolid, Sparta and Messenia, apparently in increasing order of desirability. The lot of Temenos was the Argolid; Prokles and Eurysthenes won Sparta, and from them was descended the dual line of Spartan kings; Kresphontes, who made sure his lot was the last, gained Messenia.

It was from Temenos that the Dorian kings of Argos claimed descent; and the idea that the Peloponnese had been divided into three lots gave rise to their claim to rule not only the Argolid, but the other places along the east coast of the Peloponnese that went with it in this division.

This, of course, is only the main element in the tradition; there are other parts of the story, recorded in different places by various authors. Pausanias for example, tells how Temenos came to the Argolid, making his base for the advance on Argos at Temenion, which was named after him. Elsewhere he tells how 'Rhegnidas, a Dorian, son of Phalkes and grandson of Temenos' made an attack on Phleious, with an army from Argos and Sikyon. The Phleiasians capitulated, accepted Rhegnidas as king, gave his Dorians a share in the land, but otherwise remained in possession. Diodorus gives another exception to the straightforward division of the Peloponnese into three: this was the territory of Corinth, which was handed over to one Aletes, from whom were descended the kings of Corinth, known after the fifth king, Bacchis, as the Bacchiadai.[5]

It appears that the story of the return of the Herakleidai contained conflicting and even contradictory elements; that the versions we possess are 'edited', compilations selected from the mass of legends and traditions that were differently preserved in the different Dorian cities. In an attempt to present a rational and logical account, in all probability much has been excluded. It has certainly been worked over much more thoroughly than the poems of Homer, which still carry the clear traces of their oral transmission, and direct descent from the Late Bronze Age. The inconsistencies and editing in the Homeric poems are well known. They exist also in the story of the Herakleidai.

It is possible to define various elements in the tradition and in the related stories that were not incorporated into the Apollodoran version. The core must be a residue of remembered truth; the process that brought the Dorians into southern Greece to settle, the events that lie behind the disintegration of Bronze Age society. To this are added the distorting elements. Romance and fairy tale, the single combat of the champions and the truce that resulted, the desire to explain local peculiarities—the dual kingship at Sparta, the origin of local names—and, most confusing of all, the deliberate desire to alter tradition to make it conform to posterity's idea of what should have happened, rather than the more sordid reality. The great difficulty must have been that the base of the legend was a story of the destruction of a flourishing civilization, and the intrusion of settlers from less developed parts of the Greek world. Moreover, some, at least, of the traditions belonging to that civilization also survived, and were developing in the Homeric poems as the universal basis of what the Greeks in general regarded as their history; the fragments of a painted vase depicting the blinding of Polyphemos, made in Argos in the early seventh century B.C. show that the Homeric stories from the Bronze Age were known even in the Dorian cities.[6] To make the Herakleidai more respectable their story had to be assimilated with those of Bronze Age Mycenae and Tiryns; Temenos, the sons of Aristodemos, and Kresphontes had to appear as successor kings in the substantial possessions of the Homeric rulers; and if there was a Homeric king of the Argolid, of Lakonia, and of Messenia, so there had to be their Heraklid counterparts.

There is no easy criterion by which to decide what elements of the story are to be retained as historical in essentials, and which to discard. The story clearly knows two distinct periods of attack, separated by a considerable lapse of time. This agrees with the suggestion, based largely on archaeological evidence, that the Bronze Age communities of southern Greece were destroyed in a series of plundering raids, culminating at the end of the thirteenth century B.C., when the Peloponnese was completely overrun by invaders, but not permanently occupied; and that the settlement of the Dorians did not begin until later. But what of the other elements? Herakles, the founder of the dynasty, was bound in service to the king of Tiryns. Is this merely an attempt to justify the intrusion of the Heraklids into the Peloponnese as a 'return' to an ancestral home, or does it indicate that Dorians were employed by the Bronze Age kings, presumably as mercenary soldiers? Is any value to be placed on the supposed chronology which equates the end of the first phase, the raid which gave the Heraklids control of the Peloponnese, with the reign of Atreus, thus putting it firmly before the expedition to Troy (though modern archaeology dates the fall of Troy at least a generation before the destruction of Mycenae, Pylos and the other Bronze Age sites of the Peloponnese)? Most important of all for the later history of Argos, can any reliance at all be placed on the Apollodoran version of what happened when the Heraklids finally occupied and settled in the Peloponnese? The idea of the 'lot of Temenos' formed the basis to real territorial claims by the Argives in historical times. What justification is there for this? Temenos appears in several guises; as one of the Heraklid brothers and leaders of the conquest, in the tradition; as the ancestor of the historical kings of Argos; as the founder hero (one presumes) of the Argive phratry, the Temenidai. The place Temenion on the Argive gulf was named after him, and there in the second century A.D. the Dorians of Argos still paid their respects at his tomb. Yet none of this makes him a historical person. The mythical or divine ancestor as the founder of a family or clan is a commonplace in Greek tradition and it is not unlikely that the family gave its name to the ancestor, rather than the reverse. The compilation of a genealogy, and particularly the linking of genealogies from different parts of the Greek world, as we have it in the common descent of all Dorian kings (even the kings of Phleious!) from the Heraklid Aristomachos is vulnerable to the processes of syncretism and the desire to discover unity where in fact there was none. If we reject the blood-relationship between the Dorian kings of Argos, Sparta and Messenia, this part of the Heraklid tradition becomes more than suspect; and we must surely reject also the joint conquest of the Peloponnese, and the division into lots.

Thus, though in certain details the Heraklid story does recall the events that turned the Greek world upside down at the end of the Bronze Age, all too obviously it has been subjected to interested, and, at times, sophisticated revision. Its account of an organized conquest of the Peloponnese, and the simple transfer of the 'Homeric' Argolid of Tisamenos to the Dorian king Temenos, as an organized and extensive realm, is suspect in the extreme. The stories retained by Pausanias, of the use of Temenion as a base for operations in the Argolid, of the much later occupation of Phleiasia by a grandson of Temenos, point to gradual and sporadic occupation and settlement.

5 The Dorian settlement

In the Late Bronze Age the Argolid was densely inhabited. Flourishing communities existed at Mycenae, Tiryns, Argos and elsewhere. Besides the great 'palace' or citadel sites there is ample archaeological evidence for other settlements, villages or perhaps farms; there are innumerable tombs. The destruction of these communities in the years around 1200 B.C. undoubtedly brought about a severe decline in the population, as people took refuge in other parts of Greece, or fled overseas. Nevertheless, it seems that at least a nucleus of population remained, at Mycenae, at Tiryns and on the Aspis at Argos.

These communities remained in existence.[1] Those at Mycenae and Tiryns continued, apparently without any discernible break. At Argos the community on the Aspis continued to bury its dead in the cemeteries on the Deiras col, which had been used before the great wave of destruction, but this practice did not last for any great length of time. By the end of the tenth century, at the very latest, a new community had grown up on the eastern flanks of the Larisa and the flatter ground below it, in the region that was to be at the heart of the Classical city. Here are the agora and the chief temple of Apollo, and the monuments and sacred spots described by Pausanias. It was surrounded by—and the area of the Classical city in part includes—the places of burial, which show clearly that in the course of the ninth century B.C. this became an important community. It was not the first to be located on this site. Underneath the remains of the first millennium B.C. the French archaeologists found houses and other traces of occupation belonging to the Middle Bronze Age (though, as we have seen, the chief Late Bronze Age occupation was on the Aspis).

The reason for the occupation of this lower site, which has remained the site of the city from the beginning of the first millennium

B.C. to the present day is presumably the presence of adequate water supply, the reason for its abandonment in the Late Bronze Age its insecurity and the difficulty of defending it from attack. The re-development of the lower town in the tenth century B.C. may indicate a return to more settled conditions, just as the Classical city of Athens developed on the more convenient ground below the acropolis. But at Athens the chief sanctuary remained on the acropolis, on the site of the Bronze Age 'palace': at Argos, though the Aspis carried its due share of religious buildings, at least in later times, the chief temple was most definitely not on the Late Bronze Age site, but in the lower town. There seems no reason to doubt that the lower town represents the area in which the Dorians settled, introducing or at least developing the worship of Apollo (in contrast to that of Hera which is more closely identified with the Bronze Age, pre-Dorian communities on the other side of the Argolid).

The precise date of the Dorian settlement is uncertain. Tombs containing pottery in the Protogeometric style have been found in the region to the south of the agora and theatre: late Protogeometric vases in the site now occupied by Argos Museum.[2] In an area excavated by the French archaeologists near the theatre, traces of habitation were found, dating back to the phase that followed the collapse of Late Bronze Age civilization, and apparently occupied for some length of time. These traces of occupation, and the pottery in the Protogeometric style, of the eleventh and tenth centuries B.C. are scanty compared with those that survive from the succeeding 'Geometric' phase of the ninth and above all eighth centuries. But there is enough to prove that the settlement to the east of the Larisa began at an interval after the collapse of Late Bronze Age Greece, that it began on a very small scale during the eleventh century B.C. and developed very slowly, over two or three centuries.

The development of this new, Dorian, Argos raises several problems. The attractiveness of the lower site may have resulted from the presence of better water supplies than on the Aspis (where rainwater had to be collected in cisterns); but the Aspis gives a better defensive position. In areas where they settled, in Lakonia and in Crete, the Dorians formed a warrior caste: presumably they were confident enough in their military prowess to invite the risks that a less easily defended site involved. The fate of the existing community on the Aspis, and its relations with the Dorian settlement are also matters of importance. The Aspis community appears to fade away at the time that the new Dorian community first develops. Two explanations are possible, that the Dorians drove out the previous inhabitants of Argos (who may have joined the other non-Dorian communities in the Argolid, or have fled overseas) or, alternatively, that the Aspis community was absorbed into the new town on the lower slopes of the Larisa. This latter is more likely. Wherever they settled in Greece the Dorians would appear to have been dependent on others as skilled craftsmen, as workers in metal and, above all, as potters. The tradition of pottery manufacture in the Argolid continued without a break from the Late Bronze Age (though the Protogeometric styles which seem significant for the foundation of Dorian Argos may be influenced by the work of potters at Athens exported to the Argolid among other parts of Greece). It is not unreasonable to suppose that this continuity required also some continuity of population. Since Argos itself developed as a centre for the manufacture of pottery, at least by Geometric times (for the French excavations have discovered pottery workshops in the immediate vicinity of the town), it follows that the population of Argos then included people of non-Dorian descent; and these are presumably descendants of those who lived on the Aspis.[3]

If this is so, Dorian Argos was from the start a town of mixed origins. That the non-Dorians were politically subordinate to the Dorian settlers is probable in view of later Argive history, but beyond this supposition it is impossible to reconstruct the early situation. The archaeological evidence confirms that the population was small and remained small for a considerable period of time, making even less likely the Heraklid tradition of an organized conquest and the immediate creation of an extensive empire. That this early community was also poor seems obvious; though not completely isolated, as the importation of Attic pottery confirms,[4] the Argolid was dependent on its own reduced and now ill-organized resources. The general level of poverty is surely reflected also in the burial customs; the valuable articles, including decorated pottery, deposited in the tombs are few, and the paucity of recognizable early graves may therefore understate the real population level of the early settlement; but it was still a small place.

6 Argos in the ninth and eighth centuries

In later times, the Greeks knew the names of a line of kings descended from Temenos who ruled in Argos. The last of these Temenid kings were certainly historical, and played an important part in the development of the city; but the existence of a king list recording the names of those who were believed to have ruled in what we would term the eleventh, tenth and ninth centuries B.C. tells us nothing of the real history of Argos in these years.[1]

The archaeological evidence is a little more helpful. In a negative sense, it shows (as we have seen) that the earliest Dorian settlement was a negligible place and remained so for a considerable period. It is unlikely that it controlled more than the immediately adjacent neighbourhood; the people living in the ruins of Tiryns, Mycenae and other Bronze Age towns were independent (for we have accounts of how they were later forced into submission) as were, most certainly, those of the more distant communities that Argos later claimed as 'the lot of Temenos'. By the ninth century, Dorian Argos, though in all probability still confined within very narrow limits, was a stabilized community. The inhabited area, to judge from the places where graves and cemeteries have been found, was still very restricted, indicating that the population was still small; but the number of graves found and recognized as belonging to this 'Geometric' phase, the quantity of the pots and other articles deposited in them for the use of the dead, indicate that the population was on the increase, and that it was becoming more prosperous. The quality of the pottery also is improved. The presence of pottery workshops just outside the town proves that these pots were made locally;[2] they also testify to the existence of a specialized class of craftsmen. The classical threefold division of Dorian Greek society is firstly into the warrior class, the Dorian citizens, whose military prowess had not only won and protected their settlement among

67

the ruins of Bronze Age Greece, but was to lead to a steady extension of territorial control; then the craftsmen who produced the tools and utensils, pots, pans and armour as essential to the maintenance of life as military prowess, but which nevertheless conferred a lower rank in the social structure (and these people, as we have seen, were probably the descendants of the Bronze Age population); and finally, the farmers, the naked ones—gymnetes—the labourers who toiled in the fields that were the property of the Dorian warriors and who were more certainly descended from the earlier inhabitants. It is probable that this class existed at Dorian Argos from its inception: it certainly existed in later times, after Argos' power had expanded.[3] It cannot be proved for the earliest period but as an institution it is so typical of Dorian society in other parts of Greece as well as Argos that it probably existed even in the restricted, early town of the tenth and ninth centuries B.C.

Dorian Sparta was ruled by kings (with varying limitations to their authority) until the second century B.C.: the later kings of the Classical and Hellenistic ages are often persons of considerable historical importance. In Argos the kings ceased to exercise any control over Argive affairs by the sixth century B.C. Their function in the earliest city, and their origin are matters as obscure as the history of the city itself at that time. The normal function of the Spartan kings was to lead the Spartan army to battle, and in the shadowy years between prehistory and history from which stories, whose confirmation is next to impossible, survived to be recorded by later scholars, we hear of Argive kings exercising that function.[4] Military command must have been the chief political function in the primitive Dorian communities both before and after their settlement at Argos and elsewhere, and this aspect of the kingship suggests that the position was traditional; that the Dorians were normally ruled by hereditary leaders; but to judge from the small size of the original Dorian settlement at Argos, 'king' is a grandiloquent word for such a leader. Early Argos was a village, its population a few hundred at the most, its ruler a village chief, descendant of the chiefs who had commanded the roving bands of Dorians as they moved south to settle.

But the settlement transformed not only the status of the settlers, but the role of the kings. The population of Argos included non-Dorians as well as Dorians. The situation that arose from this was inevitably more complex. Were these non-Dorians directly subject to the authority of the king? The authority of the king depended on the acceptance of him by the Dorians. If, as seems inevitable, the non-Dorians were in a subordinate position politically, they would be bound to accept the authority of the king as imposed on them; but their subservience might well be organized (since this appears to be true in other Dorian communities, such as Sparta and the cities of Crete) through the intermediary of Dorian citizens, in family groups; so that each Dorian family 'controlled' its own non-Dorian families. Thus, inevitably, a dual authority grew up; the traditional authority of the king, and the more limited authority of the Dorian head of family over his non-Dorian 'subjects'.

A further complexity was caused by religion. The well-being of a Greek community depended on its having proper relations with the gods who were particularly concerned with it. The maintenance of these relations through the medium of sacrificial offerings was, like the military defence of the community, by tradition the concern of the king. Even where the secular political authority of the king was successfully challenged and overthrown it was felt to be essential to maintain the title (usually given to a person elected to serve for one year) so that the proper religious observances could still be carried out by a king. Though the origins of the cults observed in the Argolid are often obscure, it is certain that many of them were in direct continuity from the Bronze Age, that is, they were essentially pre-Dorian.[5] Through them the king also assumed a direct link with the interests of the pre-Dorian people.

We do not know enough about the earliest history of Dorian Argos to say whether these problems were then anything more than the potential complexities with, as yet, no real effect on the society of the state. So long as the state was itself small, impoverished and simple in character, the authority of the king was likely to have been real and effective; simple communities, based on the binding acceptance of tradition are likely to have uneventful histories and to be politically stable. Argive history begins when this simple situation breaks down as a result of stress and strain imposed on it.

As in other parts of the Greek world, the eighth century B.C. saw a crucial development in Argos, which is reflected in what we know of her history. The Dorian city became involved in wars, apparently aggressive conquests, which altered the character of the state, while leaving in the memory of the Argive people some details of the course they took. These details are usually insufficient to reconstruct the full history of the wars, and their chronology is notoriously problematical, for they occurred at a period when no regular system had yet been devised, but the nature of the transformation, and some at least of its immediate consequences, are discernible.

By the eighth century B.C. the city had obviously made considerable progress within itself. It was larger, and its population had become much more numerous, to judge from the increasing number of tombs that have survived as time passes. The level of prosperity had risen slightly but significantly; the total number of pots deposited in the graves is much larger, and proves the existence of industrial activity on what was for early Greece a substantial scale; but the improvement should not be exaggerated. Argos was still, in comparison with what she and other Greek cities were to become, a small place, a village in one corner of the Argolid.

By the end of the century a transformation had been accomplished. The pottery industry produced a mass of exuberant—perhaps over-exuberant—vessels with a riot of decorative motifs which seem in themselves to be tokens of a changing world.[6] For two hundred years Argive pottery had been decorated with a slowly developing series of sober, simple geometric patterns, in which plain lines alternated with larger bands of dark paint, with perhaps fragments of maeander or other simpler devices used as highlights and to break some of the monotony. Now the simplicity was overwhelmed by a complex pattern of jazzy design; a patchwork of panels, linked by zig-zags, maeanders and the other elements of the older designs, but now broken and re-arranged in what appears at a casual glance a completely haphazard and random arrangement, but which on closer study appears rather as a system so complex that the complexity disguises and conceals the existence of the system. Figure decoration forms an essential part of the new designs; the older styles had been severely abstract, figures rare in the extreme and, when they did occur, more often than not hidden in the less obvious parts of the decoration, concealed under the handles, and so forth. The figure motifs now used include human beings, male and female, singly and in dancing choruses; they include animals, especially horses, birds and fish. A particular favourite is the combination of man and horse, a man leading a horse or heraldically posed between pairs of horses. There is as yet no attempt to depict recognizable scenes from Greek mythology and tradition—that was to come in the next century—but it is difficult to avoid the impression that the choice of motif in the figure and animal groups has a significance deeper than that of mere repetitive decoration. The horse, for example, is in archaic and Classical Greek society a symbol of aristocratic wealth. Only those families with favoured estates could afford to breed and maintain such expensive animals. They are, by tradition, the 'cavalry' (though often their horses were used only as a means of transport, and the aristocrat descended from his horse on the field of battle to fight as an infantryman). Possession of horses qualified the young aristocrat for participation in the most prestigious event in the athletic contests such as the Olympic games, the chariot race. The pottery, surely, is decorated with the taste of this class in mind (and, no doubt, much was made for them).

Late Argive Geometric pottery is easily recognizable as a separate and distinct style. Yet this development did not occur in isolation.[7] The Late Geometric pottery of Athens, though recognizably different from that of Argos, also introduced new motifs, particularly figure scenes; horses and chariots appear among these. Earlier vases, though decorated, were essentially designed to be used (even if they were deposited in graves). Late Geometric vases, at Athens and in the Argolid, include exaggerated, large and expensive pieces conceived only as ostentatious offerings to the dead. At Corinth, though the Late Geometric style remains, by comparison, simple, it gives way to the style called proto-Corinthian, which includes figure and animal designs of a type not encountered on earlier Greek vases, and which betray a foreign influence. These developments reflect the changes that the Greek world now underwent.

At Argos, the archaeological evidence consists of more than the pottery and the evolution of the Late Geometric pottery styles, important though these are. Among the eighth century tombs excavated, one stands out by virtue of the grave goods it contained. This is the 'Panoply grave' which dates, judging by the pottery in it, from the last decade of the eighth century.[8] It is the grave of a young man, a warrior, for his suit of armour was buried with him; this included a bell-shaped corselet, and a helmet that appears to derive from a Near Eastern type used by the Assyrians. By itself, the suit of armour would tell us little concerning the military history of Argos, though, as we shall see, it is perhaps another clue that enables us to discern something a little more definite in the shadows of early Greek history in this respect. But it does indicate that Argos was sharing in the general resumption of contacts between Greece and the east Mediterranean that is typical of the eighth century B.C., and that one family at least in late eighth century Argos was wealthy enough to bury an expensive, and modern suit of bronze armour in a grave. Equally significant was the inclusion among the offerings in this tomb of a pair of fire dogs (metal stands on which rested the spits used for roasting meat) in the form of stylized warships. In themselves, these indicate at least an interest in the sea; but there is also again a connection with the eastern Mediterranean, for the only close parallel for the depositing of ship fire dogs in a tomb comes from the island of Cyprus,[9] a primary source of copper.

It would thus seem that at Argos, as at Corinth and Athens, a certain section of the population was becoming substantially wealthier in real terms than it had been in the preceding ninth century. The great development in the pottery styles suggests not only new artistic influences coming into the Argive world, but a considerable increase in the market for pots and presumably, other manufactured articles. Moreover, there are indications that goods were now being imported from overseas, particularly the eastern Mediterranean. These are the visible signs of increasing wealth; in all probability there were other indications which have not survived in the archaeological record. The historical problem is to discover the basis of this increased prosperity. The essential economic basis of the ancient world was always agriculture. Manufacture and trade could increase the wealth of certain individuals or communities, but there was nothing remotely approaching a modern industrial society. The prosperity of Greece arose from her position as middleman in the trade routes between east and west Mediterranean, a source of wealth that almost certainly has been exaggerated in its extent and effects; and from the ability of the Greeks to export their own products overseas (a third source of prosperity was political, not economic; the ability to exact a tribute from overseas dependents). Eighth century Argos, as far as we can tell, was not a major trading community, as the Bronze Age Argolid must have been; the Euboean cities of Chalcis and Eretria seem to have held the first place in this respect, followed later in the century, perhaps, by Corinth.[10] Nor can there have been a great overseas demand for the manufactured articles produced in the Argolid, which would have had little attraction to the more sophisticated societies in the eastern Mediterranean; Argive Geometric pottery is an essentially local style, and does not travel far from this region where it was produced (unlike the pottery of the Late Bronze Age). Thus the increase in Argive prosperity more than likely resulted from a rise in the basic agricultural production controlled by the Argives than anything else. Probably the situation in the years following the collapse of Bronze Age civilization had meant that agriculture in the Argolid was on a considerably reduced scale; so there was much leeway to make up, land that had gone out of production to be farmed once more, now the incentive to produce more than could be consumed locally had returned. It is unlikely that there was any improvement in farming methods; throughout antiquity there was little development in what was an essentially conservative art, and there were fixed limits on what the land could produce. The surplus cannot have been very great, for many Greek cities often had to be importers of agricultural produce to keep their populations fed; and if the return of prosperity brought about an increase in population, then the surplus was likely to diminish rather than increase. Further, once the taste or need for imported articles was established, the desire for personal wealth would increase the demand made on the economy by a significant section of the Argive population.

Thus the archaeological evidence for economic development also demonstrates the likelihood, by cause and effect, of political development, and though our factual information on the early political history of Argos is scanty, it would seem to bear out such a sequence.

The eighth century B.C. sees the formation of larger political units out of the divided communities which had existed in Greece since the disruptions of the Late Bronze Age; the memory of this, the first significant historical development since that time, survived to be recorded by later historians and antiquaries. In such memories, the record of time is always most imprecise, the normal reckoning being by generations of kings; though in the form in which they have come down to us, transmitted by Hellenistic and later scholars, such indications more often than not have been translated into precise dates calculated on the quadrennial cycle of the Olympic games. Such precision may be deceptive and these dates are best treated as approximations only; moreover, a precise correlation between apparent dates for events in different parts of the Greek world based ultimately on different genealogies may be quite inaccurate in reality. Even so, a general pattern of development emerges that seems to belong to the second half of the eighth century. It includes the foundation of colonies overseas, where the record of the foundation date is more likely to survive with a degree of accuracy than that of an incidental event in the history of an established community;[11] and since this movement can be related to the formation of the larger units in the older Greek world, we might see here some confirmation of a comparable date.

Among the communities that develop are Sparta, which extended her control over the whole of the Eurotas valley in which she was situated and then, apparently before the end of the century, achieved at least the partial subjugation of Messenia on the other side of the substantial mountain barrier of Taygetos; Corinth, which occupied territory up to the watershed that divides the Corinthia from the Argolid, and also briefly subjugated the Megarid; and Megara, which unified itself out of five constituent villages as a counter measure to Corinthian aggression. Sparta (as a consumer, if nothing else) and Corinth are both involved in overseas trade; since there the territorial expansion and the trading are coincidental in time the interconnection is certain; both, at about this time, sent out colonies to the west to get rid of unwanted or undesirable inhabitants (rather than 'surplus' in the crude sense). In Sparta and Corinth the expansion is clearly to the economic benefit of the aggressors. The citizens of Sparta, the Spartiates, began to draw their wealth from distant estates worked for them by their helots; there is no reason to suppose that at this early stage the new estates were taken over merely to ensure the basic essentials of life. Even when the much stricter regime of Classical Sparta developed, in which wealth and the slightest signs of luxury were rejected, at least in theory, the Spartan citizen was still able to live on the labours of others. In Corinth, the new-found prosperity and the fruits of trade were the prerogative of the corresponding ruling class, the clan of the Bacchiadai,[12] who were able to exact some form of tribute from the people of the adjacent Megarid. The resumption of trading contact with the Near East had made political domination of the weaker by the stronger more economically desirable than it had been in previous, more isolated times.

Argos experienced the same pressures and developments. The concept of a politically subservient population whose labours benefited their Dorian masters already existed in the craftsman element of Argive society and, probably, in the labourers who worked on the land. It was a simple matter to extend the principle to the other communities of the Argive plain. This suggests that not only was Argos already the largest and most powerful community in the Argolid, but that she alone possessed a military aristocracy of Dorian origin. This would, in part, explain the reversal of fortune that saw the shift of power and wealth from the eastern Argolid (where it had clearly rested in the Late Bronze Age) westwards to Argos. The new pattern in the Peloponnese was essentially that in which a subordinate population supplies the needs of a military caste who are freed from the more mundane responsibilities of working for their living. This was the Dorian pattern, and it was the Dorian nuclei settled in the different regions that provided the impetus—Spartans at Sparta, Bacchiadai at Corinth, Dorians at Argos, none of whom were based on the old Bronze Age centres.

The process of expansion covers two essential stages, first the subjugation of the Argive plain, followed by the extension of authority to the separate, distinct regions adjacent to it. The chronology of the first stage cannot be recovered since it was more distinctly a matter for Argive history alone, but it ended, and heralded the beginning of the second stage, with the conquest of Asine; and that provides a point of contact with the history of Sparta. As we have seen, the Asinaia is a distinct region, though immediately adjacent to and easily accessible from the Argive plain. Its assimilation by an aggressive Argos is natural and inevitable, but such a move presupposes that Argos had already taken over Midea, Tiryns and Nauplia, which are situated in that part of the Argive plain closest to Asine. An extension of control by Argos into the Asinaia without the prior subjugation of these other communities is unreasonable. Further, Asine, as the archaeological evidence suggests, and its geographical position makes more than likely, was a substantial community which would do its best to defend itself. Thus there was likely to be a pause, of uncertain duration, between the subjugation of the Argive plain and the conquest of Asine. The fragmentary historical information that we have bears this out. The final struggle between Argos and Asine was a bitter one. When the Argives won the ultimate victory Asine was totally destroyed and the population expelled.[13] This destruction is proved archaeologically by the excavations at Asine, and dated securely towards the end of the eighth century.[14] Faced with the prospect of this destruction at the hands of a more powerful neighbour, the people of Asine had looked for help; significantly they turned to Sparta. The Spartans sent

75

an army under their king Nikandros, which attacked and ravaged the Argolid but achieved little else. When the Spartans withdrew, the Argives retaliated against Asine, and though the struggle was apparently protracted, the Spartans failed, or were unable to intervene a second time. When Asine eventually fell, all the Spartans could do was to offer its expelled populace a place of refuge in Messenia.

The involvement of Argos and Sparta, states separated from each other by many miles and high mountains, marks quite clearly the development of a new phase in Greek history. This rivalry continued throughout the Classical age, and is fundamental to Argive history. Its origins are therefore of some significance. The first collision occurred, perhaps, in the Thyreatis, the region that was to become the chief cause of contention between Argos and Sparta in Classical times; a battle was fought there at a date which later scholarship calculated to be 719/8 B.C., unless this is a projection back in time of the later, historical conflict.[15] In the reign of King Alkamenes, the Spartans attacked Helos on the coast of Lakonia, and captured it, despite help brought by the Argives. The evidence is again imprecise, a local tradition recorded by Pausanias in the second century A.D., but it at least provides a reason for the otherwise inexplicable subsequent intrusion into Argive affairs by the Spartans. The Argives retained memories of an extensive empire that they once possessed, including the east coast communities of the Peloponnese and the island of Kythera. Herodotus, who of course lived much nearer to these events than Pausanias, regarded the loss of this empire as a cause of the strife which existed between the Argives and the Spartans about the middle of the sixth century B.C.

The interpretation of this fragmentary information is fraught with difficulties. Chief among these is the undoubted confusion which it is likely had already entered into the account by Herodotus' time. The major sources of error need to be considered. First of all, the traditions were recorded after Sparta and Argos had finally emerged as major, developed and expanded city states, controlling more or less distant territory and including in their population the inhabitants of other towns and communities which had become politically subject to them. Doubtless there was a tendency to regard this as the normal and natural situation, and the existence, and loss of an early Argive empire might then seem the logical explanation of the conflict between the two communities. Secondly the developed city states of the Classical period were, in a sense, anticipated by the Late Bronze Age communities, with their complex organization; the memory of this prehistoric organization might have been confused with, or, rather, supplanted the far less spectacular early history of the Dorian villages. If the argument, that extended territorial control only makes sense in an atmosphere of economic development, is accepted, no Argive empire is likely to have existed before the archaeologically attested expansion of the eighth century. Thus the early Argive empire becomes a most shadowy creation, and a more modest interpretation of these early events seems desirable. They were, perhaps, more in the nature of piratical raids, of the sort in which the warrior of the Panoply grave, with his up-to-date armour and interest in the sea, may have engaged and lost his life.

The geographer Strabo, writing in the first century B.C., mentions cities laid waste by Argos, 'because of disobedience'.[16] Those named are Tiryns, Asine and Nauplia; a fourth name has been lost from the manuscripts, probably Midea. Strabo gives no indication as to when this happened. By the time Pausanias was writing all these places were deserted; this may have been their condition in Strabo's time, and he is merely explaining their present condition; but by Hellenistic times all three (four if we include Midea) had been firmly incorporated into the Argive state; the population of Asine consisted of Argives, not the original Asinaians.[17] The Naupliadai were citizens, and 'disobedience' resulting in such savage punishment is difficult to understand; in fact, the abandonment of these sites is more the gradual result of social and economic pressures than savage political repression. This savagery is more directly involved in the original conquest of Asine, and this suggests that, whatever Strabo himself may have believed, the 'disobedience' which was remembered in the Argolid was the original reluctance of Asine to become subject to Dorian Argos. This in turn may be an indication (but nothing more) that the expansion of Argive control into the Asinaia was associated with its extension to the eastern side of the Argive plain, and, presumably, not that far separated from it in date.

It seems preferable to suppose, then, that the creation of the larger Argive state did not begin much before the middle of the eighth century; and the involvement of Argos with Sparta should be related to this. We can, indeed, detect two parallel developments taking place at the same time, in not dissimilar circumstances, and under similar conditions. Sparta felt the same pressures as Argos at about the same period in her history, and reacted in the same way, gradually overrunning the other communities of the area in which she was situated, the Eurotas valley. Argos, meanwhile, having unified the Argolid under her control, was extending her influence among the small communities on the east coast of the Peloponnese, which were more easily accessible by ship from the Argive gulf than by land from Sparta. These communities would be particularly relevant to Argos at a time when overseas trade was being resumed, though an earlier phase of piracy is more than probable; they were also on the direct route to Crete, with which Argos can be proved at a later date to have had close connections, and which may have acted at this stage as the middleman in trade contacts between Argos and the Near East.

When Helos was threatened by Sparta, the subjugation of the Eurotas valley had not been completed. Since Argos intervened, and since Helos could turn to Argos in the first place for support, it would seem that the subjugation of the Argolid was already complete, and that Argos had extended still further. Assuming that both movements began about the same time, this can best be explained by the fact that the Argolid is the smaller of the two regions. In any case, the difference in time is likely to have been slight, because the clash came at a moment when Argos had not yet taken over Asine, and cannot have been that distant in time from the movement of Sparta against Messenia. In conclusion, it seems preferable to regard this phase of Greek history as something which developed suddenly and rapidly, rather than as a process that resulted from protracted and small scale movement. A period of fifty years or, at the very most, a century seems sufficient to bring these powers from their simple original state to one of crisis.

7   Pheidon of Argos

The Argive intervention at Helos, and the Spartan attempt to avert the fate of Asine, unsuccessful though they were, mark the beginning of the long-lasting conflict between Argos and Sparta. In the seventh century B.C., when both states had extended their authority beyond the normal, restrained geographical limits of a Greek city state, the conflict first reached serious proportions. By this time their territories had extended so that they came into contact, with only the hilly wilderness of Mount Parnon between them; so that their border disputes began to take on a more international character. Later Greek historians saw the conflict in even more fundamental terms; it was a struggle for leadership over the whole Peloponnese, and for a time the Argives succeeded in wresting that leadership from the Spartans, who, by the fifth century B.C. when things were first written down, must have appeared to hold such leadership almost by ancestral right. The phraseology is possibly an anachronism; although the struggle extended further over the Peloponnese, there are no real signs that Argos was trying to establish total domination. On the other hand, the Spartans had already assimilated, if not finally digested, the extensive area of Messenia, and the fact that the crucial battle was fought in Argive territory suggests that they were the aggressors.

This battle was at Hysiai, in an area which in later times was the scene of other combats with the Spartans, which was at times ravaged by them, but which (unlike the region next to the south, the Thyreatis) remained firmly Argive territory. It must have been incorporated into the Argive state in the eighth century extension of Argive authority. It is possible to calculate an apparently precise date for the battle. Pausanias says it was fought in the third year of the Olympiad in which Eurybotos the Athenian won the stadion race.[1] Pausanias also gave the number of the Olympiad in which Eurybotos won his victory, but the figure accidentally has been omitted in the manuscript, a failing in the transmission of Pausanias' text which undoubtedly occurs elsewhere, with important consequences for the reconstruction of Argive history. Fortunately another late author, Dionysius of Halikarnassos, records[2] that Eurybates (who is presumed to be the same man as Pausanias' Eurybotos) won the stadion race in the Olympic games, which according to our era were held in 672 B.C. The battle, therefore was fought in 669 B.C. Such a date has to be taken on trust, but there is no good reason to contravert it, and it can be correlated with other developments in Spartan history.

This was not apparently the first time that Sparta had attempted an invasion of Argive territory in her own interest, though again the reliability of the late authority that is our sole source of information cannot be proved. According to Eusebius[3] there was a battle between Argos and Sparta in the Thyreatis in the year 719/18. As we have seen, the accuracy of this information cannot be checked; but the Thyreatis, which is directly accessible from Lakonia is the obvious first point in Argive territory for the Spartans to attack; a raid here at some date prior to the invasion of Hysiai is logical. While the Argives claimed that originally it was theirs, it is possible that such a clash developed when both Argos and Sparta were extending their interests into regions that properly belonged to neither of them. The Thyreatis later became Spartan territory, but there is no reason to suppose that the Argives lost control of it as a result of this very early battle. This is very much a border dispute over territory distinct from and lying between two major powers.

The invasion of Hysiai suggests a further development. Though it is possible to enter the district from Lakonia through the passes of Mount Parnon, the simplest route is by way of Arcadia, through the territory of Tegea. A Spartan intrusion into the district of Hysiai would serve to isolate more completely this part of the central Peloponnese. The Spartans had already isolated Tegea from the south-west by their intrusion into Messenia. How Tegea reacted to Sparta at this stage in history cannot be discovered, but if Argos had priority as an enemy for Sparta it would seem to follow that relations between Sparta and the southern Arcadians were satisfactory from the Spartan point of view. Another possibility is that Argos had already become an ally of the Arcadians who were worried by the aggressive policies of Sparta in the late eighth century, and that Sparta's action against Argos, at Hysiai and, perhaps, earlier in the Thyreatis, was intended to weaken the threat that such a combination posed to her.

The consequences of the battle of Hysiai were serious enough. As a result of Argos' victory, Argive control was confirmed, not only over Hysiai but, for some time at least, the Thyreatis as well. Sparta's military prestige was shattered, and the Messenians, whose initial subjugation had been a long-drawn-out process immediately rebelled. Spartan domination in the southern Peloponnese came to an end, and, in this sense at least, it is possible to see how later history credited the Argives with wresting the leadership of the Peloponnese from the Spartans. It was many years before the Spartans were able to renew the struggle with Argos; but the memory of the rebuff they had received went deep.

Behind all these events looms the shadowy figure of the Argive king Pheidon. That Pheidon was a major figure in early Argive, and indeed, Peloponnesian history there is no reason to doubt. He is mentioned by Herodotus, as well as the later historians.[4] Aristotle knew something about his political activity, even if he mentions him only in one brief passage of the *Politics*. He was a descendant of Temenos, and Diodorus, in a passage of his seventh book, gave two versions of his genealogy. But all this only adds up to a series of disjointed scraps; there is no full, factual, coherent account of the man and his achievement, and in certain critical respects the information we have about him is contradictory. Part of the confusion seems to result from the probable existence of several people with the same name, for Aristotle knew also of a Pheidon of Corinth, and Herodotus appears to confuse him with another Pheidon who lived around 600 B.C.[5] The greatest problem concerns the date at which he lived and ruled Argos, because to understand his achievement it is essential to put him in his proper context as far as Argive history is concerned. He was remembered for abrupt and violent action, for illegally seizing control of the sanctuary at Olympia and making himself president of the Olympic games, for interfering in the internal affairs of Corinth, and perhaps of other states in the vicinity of Argos. His achievement was described as 'restoring the lot of Temenos'. Aristotle refers to him as an example of a man who, inheriting limited constitutional powers as king, extends his authority in an arbitrary and unconstitutional fashion, becoming a 'tyrant'. The most precise date for these activities is given by Pausanias,[6] who says that Pheidon interfered in the celebration of the eighth Olympic games, that is, in 748 B.C. This date can be equated, roughly, with the indications of the Temenid genealogy, which makes Pheidon tenth in descent from Temenos, and such an eighth century date for Pheidon has been defended.[7]

Another theory seeks to link Pheidon with the battle of Hysiai in 669 B.C. (although Greek history remembered Pheidon, and remembered the battle of Hysiai, the two were never connected by the ancients). Such a victory would have made possible Pheidon's march across the Peloponnese to Olympia, and the date in Pausanias can easily be explained away as the result of a faulty transmission of the text in the manuscripts: the figure 8 should in fact be 28 (that is, 668 B.C.), the Greek equivalent of 2 having dropped out of the text (we have seen another example of Pausanias' manuscripts omitting numerals). In addition, the story that Pheidon met his death at Corinth when he was involved in political strife there could be equated with the struggle which led up to the establishment there of Kypselos as tyrant, for which the conventional date recorded by the later Greek historian (Diodorus) is the equivalent to 657 B.C.

Because of the inadequate evidence, the truth will never be known for certain; but it could be argued that Pheidon's activities fit the Argos of the seventh century better than the Argos of the eighth. The concept that Pheidon restored the lot of Temenos, if it means anything, suggests either that he was responsible for the reunification of the Argive plain under Argos, that is, the first phase of Argive development, or that he was responsible for the wider extension of Argive authority, the second phase of Argive development. His involvement with Olympia seems to point to the second rather than the first phase. The argument that, archaeologically speaking, Argos seems more prosperous in the eighth century than the seventh, which has been used to support the earlier dating, is irrelevant,[8] for the sort of imperialism implied by Pheidon's involvement at Olympia and the description of him as a tyrant suggests more desperate activity at a time of over-extension in the economic sphere; tyrants come two or three generations after the great trade expansion, and as a consequence of the establishment of local domination of the sort that Argos achieved in the first phase of her development.

At the middle of the eighth century Sparta and Argos were almost certainly still involved in the establishment of their local authority.

The direct, military involvement of either in the affairs of Elis at this point of time seems anachronistic. By the seventh century the situation had changed. In order to reach Olympia Pheidon must have marched his Argive army right across the Peloponnese. Whether or not they had the prestige of victory at Hysiai, such a march would have involved the Argives with other states apart from Elis. The Arcadian community of Mantinea emerges as an ally of Argos on several occasions, just as Tegea to the south becomes, eventually, a close associate of Sparta. Pheidon's route to Olympia would have taken him over the passes of Artemision and through Mantinean territory. In the great rebellion of the Messenians against Sparta, which, with virtual certainty, was a consequence of Hysiai, they found support among the Arcadians, from Aristokrates, who was possibly king of Orchomenos (which lies next to Mantinea on Pheidon's route to Olympia) and from Pantaleon of Pisa, the community in which Olympia was situated, and which, according to Pausanias, had invited Pheidon's intervention. It would not be surprising if Sparta's original intrusion into Messenia had caused alarm amongst other Peloponnesian states; and that some form of agreement (formal alliance is perhaps too strong a term, and, as always, the evidence is too scanty for certainty) had been entered into by them, an agreement in which the king of Argos played a prominent part. If such an agreement was developing, it can only have caused some alarm at Sparta; the friendship with Tegea and Elis may have been the result. It is thus possible to put the battle of Hysiai in a more intelligible context. It was memorable because the battle was fought as no mere border dispute, but as a political act, an attempt by the Spartans to strike at the heart of an Argive alliance which threatened their interest. Spartan fears, which recur again and again in later Greek history, of what could be achieved by Argos as the leader of a rival Peloponnesian alliance to her own, were surely rooted firmly in the history of seventh century Argos. It seems not unreasonable to attribute this, the true restoration of the lot of Temenos, to his descendant Pheidon.

Argos gained surprisingly little from her victory at Hysiai. The anti-Spartan coalition, such as it was, never acted effectively. The Messenians seem to have maintained their independence for a time, supported by Aristokrates the Arcadian; but at the final battle he deserted them and, in isolation, the Messenians were once more forced under the domination of Sparta.

It would seem that Argos' actions up to Hysiai were essentially defensive; but there were certainly people in Argos who were more ambitious for their city, who wanted her to take upon herself a role similar to that of Sparta. The grandson of Pheidon, Meltas, who was the last of the Temenid kings to rule in Argos, was driven from the city because he gave land to the Arcadians that the Argives wanted for themselves. We may discern here an attempt by the king to thwart the territorial ambitions of the Dorian aristocrats of the city, and their angry reaction to this. The chronology of this event is, naturally, as obscure as that of Pheidon himself. Much clearer is a distinct anti-Argive reaction in the north-east Peloponnese. The Argives had apparently involved themselves in the internal affairs of Corinth, in events which led to the death of Pheidon, and this would appear to have roused suspicion concerning Argive policy. Perhaps the suspicion went even deeper. In 657 B.C. (again, a traditional date the authenticity of which cannot be checked) the Bacchiadai, the Dorian aristocratic clan that ruled Corinth, were overthrown by Kypselos, who set himself up as a tyrant. The cause of this is to be sought in the internal affairs of Corinth, but it is noticeable that Kypselos' son Periander was married to Melissa, grand-daughter of Aristokrates of Arcadia. The name of Kypselos' father Aetion also has possible connections with Arcadia, and his identification as a 'Lapith' may equally betoken some kinship with the non-Dorian peoples of the central Peloponnese. The revolution at nearby Sikyon had a definite anti-Dorian, anti-Argive aspect. Kleisthenes, the tyrant in the early sixth century, renamed the Dorian tribes Pigmen, Assmen, Swinemen (while his own, non-Dorian tribe became the Archelaoi, the rulers of the people).[9] He also attempted to get rid of Adrastos, an Argive, whose shrine was situated in the agora of Sikyon and formed the centre of a cult. There was also a tyrant at Epidauros, Prokles, who was the father of Periander's wife Melissa, and also related to Aristokrates.

In effect, these developments mark the end of Argive territorial ambitions at least until the fourth century B.C. From this time until the very end of the Classical era Argos was more concerned to hold what was already hers. Only Sparta permanently controlled what was in reality a separate region of Greece, and held it in subjection. The strain profoundly affected her character as a city state.

When Messenia was eventually subdued the Spartans made, in the next century, one more half-hearted attempt at territorial aggrandizement, at the expense of Tegea. It failed dismally, though strangely the failure did not, as far as we know, have the same effect as Hysiai in undermining Spartan supremacy in Messenia. From this time also, Sparta had learnt the lesson; the acquisition of additional territory by reducing an erstwhile free Greek population to subject status was not practical politics on the Greek mainland, and though Sparta was to fight Argos again, and on at least one occasion inflict a devastating defeat on her, she never attempted to destroy Argos as a state, or incorporate her territory into her own, except for intervening territory on her immediate borders.

With the gradual evolution of a *status quo* in mainland Greece, there was a growing tendency towards more egalitarian regimes in the city states. The demand for a redistribution of land, its more equal sharing among the populations, begins to feature in Greek political life. This is particularly noticeable in the cities which were governed for a time by tyrants. At Corinth, for example, the tyrants expelled the land-holding Bacchiadai, whose estates were presumably forfeited and redistributed. There are other signs of egalitarianism at Corinth. Wealthy women were prevented, by force if need be, from wearing luxurious clothes; there was a commission, or so we are told, to prevent people living beyond their means; migration to the city (in search of work, presumably, the sign of a dispossessed peasantry) was forbidden, so that the poorer inhabitants would not sell out their land in the hope of finding lucrative employment in the city. Even when the tyrants eventually outlived their usefulness, there was no attempt to return to the previous situation, where one group controlled all the affairs of the city; instead, a new system of tribes was devised not apparently based on the old Dorian divisions, but artificially created to unite citizens of different origins.

This did not happen at Sparta. The Spartans, notoriously, were opposed to the tyrants, at the end of the sixth century, at least, suppressing this form of administration wherever possible. Sparta remained, unlike the cities of the tyrants, a state in which a minority had citizen privileges, and ruled over a subject majority. The Spartans successfully withstood pressures towards egalitarianism. In the end, more and more effort had to be devoted to this purpose, and for this reason the Spartan regime, with its emphasis on military skill and preparedness, was strengthened and maintained.

Thus we have two extremes—the 'tyrant' states on the one hand in which distinctions of status appear not to have been too extreme, and Sparta where they most certainly were. To which pattern does Argos belong? We have seen Argos develop in much the same way as Sparta, indeed possibly forming a precedent and prototype for the extended Spartan state. By the fifth century, Argos became the ally of democratic Athens, but this alliance resulted more from Argive hostility towards Sparta than out of any sympathy the Argives of the fifth century might have felt for democratic principles. At Argos there is no artificial redivision of the tribes to obscure the distinctions between Dorian and non-Dorian. Hylleis, Pamphyloi and Dymanes still occur in the inscriptions of the Hellenistic Age so there can have been no attempt to obscure them in the seventh or sixth century. When non-Dorians at last acquired citizen status, they were enrolled in a separate, fourth tribe, the Hyrnathioi. It is possible that Pheidon extended the basis of recruitment for the Argive army, enrolling non-Dorians into a new military system (see below p. 180). This might have provided a starting-off point for a political re-organization, but if so, it hardly outlived Pheidon's death, the consequence of which would seem to have been a reaction to the pre-Pheidonian system. Argos remained in the seventh and the sixth century, like Sparta, a state of Dorian domination, where there was a privileged citizen body, and a subject population, even within the Argolid itself. The distinction is only one of scale; Sparta controlled wider territories, and, by the sixth century, had a subject population proportionally much larger in comparison with the citizen numbers than Argos. Though Argos gradually lost ground to Sparta, she was still a flourishing city, in which the arts flourished (as can be seen from Chapter 21). She should not be judged, as has been done, by the decline of her pottery industry in the face of Corinthian competition.

8 Argos from the end of the seventh century to the Persian wars

No significant change can be seen in the fortunes of Argos during the remainder of the seventh century. The chronological distinction into centuries is, of course, quite artificial, depending on the Christian era, and in itself is meaningless in the context of early Greek history; yet there is a difference between the centuries, and particularly between the seventh and the sixth, that is relevant to the historian. One difference is artistic: the sixth century, all over Greece, marks the full flowering of archaic art. Life-size sculptures became an important part of Greek artistic achievement. Stone temples are built in the principal towns and sanctuaries. There is a discernible change in the quality of the historical record. Herodotus wrote his history of the Persian invasion of Greece about the middle of the fifth century B.C. He was naturally concerned to give an account of events leading up to that conflict, and this involved him in some discussion of the history of Greece in what we term the sixth century B.C. Moreover, by questioning people older than himself he could speak with a generation actually born in that century, and who had themselves heard of the earlier doings of that century at first hand. Thus the sixth century is much closer to recorded history than the seventh; events begin to take on a clearer significance, even if there is still much obscurity.

Unfortunately, as far as Argos is concerned, the obscurity is almost impenetrable. Argos kept aloof from the Persian wars, and Herodotus did not have to seek far for the reason; her implacable hatred of Sparta, which had been heightened by the catastrophic defeat the Spartan king Kleomenes had inflicted on her at the battle of Sepeia. Into the causes of that battle, Herodotus made little enquiry. Yet it is a culminating point in a long-drawn-out dispute, whose origins we have discerned in the events that led up to Hysiai and whose consequences continued to exert their influence on Greek history for several centuries to come. Herodotus first mentions the conflict in the first book of his *History*.[1] Kroisos, king of Lydia, engaged in war with the newly-formed Persian empire and besieged in his capital Sardis, looked to Greece for help. He approached Sparta who, Herodotus tells us, at that time (that is, at about the middle of the sixth century) was in strife with Argos over the Thyreatis. It is at this point that Herodotus describes the full extent of the Argive empire, including the east coast of the Peloponnese down to Cape Malea, the island of Kythera and 'the other islands', though the significance of this description is not that Herodotus believed that the Argives actually controlled all this immediately prior to the events of the mid-sixth century, but that this was in previous time the full extent of Argive power, which already, perhaps, had been eroded somewhat, and which might even belong to the epic days, not of Dorian Argos, but of Agamemnon.

In pursuit of this conflict, the Spartans had already seized the Thyreatis, which was part of the Argolid. The Argives sent an army to recover it, but instead of fighting a pitched battle with their full forces, came to an agreement with the Spartans that three hundred champions should be selected from each side and that the land should be given to whoever won. In the battle all but two of the Argives were killed, all but one of the Spartans. The Argives therefore went back to Argos, claiming the victory: the one Spartan remained, and claimed that since he had been left in possession victory was his. Both the armies came out again, since the victory was disputed, and after many on both sides had died, the Spartans were victorious. As a sign of mourning, from that time the Argives cut their hair short (and Herodotus implies they still did in his time) and forbade their women to wear gold ornaments, while the Spartans on the contrary, from that time began to wear their hair long. Othryadas, the sole survivor of the Spartan three hundred, was ashamed that he had lived when his companions had all died, and refused to return to Sparta; he remained in the Thyreatis.

Such a story appears to have been romanticized. The idea of two Greek cities of the sixth century deciding a territorial dispute by a battle of selected champions is, to say the least, odd. There are close parallels with the Spartan rearguard action at Thermopylai, where three hundred picked men—the royal bodyguard—fought to the last (actually combing their long hair before battle), only one surviving, and he, too, refusing from shame to return to Sparta. His shame was real; his companions had been trapped, and the fight then was to the death, but it is difficult to see why Othryadas should be so ashamed of his survival, especially as his trick enabled the Spartans to win land they had otherwise lost.

Even if we assume that the reality was much simpler, and that something which started as little more than a small-scale border raid by a regularly sized sub-division of the Spartan army was subsequently rendered more serious by the clash of the main citizen forces of Sparta and Argos, it is necessary to see why this romanticizing came about, especially as Herodotus appears to date the dispute to the years around 550 B.C. (that is, almost within living memory of the time he wrote). It is obviously true that Herodotus' information about affairs in the Peloponnese that did not involve Athens is comparatively scanty. In several important topics he is confused—the dating of Pheidon and his son is one of them—and he often appears to have had access to romanticized, folk-tale versions of events rather than personal or family traditions handed down factually within a limited circle—the stories he attaches to the history of Kypselos and the tyranny at Corinth are good examples of this. Yet these belong to remoter times than the mid-sixth century. Certainly the attribution of what would seem to be long-standing customs (such as the length of Argive and Spartan hair) to single and relatively recent events in history, which has parallels elsewhere in Herodotus, appears to be an anachronistic simplification caused by a desire to rationalize and explain all historical phenomena within the limited range of his knowledge. If it is possible that Herodotus' Argive empire belongs to a more remote period of time than the context in which it was mentioned, then we might also translate the 'battle of the champions' back into the remoter origins of the dispute over the Thyreatis. The main battle is a different matter. Argos seems to have suffered defeat and the Thyreatis passed under Spartan control.

In the sixth century, the position of Sparta in the Peloponnese had strengthened. With Messenia now firmly under her control, her citizens could devote themselves entirely to the arts of war. The freedom they now possessed from the need to till their own lands was not simply a release from degrading and unmilitary occupation—Athenian hoplites did not fight less well for being recruited from the peasant farmers of Attica. The crucial difference is rather the amount of time they could devote to training and preparation, and the cohesion of the Spartan hoplites as a fighting force derived from this. Early in the century the Spartans had been involved in the war with their Arcadian neighbour Tegea; they suffered a surprise defeat, and the fetters in which the Tegeates bound their Spartan prisoners were preserved in their chief temple and shown to later visitors.[2] Spartan purpose in fighting this war was still, it would seem, the desire to subjugate even more territory to their domination, for the fetters had been brought with them by the Spartans, who expected to turn the Tegeates into helots. The fact of the defeat is a surprising one; perhaps the expedition, like that to the Thyreatis, consisted only of a sub-division of the Spartan army. Otherwise we must suppose that Sparta was opposed by a much larger force than that mustered by Tegea alone; for never again could Tegea, from her own resources, successfully withstand the Spartan military machine. In this case, a wider Arcadian alliance, perhaps still supported by Argos, is the easiest explanation of the victory and it is certainly the easiest explanation of the otherwise surprising fact that Sparta did not seek vengeance for the setback, but contented herself with making Tegea her ally; it was enough to detach Tegea from the anti-Spartan alliance, to divide the Arcadians amongst themselves.

The drive against Argos is similar in pattern, and some sympathy of interest between Argos and Tegea is natural in these circumstances. Possession by Sparta of the Thyreatis helped her to dominate Tegea, isolating her more abruptly from the sea, and this also fits a time when Spartan policy was still one of territorial aggrandizement. The capture of the region was a distinct blow to Argive prestige and it is not surprising that Tegea was, on the whole, confirmed in her loyalty to Sparta. From this time, the Spartan land greed seems to have been satisfied, and there are no further extensions of territory. As in the tyrant-ruled cities the need for extra land was held in check by restrictions on the acquisition of luxury articles. The archaeological evidence suggests that the notorious Spartan austerity began during the sixth century B.C.[3] The policy of territorial expansion had strangled itself; the subject people had to be held under control, no more land could be assimilated into the Spartan system and held, and the desire for luxuries had to be restrained. The wealth of Sparta now had to be devoted to the upkeep of her professional citizen army.

In place of territorial expansion a struggle developed for leadership and the formation of alliances. Sparta sought to protect herself from the dangers of war with external armies by alliances in the Peloponnese. Friendship with at least some of the Arcadians was the cornerstone of this policy. This meant that the Messenian helots had little hope of assistance should they rebel, while the danger of a substantial anti-Spartan alliance between Argos and the Arcadians was averted. It was now Spartan policy to maintain this situation. Conversely, Sparta was threatened not only by the danger of a helot rising, but also by the possibility of a successful anti-Spartan alliance, based on Arcadia and Argos. The need to restrict the risks of such an alliance were now far more important.

Argos in her turn was able to tolerate neither the risk of potential isolation nor the loss of territory which had been hers, perhaps since the close of the eighth century, if not before. She sought allies elsewhere. There had always been tenuous connections with Athens. From early time Argive potters seem to have been aware of developments made by their Athenian counterparts. This is certainly true in Geometric pottery and there are possible connections between post-Geometric pottery in Attica and the Argolid. In the sixth century, there is definite evidence that Argos sought a counterbalance to Spartan supremacy by an Athenian alliance, a policy that was to recur in the fifth century. In his final return to power the Athenian tyrant Peisistratos was aided by soldiers hired from various parts of the Greek world; they included soldiers from Argos.[4] It is unlikely that these were mercenaries in the conventional sense, individuals who hired themselves out for foreign military service; more likely the Argives sent troops on the understanding that their expenses would be met from Peisistratos' private fortune. The date of Peisistratos' tyrannies are a notorious crux of sixth century history, though the final return cannot be earlier than 546 B.C., and some scholars have suggested a later date. Whenever it was, the loan of mercenaries came after the loss of Thyreatis. Argos may then have had population problems (though the loss of life in the struggle for the Thyreatis must have been heavy) but it is surprising that these troops were hired to another power rather than used for a war of revenge in the Peloponnese. Perhaps the risks were too great, Sparta too powerful and the potential rewards of friendship with the ruler of Athens greater. Peisistratos also had more personal relations with Argos; the man he appointed tyrant of Sigeion (in the Hellespont) was Hegesistratos, his bastard son by 'an Argive woman'. It is possible also that Argos was ruled at this time by a tyrant called Perilaos.[5] Sparta's antipathy to tyrants was notorious, and would seem based on practical, rather than ideological grounds. The tyrants were opposed not merely because they were tyrants, but because they were associated with the reaction against Spartan leadership.

The Athenian tyranny was overthrown in 510 B.C. through the intervention of Kleomenes, the Spartan king, and a small Spartan army. Kleomenes' subsequent intervention in Athens and his expulsion are irrelevant incidentals to his career; the first intervention was more serious. Kleomenes' whole policy seems concerned to strengthen the claims of Sparta to the leadership of the Greek mainland, the cause being not so much the return of Spartan greed and desire for aggrandizement, as an awareness of the need to unite the Greeks in the face of the growing menace of Persia. The first Persian invasion of Greece was the campaign of Marathon in 490 B.C., but the reality of the Persian menace had been obvious ever since the destruction of the Lydian kingdom in 546, and the absorption of the eastern Greeks into the Persian empire. In the 520s Persia had conquered Egypt, and removed Polykrates, tyrant of Samos, whose fleet constituted one of the chief barriers to Persian expansion by sea across the Aegean. Subsequently Sparta is credited (in a curious list that records the successive powers that controlled the seas[6]) with a naval policy that led to her dominating the Aegean. It suggests that she was already making preparations in the face of the threat from Persia.

After his expulsion, the Athenian tyrant Hippias, son of Peisistratos, found refuge in the Persian empire. When the Athenians were threatened with further unwanted Spartan intervention they looked for help to Persia, even though, in the event, the terms on which it was offered made it unacceptable. Already the distant power of Persia was being suggested as a possible counterbalance to Sparta. In the first decade of the fifth century she had moved into Thrace and Macedonia. She was on the borders of mainland Greece itself, she had a powerful fleet, and the danger of invasion was increasing. The prospects to be gained from collaboration with Persia must have been very tempting.

Kleomenes went to some lengths to win the support of the Peloponnesians who had looked, perhaps, to the existing government of

Argos for leadership. At Athens he had proclaimed himself to be not a Dorian but an Achaean,[7] stressing his descent from the Herakleidai, who, by tradition if not by fact, were, as we have seen, assimilated into the Achaeans of the Bronze Age Argolid. This has been interpreted as a reaction against Dorian supremacy, even at Sparta itself. Kleomenes certainly died in disgrace, ousted from his office as king, and possibly involved in an attempt to rouse the Messenian helots in rebellion[8] (whether or not he was actually successful); but these stories may result only from the hostile accounts of him circulated by his enemies after his fall from power. It is unlikely that Kleomenes would have dominated Spartan affairs for so long if he had been essentially anti-Dorian.

At this moment, almost certainly in the year 494 B.C., Kleomenes struck at Argos.[9] With the Spartan army, he set off for Argos by the obvious, direct route. At the river Erasinos he was checked, according to Herodotus, because the sacrifices he made did not have a satisfactory outcome (a more prosaic explanation might be that his advance along the narrow section of plain between the mountains and the sea was here checked by the Argive army). He was therefore forced to withdraw, back to the Thyreatis. He was then able to transport his army by sea, across the gulf of Argos to the territory of Tiryns and Nauplia, where he disembarked. Herodotus remarks subsequently that the Argives had a quarrel with the people of Aigina, because of the help they had rendered to Kleomenes in this campaign. Since at the Battle of Salamis in 480 B.C. the Aiginetans had the next largest fleet after the Athenians (whose fleet had been built only in the years immediately preceding that battle), the service the Aiginetans rendered the Spartans on this occasion was presumably the provision of warships to transport (or at least escort) the Spartan army to Nauplia. The Argive army took up position at Sepeia, close to Tiryns. For some time the armies faced each other, until Kleomenes realized that the Argives understood the signals made to the Spartan army, and were acting in accordance with them. He therefore ordered that when next the signal for breakfast was given, the meaning would be changed; instead the Spartans were to take up arms and charge the Argives. This happened. The Argives, expecting the Spartans to be at breakfast, and so taking theirs also, were caught completely unawares. Many were slaughtered, more fled to a sacred grove (called, confusingly, Argos) where they were trapped by the Spartans. Fifty of them were induced to leave, on being given the false news that they had been ransomed (at the standard Peloponnesian rate of two minas per head) and were put to death, before the remainder found out what was happening. Kleomenes then forced his helots (so that he should not himself be guilty of sacrilege) to set fire to the grove.

The battle and the subsequent un-Greek acts of treachery and sacrilege gave Kleomenes complete control of the Argolid. He was able to send home the bulk of his army and, escorted only by a thousand picked men, went to the Heraion to sacrifice. Here he was forbidden by the priest (not, notice, the priestess) on the grounds that it was not lawful for a foreigner to sacrifice. Again Kleomenes committed sacrilege: he ordered his helot attendants to whip the priest from the altar, and conducted the sacrifice himself. He then returned home.

This is the account of Herodotus. Pausanias gives some additional details.[10] After the battle, and the massacre in the grove of Argos, Telesilla, a distinguished Argive poetess, organized the resistance in Argos town. She gathered the slaves, and the 'old and young' citizens, those of the age group which did not fight in the field, and armed them with the weapons that had been deposited in the sanctuaries and elsewhere. In addition she armed the women, and placed them where it was anticipated that the Spartans would attack. The Spartans were nonplussed, not so much by the spirited signs of resistance, but by the disgrace that would attach to them if they were known to fight women (as if their previous activity had not been disgraceful enough) and so they withdrew. This, says Pausanias, is the explanation of an oracular response made jointly to the Argives and the Milesians and recorded by Herodotus, whether he understood it or not.

The role of Telesilla may have been exaggerated. It was not abnormal, when a direct assault on a city was threatened, for the women to participate in a last ditch defence[11] (the terror and timidity shown by the Spartan women when Sparta herself was at last threatened was commented on). That the Spartans hesitated to attack Argos town is not surprising; hoplites were ill-suited to house to house warfare, and the danger of missiles being dropped from house roofs was something no hoplite could adequately guard against, as we shall see later, when the Epirote king Pyrrhus tried to storm Argos itself. If Argos was walled at this time, a direct attack would be next to impossible, but although Pausanias mentions walls, there is always the possibility this is an anachronism made by an author writing when Argos had been walled for many centuries. In short, the activities at Argos are what would be expected, and, were it not for the unexplained oracle in Herodotus, there would have been no need to devise the explanation that Pausanias gives.

More difficult to explain is Kleomenes' behaviour. In the end, Kleomenes was to be driven out of Sparta, and explained away as a madman.[12] The emphasis placed in Herodotus on Kleomenes' sacrilegious and other unbalanced acts suggests that this is part of the Spartan apologia—he was not even man enough to commit sacrilege himself, but ordered his helots to do it on his behalf. Kleomenes' activities could easily be interpreted, or misinterpreted, as a bid for personal power. At Athens, he claimed the right to sacrifice to Athena, at the Argive Heraion; after the battle of Sepeia, he assumed by force the right to sacrifice to Hera. His claim to Achaean ancestry, when challenged as a Dorian intruder by the priestess at Athens, may only have been a polite witticism; but the argument that lay behind it was that of the single descent of the Heraklid kings; and since the Spartans had eliminated the Messenian royal family, and the Argives had themselves driven out the descendants of Temenos, the Spartan kings alone represented the Heraklid line. Certainly somebody at Sparta suspected his ambitions and the opposition to him was eventually successful; but even after his disgrace and death the policy that he represented, the establishment of Spartan hegemony over all Greece, was accepted by at least a significant section of the Spartan people, even though, for reasons beyond Spartan control, it was impractical in the changed circumstances caused by the defeat of the Persians. That defeat, moreover, was achieved by those Greeks who were, for whatever reason, unified under Spartan leadership. Whatever Kleomenes' personal motives, there can be little doubt that his policies were correct, and the basis of Greece's salvation.

In 494 B.C. the Ionian rebellion against Persian domination was coming to an end. The Persian military machine had suffered some setbacks but its inexorable strength had retrieved the situation. The future of Greek independence must have seemed dubious in the extreme. How far the Persians were already involved in negotiations with the free Greeks is not known. Such negotiations would doubtless be secret and unofficial, with prominent individuals rather than governments, and conducted by unobtrusive intermediaries. That the Greek and Persian worlds were free from contact of this sort is unthinkable, even if the historians know next to nothing about them. The idea of seeking Persian subvention to redress the balance in Greece was established; and to Argos, whose authority and territory had been eroded by Spartan success in the sixth century, the temptation of Persian support was doubtless considerable. If Spartan policy was to strengthen Greece, Argos had to be considered. That Argos would sink her differences with Sparta was unthinkable, except on conditions that would cause such loss of prestige to Sparta that they could not be countenanced; when, at the eleventh hour, the Spartans proposed co-operation, the Argives insisted on joint leadership of the Greeks.

The alternative was to eliminate Argos as a source of danger. Kleomenes' harshness towards the Argives, his ruthless pursuit of the beaten Argive army, are due to more than a cruel and unbalanced element in his personal character. The impression given by Herodotus is that the Argive army before the battle was regarded by the Spartans as virtually equal to their own; Kleomenes had to take advantage of a surprise to gain the upper hand, and if the failure to cross the Erasinos was due to more than religious obstruction, the Argive army was probably the cause. The policy was to neutralize Argos militarily and politically, but not to destroy her completely, for such an act would have outraged even those Greek states which regarded Argos as an enemy; particularly it would have upset the Athenians, who were not wholeheartedly anti-Persian, and whose co-operation was vital.

The Argive losses at Sepeia were put at six thousand; comparison with the size of the armies put into the field by Athens, Sparta and Corinth during the Persian wars suggest that this represents the entire body of male citizens of military age. That the loss was as total as this has been doubted, and with reason,[13] but that the real loss, whatever it was numerically, represented a major catastrophe for Argos there can be little doubt. Though fourteen years were to pass before the Persians confronted the Spartans and their allies with a major army, when that happened the Argives were still powerless to intervene. By that time the age group that was too young to fight at Sepeia constituted half the normal numbers of the Argive army; the implication is that the losses in the older age group were very serious indeed. From the wider point of view, the presumption must be that this was beneficial to the Greeks, where resistance to Persia would have been seriously impeded if Argos had remained an effective force in Greek politics at the time of the invasion.

As it was, Argos was unable to retain control even over the Argolid. Exactly what happened is obscure. Herodotus gives a brief account of the consequences, all of which he sets in the period before the Persian invasion of 480 B.C. Argos, he says, was 'emptied of men', with the result that 'the slaves' ('douloi') controlled everything (these, presumably, the same slaves that Telesilla is supposed to have armed in the last ditch defence of Argos town). They ruled and administered the state, having married the widows of the Argives killed in the battle until the children of the Argives slaughtered at Sepeia came of age. When this happened, the 'slaves' seized Tiryns after a fight, and set themselves up in independence. For a while there was friendship between the slaves and the Argives, until the prophet Kleander, who came from Phigaleia in western Arcadia, urged the slaves to fight their masters. As a result there was a long period of war which the Argives eventually won.

The problems that Herodotus' narrative creates are considerable. The chief difficulty is the identification of the 'slaves'. It would appear from the manner in which they were organized for the last ditch defence of Argos (whether or not it took a poetess to achieve this) that at the time of the battle they were at Argos town, along with the 'old and the young'. It would also seem that they were unarmed; that is, they belonged to a class not allowed to possess hoplite weapons nor able to afford them, and they had to be given these from the sanctuaries (which in other cities also, such as Athens, served in effect as reserve armouries). At the time of the Persian invasion of Greece both Tiryns and Mycenae were able to act independently of Argos, and sent small contingents of hoplites (a total of four hundred men) to the allied army. Herodotus has perhaps confused this assertion of independence with events in Argos itself. Quite clearly the war between the slaves at Tiryns and the Argives had not ended at the time of the Persian invasion, though Herodotus may have been anticipating the eventual outcome after the invasion when he wrote this section—the strict chronological context of the passage should not be pressed. Aristotle,[14] referring to these events calls the people who took over the government of Argos the 'perioikoi'. This is a term which elsewhere[15] applied to the

97

Cretan cities, he equates with the helots of Sparta. At Sparta the term 'perioikoi' came to be applied (but not by Aristotle) to the citizens of the outlying town, which did not have full citizen rights, but were certainly not reduced to the status of helots. This has perhaps added to the confusion. In theory it is possible to distinguish between the agricultural labourers, 'slaves' of the Argive citizens, who worked on the farms that surrounded Argos town[16] and, on the other hand, the inhabitants of outlying districts such as Mycenae and the other communities of the eastern Argolid. In Hellenistic times Mycenae can be proved to have possessed its own political institutions, assembly of the people and magistrates; unfortunately these cannot be traced back to the early fifth century B.C. (even though they are denoted in the later epigraphic evidence by the traditional terms so it is not possible to say whether these institutions are a continuation of the early system, or a revival. The archaeological record at Mycenae, Tiryns and Asine suggests that the towns, as urban centres, were abandoned, and Herodotus' account of how the 'slaves' seized the citadel at Tiryns bears this out. There is thus a probability that, along with the urban centres, the political institutions of these communities were extinguished by the Argives, so that their people became, in political status, indistinguishable from the agricultural 'slaves' of the Argives. To Aristotle therefore, they were 'perioikoi' in the 'Cretan' sense, to Herodotus they were 'douloi', and both meant, despite the differing terms, the same thing.

Plutarch, however, 'corrects' Herodotus.[17] The people who took over Argos, and married the husbandless women of the dead citizens were not slaves but 'perioikoi' in the more usual sense, the citizens of the outlying communities who possessed local political rights. Plutarch, of course, was writing long after these events, and after profound changes in the social and political organization of Greece: to him, 'slave' meant a purchased slave, bought in the international slave markets and normally of non-Greek origin. Such people had fought for Athens, as rowers in her fleet at the desperate engagement of Arginousai, in the closing stages of the war with Sparta, so it was not unthinkable (to a later writer) that comparable people should have been armed to fight for Argos in her hour of need; but it was unthinkable that they should marry the proud women of Dorian Argos, and so Herodotus (argues Plutarch) was incorrect in describing them as 'slaves'. The identification of the slaves with the

Argive equivalent to the helot class obviates this difficulty. It is equally possible that Plutarch was misinterpreting Aristotle, in accepting his term 'perioikoi' as a correction of Herodotus' 'slaves' rather than its equivalent.

Yet even if there is no political distinction between the two groups, there may have been a social one. The Dorian citizens of Argos possessed landed estates, which varied in size. The largest, belonging to the most prominent citizens, must have been worked for them by labourers (though the lesser citizens still probably tilled their own fields); these labourers are, of course, the 'slaves', and are certainly included in those who were involved in the last ditch defence of Argos after Sepeia. It is also possible that some 'slaves' possessed their own estates, at least in the sense that they had tenure of occupation, and that this normally passed from father to son on a hereditary basis, paying a proportion of their produce to a Dorian 'landlord'. The slaughter of the 'landlord' class at Sepeia thus created an abnormal situation for these people, and it has been suggested, not only that the solution to this was the marriage of these 'slaves' to the womenfolk of the deceased 'landlords' (so that children might be born who would then inherit the title to the land) but that such marriages were part of Argive law, a traditionally enforced solution to a problem which no doubt recurred on a smaller scale throughout earlier Argive history, but which became particularly prominent after the abnormal losses of the Dorian citizen body following Sepeia.[18] If 'douloi' of this class were more numerous in the areas of the outlying communities, which seems implied in Aristotle's use of the term 'perioikoi' to describe them, then the source of the confusion is more easily appreciated.

It would seem, then, that the outlying population took over Argos, in at least the sense that they dominated the city in numbers, for they had suffered no losses in the battle. This domination declined, not so much perhaps when the children of any marriages they had contracted with the womenfolk of the Dorians came of age, but when the existing younger generation of Dorians born before the battle came to maturity. The consequence of this was that instead the 'slaves' asserted the independence of the original communities to which they belonged, those of the eastern Argolid.

About the time of the Persian invasion of Attica that ended with the battle of Marathon—in other words, not long after Sepeia— the island of Aigina, faced with an attack mounted by the Athenians appealed to Argos as an old ally for help. The Argives refused, not on the ground that as a consequence of Sepeia they were powerless to intervene, but because the people of Aigina had helped Kleomenes at the time of that battle. Nevertheless, there was a certain section of the Argive citizen body which was dissatisfied at this decision, and volunteered, to the numbers of a thousand, to go to the aid of the Aiginetans. There they were all caught and killed. If Sepeia was so disastrous, it seems strange that Argos was still considered a potential source of help in a foreign war. That the Argives went to Aigina to the number of a thousand is not quite incompatible with severe loss at Sepeia, since some of the young men would now be of military age. But if the figures for the soldiers available to Mycenae and Tiryns are correct, even a thousand young men should have been sufficient to reduce the rebels once more to submission; it seems strange that they should choose instead to lose their lives in a campaign that would be of little benefit to Argos. The fact that their intervention was voluntary suggests a political division in the state; on the other hand, contingents of a thousand are the normal size of units sent officially by the Argive state to help her allies.[19] In addition it is hard to see why, if the rulers of Argos were still the 'slaves' who had been put in power by the consequences of Sepeia, they should choose to ignore the appeal of Aigina because Aigina had helped to bring that situation about. If the thousand volunteers had come from the former Dorian predominant class their hatred for the ally of their destroyer Kleomenes should have discouraged them from going to Aigina's aid, rather than the reverse; yet, as the suppression of Aigina in its turn had the backing of Kleomenes, their willingness to help is perhaps not so surprising. Indeed, it is possible that the 'volunteers' went with the approval of a city which was prevented against its will from official intervention; and that, despite the upheaval in Argos, the introduction of a new element into the governing classes did not in the least lessen Argos' hatred of Sparta. The losses on Aigina would have set back still further Argos' recovery, and her abstention from active support of Persia a decade later is the more easily understood. The immunity of Mycenae and Tiryns from attack even at the time when Argos could raise an army of a thousand can best be explained by these states having a defensive alliance with Sparta, which in turn led the little towns to offer their help at the time of the Persian invasion.

After the Persian defeat, Sparta was mistress of Greece.[1] Under her leadership, the fleets and armies of the allied Greeks had saved the Greek world. Nobody was in a position to challenge her authority. No state in Greece had a better army, and although the military victory over Persia had been made possible only by the size and fighting qualities of the Athenian fleet, on which the Greeks continued to depend, Athens herself had been destroyed by the Persians, lying ruined and unfortified. It was hardly an opportune moment for Argos to challenge Spartan supremacy, even to the extent of attempting the re-unification of the Argolid.

Spartan policy naturally was to maintain her supremacy. This supremacy depended on three circumstances. First of all, it resulted from the high quality of her citizen hoplites, backed by the perioikoi (serving as soldiers) and the helots. Secondly, given that her army could never be numerically superior to the rest of Greece, Sparta needed the local support of allies. Thirdly, it was desirable that states which were enemies or potential rivals for power should be kept as weak as possible so that any threat they represented would not become an actuality. We have seen how this policy was carried out in the case of Argos. So long as Sparta's interests were confined to the Peloponnese, there appeared no serious challenge. The difficulty was caused by the extension of her affairs to include the defence of Greece against the expected renewal of the Persian onslaught. This in turn made it essential for her to have the continued support of the Athenian fleet, and to take Athens, a major city lying outside the Peloponnese, into her sphere of influence. Athens was nominally an ally; but the alliance had been formed for the defence of Greece, not the advancement of Sparta, and unlike the other Spartan allies she was potentially (if not in the actual circumstances of 478) Sparta's equal. Indeed, possession of the largest fleet in Greece made her in certain directions Sparta's superior, a fact that was obvious both to Sparta and Athens herself. So the third cornerstone of Sparta's policy had to be applied. Athens was a potential rival, and had to be kept as weak as possible. The device was the request that Athens should not rebuild her walls, leaving her exposed to the risk of Spartan punitive action. As soon as these walls were rebuilt (an achievement which Thucydides credits to the wiles and diplomacy of Themistokles) and as soon as it became obvious that the eastern Greeks would not allow themselves to be evacuated back to the mainland, as Sparta wanted, but would instead join a naval alliance led by Athens, Sparta's brief moment of complete supremacy had slipped from her. From this time on the most she could hope for, until circumstances changed at the end of the century, was for a divided leadership, Athens superior by sea, but recognizing Sparta's right to dominate in the Peloponnese. Spartan authority had declined a little, but so long as Athens was prepared to accept this division of leadership, the hopes of Argos were not very good.

Nevertheless, Argos began to stage a surprising recovery. This belongs essentially to the period after the Persian wars, and ends in 451 B.C. During this time Argos undertook a successful war against Mycenae and Tiryns, which ended in their subjugation; the Argolid was now reunified under Argive control, and remained so. Argos also became involved in an anti-Spartan alliance in the Peloponnese, involving 'all the Arcadians except Mantinea' and in which Tegea played a prominent part. As a result the Spartans were forced to fight two battles, one near Tegea against an army comprised of Tegeate and Argive troops, the other, at a place called Dipaia, against Arcadians only, without Mantinea and without Argos. Although at the end of the period Argos was forced to make peace with Sparta, in a treaty which was to be valid for thirty years, her position was then little different from that which she had held before the disastrous battle of Sepeia, and though she was still deprived of the Thyreatis, the region immediately to the north of that district, the valley of Hysiai, was clearly once more an Argive possession.

The recovery depended on several factors; the return of internal stability to Argos; the increasing involvement of Athens and Sparta which gave Argos a potential ally of major importance; and, above all, the fatal earthquake which devastated Sparta at a crucial period in her history, and decimated her citizen population and her army. There can be little doubt that this last event was the turning point in the fortunes of Argos.

In the period before the earthquake Athenian policies are for us centred on the personality of Kimon. Kimon was a member of one of the wealthiest aristocratic families at Athens, and though anxious to promote the well-being and strength of his own city—for his patriotism is never in doubt—he was also well disposed to Sparta, for whose aristocratic system he had a natural sympathy. He was prepared to recognize Sparta's claim to supremacy in the Peloponnese, and so long as the Athenians approved these policies, Argos' attempts to dispute that supremacy were not likely to make much headway.

Athens' success in preventing her own total subservience to Sparta once the Persians had finally withdrawn had been achieved largely through the machinations of Themistokles.[2] But as Kimon, or the policies associated with his name came to be accepted by the Athenians, Themistokles was pushed to one side and eventually ostracized, that is, banished from Athens for a ten year period, without loss of citizenship, as a result of a vote taken against him by the Athenians. The reasons for this appear to be connected with his advocacy of a more complete form of democracy than that current at Athens in the 470s. In 472 the tragedian Aeschylus produced his play the *Persai*, the effect of which was to remind the Athenians of their great naval victory at Salamis barely ten years before, a victory which had been made possible by Themistokles' policies, in particular the construction of a substantial fleet. The production of the *Persai* was financed by the young aristocrat Perikles, who went on to become, in effect, Themistokles' political heir, when the advanced democracy was at last established at Athens. Themistokles' 'crime', then, which led to his ostracism seems to be compounded from personal opposition to Kimon, as the dominant figure in Athenian politics, an anxiety to further the democratic constitution in the city, and a desire to commit her to an overt struggle for power and supremacy with Sparta.

Under the terms of ostracism, Themistokles was allowed to live in any place of his choosing beyond the limits of Athenian territory. He went to Argos and there seems no good reason to doubt that this was because he saw there the opportunity of furthering at least one of his aims, his determination to weaken the supremacy of Sparta.

103

What he achieved at Argos in real terms is debatable,[3] and must be considered in relation to Argive policies at this time; but there is no doubt that he made himself obnoxious to the Spartans who were able to persuade the Athenians to condemn him, in his absence, to the more severe penalty of full exile and deprivation of citizen rights. Moreover Sparta and Athens jointly sent agents after Themistokles (a most un-Athenian act, for they were normally prepared to allow citizens who were involved in capital offences the alternative of seeking exile and life). The threat these agents represented was sufficient to drive Themistokles from Argos.[4] Clearly at this stage Argos was not yet able overtly to ignore Spartan demands.

Diodorus relates the ostracism, the exile and the hounding of Themistokles with the events of the year 471–470 B.C., in accordance with his habit of narrating events spread over several years under the year in which they began.[5] The production of the *Persai* in 472 B.C. suggests that the ostracism was then imminent, and that Diodorus chose the next year for his account of Themistokles' adventures because it was in fact the year in which he was ostracized. More important for the history of Argos is the date of his arrival there, and his hurried departure. He need not have gone to Argos immediately, though it is usually implied that he did. His adventures ended with his arrival within the jurisdiction of the Persian king, at about the time that Artaxerxes succeeded to the throne in 465 B.C. How long his flight across Greece occupied him is less certain; he may still have been in Argos in 466 B.C., but it is usually supposed that he had left before that year.

Diodorus[6] dates the conquest and destruction of Mycenae by Argos to the year 468/7 B.C. Here again, there is no way of checking the accuracy of this statement; presumably this year has some significance for the campaign against Mycenae and Tiryns, but it is possible that it marks the beginning, rather than the end of a protracted campaign. In any case Diodorus clearly believes that the Argives were able to proceed against Mycenae only because the Spartans had by that time suffered the great earthquake, and the consequent rising of the Messenians and helots, which he dates to the previous year 469 B.C. This, he argues, prevented the Spartans from intervening to protect their friends and allies the Mycenaeans. This seems inaccurate; a later date for the earthquake is generally preferred, and it is much more likely to have happened in 465 B.C.[7] If so, we must assume either that the date for the war against

Mycenae is also incorrect, or that Diodorus is mistaken in placing that war after the weakening of Sparta that resulted from the earthquake. This is the more likely; and since Diodorus does not appear to be capable of developing such theories of cause and effect for himself, it looks as though he took this sequence from an earlier historian, who, puzzled by the inability of Sparta to save Mycenae, supposed the well-known earthquake and the consequent Messenian rising to be the cause of this. If there is another reason—which there is—the sequence of cause and effect and therefore the relative chronology does not hold. The implications are serious. Diodorus appears to derive his knowledge of the fifth century ultimately from the fourth century historian Ephorus, who wrote with the intention, here, of filling in the details omitted in Thucydides' brief résumé of the principal events that occurred between the Persian and Peloponnesian wars. If the idea that Argos was made free to attack Mycenae by the earthquake at Sparta also derives from Ephorus, it would appear that the historian had very little precise information on which to draw to supplement Thucydides. From this it would seem that the history of Argos was not properly recorded at all at least until the fourth century B.C. It is not surprising that our knowledge of Argive history is so scrappy and confused.

Behind these events looms the campaign of Tegea and Dipaia. Diodorus knows nothing of this, which is surprising, since the battles were mentioned by Herodotus (who, indeed, remains our source of information about them).[8] It is strange that they made no greater impact on the accounts of Greek history in the fifth century B.C. They occur in Herodotus in a digression, in which he tells about the seer Teisamenos of Elis, who demanded Spartan citizenship in return for his religious activities on Sparta's behalf. Herodotus says that Teisamenos performed the necessary religious ritual before five battles in which the Spartans were involved: Plataia, Tegea, Dipaia, Ithome, and Tanagra in that order. Plataia, in 479 B.C., and Tanagra, in 458 B.C., are certainly intended to be chronologically the first and last of the series, and there is therefore a strong presumption that the others are listed in the order in which they occurred. Ithome represents the campaign against the Messenian rebels; what part of the campaign, which was very protracted, this signifies is uncertain, but it probably refers to the closing stages, when the rebels were pinned down in their stronghold there. Tegea and Dipaia therefore were fought before the final stage of that rebellion. The crucial question, since it concerns the policies of Argos, is whether they were fought because of developments caused by the earthquake, or whether they happened before the earthquake, and are therefore completely unconnected with it.

The significance lies not so much in the battles themselves as in the diplomatic rumblings that caused them. Quite clearly they are caused by an alliance of the Arcadian cities, backed by Argos, and aimed against Sparta. It is possible that this was a result of the earthquake; that the Arcadians saw an opportunity to gain an advantage over Sparta. If this is so, it is surprising that they were not more successful, that Sparta was able to act against them effectively, and that there was no attempt to collaborate with the rebellious Messenians. The fact that Sparta moved against the Arcadians suggests that the Messenians were not yet in rebellion; and on the whole it looks as though this alliance and the battles it caused occurred before the earthquake. If so, it is likely to have coincided with the time that Themistokles was in Argos. Since Themistokles was renowned as an intriguer and an opponent of Spartan supremacy it is not fanciful to see a direct connection between his presence there and the development of a new anti-Spartan Peloponnesian alliance. Thucydides states that Themistokles did not stay in Argos, but travelled about the Peloponnese. There is no reason to suppose that he was engaged in mere sightseeing. At the same time Pausanias who, as regent, had commanded the Spartan and allied armies at the final battle with the Persians was put to death by the Spartan authorities. Pausanias had already been suspected of excessive personal ambition in his conduct of the allied cause after the Persians had left Greece. Now the Spartans believed (or let it be known that they believed) that Pausanias was intriguing to re-establish himself by offering freedom to the helots if they would support him. The Spartans quite clearly felt that they were being undermined in the Peloponnese; and they linked Pausanias' intrigues with those of Themistokles, for it was as a result of what they had discovered in dealing with Pausanias—or so they told the Athenians—that they asked them to punish Themistokles.

What sort of influence Themistokles had at Argos, as a person banished from his own city, is debatable. There is no doubt that he had won international respect for the part he played in the Persian Wars: this respect even extended to Sparta, and he was able to make use of it in the negotiations he conducted there while the Athenians were rebuilding their walls. His reputation was not confined to Athens and Sparta, and the knowledge that he had successfully thwarted Spartan attempts to maintain complete mastery over the Greeks would have endeared him to Sparta's Peloponnesian enemies. Themistokles had no authority at Argos. He was not a citizen; he could not hold office, and he could not even speak in the assembly. But he doubtless had friends, with whom he could not only discuss the situation in general terms, but urge his fundamental policies; he could convince them of his ability to win support among the Arcadian cities, and it could even have been his initiative in the first place that set these affairs in motion.

The battles of Tegea and Dipaia illustrated that the Spartan army had as yet lost none of its effectiveness; but we learn nothing of the consequences. The first battle was fought against Tegea and the Argives alone; the second against all the Arcadians except Mantinea and without, it would seem, Argos. The reasons can only be based on speculation. Were the Argives forced to come to terms with Sparta? Did they withdraw of their own accord, and was that the result of prudence, their losses at Tegea, or because they were otherwise pre-occupied? It would seem that the political situation in Argos was now in the balance, with some families in favour of co-operation with Sparta, others favouring an anti-Spartan policy. The balance could easily be tipped either way, by the presence of a Themistokles in favour of an anti-Spartan alliance, by the slight setback in battle in favour of breaking the alliance. At least we do not hear of active Spartan intervention at Argos, except indirectly, in getting the Athenians to drive out Themistokles, if the sequence of events is properly interpreted. Perhaps the Spartans intended to return to the attack against Argos later, after dealing with the Arcadians and perhaps already an incipient helot rising; and perhaps the earthquake intervened before any of this could be put into effect.

Such is the background to the recovery; confused, uncertain, and overshadowed by the greater significance of Spartan and Athenian history. Somewhere into this confusion fits the most important part of the recovery, from the Argive point of view; the restoration of the Argolid, the subjugation and destruction of Mycenae. Perhaps this was begun at an early date, with the risk of Spartan intervention, and the Argives becoming emboldened when that intervention did not take place. Perhaps the Argives used Themistokles and the Arcadian alliance as a smoke-screen behind which they prepared their own affairs; possibly preoccupation with the Argolid itself explains the absence of an Argive contingent from Dipaia. But whatever the reason, when the Argives were at last ready to crush Mycenae, the Spartans did not interfere. In the final attack, Argos was helped by Kleonai; the old Argos, whose influence went beyond the immediate confines of the Argolid was restored, and in terms of international politics, the consequences of Sepeia were at last annulled.

The effects of the earthquake at Sparta were even more serious, but the Argives do not appear to have taken full advantage of them. Again, it is impossible to estimate the losses to Sparta, either in terms of casualties or in the economic sense. Since the town of Sparta was itself badly hit there must have been loss of life particularly among the full Spartiate citizen families of all generations. For a time, Sparta had to fight hard for her survival, at least in the form in which the state had been organized for over two centuries; the rebellion of the Messenians at once deprived her of a large area of territory and the economic strength which she drew from it. The misfortunes of Sparta were, of course, a great opportunity for her enemies. If Argos had not yet in fact recovered Mycenae, then, as Diodorus, or his source suggests, that campaign could have been made possible by the knowledge that Sparta was now unlikely to intervene. If Diodorus is not correct in his correlation of events here, then Argos was surprisingly quiet when Sparta was involved in the suppression of the rising of Messenia. At the least, this would seem to afford an admirable opportunity to recover the small communities along the east coast of the Peloponnese, and in particular the Thyreatis which Sparta would not be in a position to defend. At the other extreme, if Argive hatred of Sparta was still intensely bitter from the aftermath of Sepeia, a new alliance with the Arcadians to bring full support to the rebels of Messenia would have reduced the Spartans to conditions of extreme desperation. As it was, even without such an alliance turned against them, the Spartans considered it necessary to apply to their own allies, and in particular the Athenians, for active military aid. It would therefore seem either that the government at Argos was not wholeheartedly anxious to take advantage of Spartan weakness, or, perhaps more likely, that the Argives were hampered by the terms of a settlement imposed on them by Sparta after the campaign of Tegea. If such a treaty had existed (and there is no record of it at all) it might have recognized the Argive right to a free hand in the Argolid, while demanding an undertaking not to interfere, by alliances or other means directly in Spartan affairs.

Whatever the cause, Argos missed her opportunity in the year of the earthquake. When the time came for more vigorous anti-Spartan activities, though there was still some hope of success, they achieved little more than a return to the existing situation.

After the earthquake, the Spartans had turned to Athens for help. The reason they gave for this was that the Messenians had fortified themselves on Mount Ithome, and the Spartans required the special skills that the Athenians were reputed to possess in warfare of this sort.[1] It was a reputation based on slender evidence, and it may be that, with their depleted manpower, the Spartans were more than anxious to commit other troops to the dangerous task of attacking a prepared defensive position, a situation in which the normal hoplite advantages were minimized, and in which there were more than the usual risks. But perhaps the political aspect was more significant.[2] Sparta was no doubt anxious to demonstrate to the rest of the Greek world (and the lesson was probably understood in Argos in particular) that the allies whose leadership and military resources, by land and sea, had served to save Greece from the immense peril of the Persian invasion, were still joined to each other in terms of treaty; in effect, to demonstrate that anyone contemplating an attack on Sparta would also have to contend with the Athenian army.

Athens at this point in her history was dominated politically by the landowning classes who seem, on the whole, to have been sympathetic to the Spartan landowners, or, if not actively sympathetic, at least apprehensive of the damage a hostile Spartan army could inflict on their estates and small-holdings. They were challenged by those political leaders who had succeeded to the position of Themistokles, who were unsympathetic to Sparta, and who sought complete supremacy for Athens, and the establishment of a full democratic government, in which authority was shared equally (or as near equally as was practical) amongst all who held Athenian citizenship. The ostracism of Themistokles emphasized the political weakness of those who held these views during the 470s, and little that happened in the first half of the succeeding decade can have altered the position. Nevertheless, there was an essential difference between this Athens and Sparta, for at Athens the citizenship was already much more widely based. The friends of Sparta were outnumbered by those whose co-operation with the Dorian city was based more on prudence than affection. These people formed the backbone of the Athenian hoplite army, and consequently of the contingent sent to help the Spartans at Ithome. Their absence possibly strengthened the democratic element in Athens; and certainly what they learnt about the true situation of the Spartans after the earthquake must have made them less anxious in their fears of what Spartan hostility could do to harm them at home. The Spartans became suspicious of their Athenian allies, sensing that their natural sympathies lay more with the Messenians whose freedom they had been called upon to suppress. Perhaps also news of an impending political upheaval in Athens reached them, and the Athenian hoplites were required at Athens if this was to be prevented. Whatever the real reason the Athenian contingent was abruptly dismissed and sent home. The disgrace, if not the inevitable tide of development in Athens and elsewhere, made the upheaval inevitable. Kimon, the political leader who was associated above all with the policy of friendship to Sparta and the shared leadership of the Greek world, who had himself commanded the Athenian contingent at Ithome, was now in his turn disgraced and ostracized, and the heirs to Themistokles' policy dominated Athens.

The change in Athenian policy was considerable. Previously she had been content to leave the domination of the mainland to Sparta. Now, she sought allies for herself among the mainland powers and strove actively to undermine any alliances that existed between Sparta and states that were useful to herself. In particular, she sought the friendship of cities whose constitutions she could recognize as democratic, if not necessarily in the same fashion as her own, or where she had some hope of establishing democratic rule. An active alliance with Argos, already hostile to Sparta, already recognized as falling into the democratic camp was a foregone conclusion, and indeed, already had been proposed as part of the democratic programme.[3] It must have appeared that Argos had at last found the champion and help she required in a war of revenge against the arch-enemy. If so, it would seem that she was sadly disappointed. The one significant battle between the army of the alliance and a Spartan army was at Tanagra in Boiotia, furthering the Athenian interest and providing only minimal benefit to Argos. In any case, the result was at best a draw, and the Spartan army was able to escape from a virtual trap, even though it suffered losses, and leaving behind on the field of battle a substantial number of Argive dead. There was no serious or sustained attempt to recover Argos' lost territories. The Argolid itself was invaded by a Spartan army which was defeated and repelled at Oinoe by an army of Argives and Athenians at about the time of Tanagra and perhaps as a conse- quence of the losses inflicted on the Spartans at that battle. From the spoils statues were dedicated at Delphi by the Argives, and the battle was commemorated at Athens by a painting in the Stoa Poikile, on the north side of the agora.[4] But by 451 B.C. Argos was ready to make her peace with the Spartans.

What went wrong? It is clear that the allies were unwilling to mount a direct attack on Sparta. The opportunity for that, if it had ever existed, had long since passed, and though the Messenian rising had not yet ended completely its effects were now contained to such an extent that a direct invasion of Lakonia would be a hazardous under- taking. Nearly a hundred years were to pass before the women of Sparta were to see the campfires of an enemy burning around their city. The best the alliance could do was to attack and eliminate Sparta's friends; perhaps in final isolation, it might then have proved possible to attack Sparta herself. The history of the years from 461 to 451 belongs more particularly to Athens. We hear more of the help given by the Argives to Athens at Tanagra, than that given by the Athenians to the Argives at Oinoe. The reason, perhaps is that the record is essentially of Athenian history, and for the Athenian historian, such as Thucydides, Argive affairs were something of a side issue. It is more difficult to reconstruct Argive attitudes to the events of these years.

Firstly, the form of the alliance. It can hardly have been formu- lated for aggressive purposes, for the active propagation of war against Sparta. If a treaty between Argos and Sparta had been made following Tegea and Dipaia, that would have been a solemn under- taking, sworn on oaths to the gods, that the two cities would not attack each other; and no change in the political situation would persuade a Greek city to the act of sacrilege involved in breaking such an oath. Even if such a treaty did not exist, or had become invalidated, it is still probable that the arrangement between Athens and Argos was one for mutual defence; it would protect Argos to a greater extent against the risk of a Spartan attack, but would not commit the Athenians to an aggressive war against the Spartans (the battle of Tanagra was fought, nominally at least, to protect Attica from violation by an invading Spartan army, and Oinoe to save the Argolid from invasion).

Athens' policy instead was to undermine the friends of Sparta, by trying to break their allegiance. The chief target was undoubtedly Corinth, even though Athenian policies were more spectacularly successful in Boiotia. Argos was, without doubt, particularly interested in Corinth, and the pressures applied to that city. Not only were the two cities adjacent to each other, but already Argive interest had extended over the geographical boundary between them, to include Kleonai.[5] In the poems of Homer, in the famous catalogue of ships in the second book of the *Iliad*, Agamemnon's kingdom extended northwards to include Corinth (as well as other areas along the south shores of the gulf of Corinth); and, though it did not include the rest of the Argolid, since Mycenae was now part of Argive territory the Argives had acquired, as it were, a traditional interest in Agamemnon's kingdom. There was now probably a significant political difference. The precise form of the constitution of Corinth, like that of Argos, is unclear and uncertain;[6] but it appears that the city was controlled by the landowning classes (or, rather, the more prosperous among them), who, like members of similar classes elsewhere, including Athens, looked to Sparta for support. It was these people who kept Corinth in the Spartan alliance just as their counterparts in Athens had maintained Athenian friendship towards Sparta. On the other hand, there was no reason to suppose that these people formed a majority of the population, any more than they did at Athens or Argos. If diplomatic and other pressure on Corinth could force her to change her constitution to a democratic form, more in tune with that of Athens or Argos, she would most likely end her support for the Spartan supremacy. In the succeeding century this political revolution actually took place, and the immediate consequence was the fusion of Argos and Corinth into a single state.[7] Argos, as a democracy, had already ended the narrow Dorian control, exercised by a limited population from a single centre over outlying communities, and already, at the end of the 460s, there was every reason why the Argives should want to extend the principle, not only to Kleonai but to the other communities of Corinthia.

Even if these dreams did exist as early as 460 B.C., they came to nothing. Athens' vision was not limited to the Peloponnese, and her involvement in an adventure in Egypt weakened her encirclement of Corinth. Corinth offered stiff resistance, and, though defeated in battle, succeeded in preventing the Athenians from applying intensive military pressure in Corinth itself (though to be fair to Athens, her main forces were engaged elsewhere). In 458 B.C. the campaign that led to Tanagra gave notice that the Spartans were not prepared as yet, whatever the difficulties, to surrender their influence over the Peloponnese and regions of central Greece. Though Tanagra did not save central Greece, Argive losses and the surprising strength of the Spartan military intervention must have caused second thoughts.

From the Peloponnesian point of view, affairs seem to reach a stalemate. The Spartans put an end to the Messenian rebellion, but only by agreeing to allow their bitterest opponents in Messenia to leave the country (they were settled by the Athenians at Naupaktos, at the mouth of the gulf of Corinth, another challenge to Corinthian interests). They were powerless to prevent Athens establishing her domination over Boiotia. They were incapable of following up their victory at Tanagra and the settling of the Messenian rising by striking effectively at Argos. It is possible that desultory fighting continued, but by 451 B.C. both Argos and Sparta were ready to end the futile war by signing peace for thirty years.

Little is known of this peace, or the precise circumstances which led to it. Thucydides does not mention it in his résumé of events between the Persian and Peloponnesian wars, though he does refer to it later, when it expired. Diodorus tells us nothing, though it is possible that it was mentioned in his account of events during the year 452 B.C., which has not survived in the manuscripts. As the time for its expiry drew near, in 421 B.C., the Spartans were afraid that the Argives would not want to renew it, unless 'someone'— the Spartans, of course—restored to them the district of Kynouria. In 451 B.C. there had been distinct signs of war-weariness. Sparta had been involved in incessant fighting against Argos, the Arcadians, the Messenians and finally Athens since the early 460s, none of which had ended with any real gain for her. Athens was still supreme in central Greece, and despite the loss of perhaps ninety ships in Egypt (and, more significantly, the renewed existence of a Persian fleet) her control of the Aegean allies was secure, though there were

signs that she wished to concentrate her efforts on the elimination
of the new Persian fleet. In 451 B.C. Kimon returned from ostracism,
and Athens began to waver from her anti-Spartan attitude. A five
year truce was signed, which gave all the contestants a breathing
space. Argos ran the risk of isolation, and would be anxious for a
settlement. Sparta would be glad of an opportunity to detach Argos
from Athens. So it is likely that the peace resulted, not from victory
of one side over the other but a more general war-weariness. It is
clear that Sparta conceded to Argos the right to control the Argolid.
The reconquest of Mycenae and Tiryns was recognized. On the
other hand, it is equally clear that the east coast of the Peloponnese,
the district of Kynouria, was not handed back to Argos, since the
Spartans feared in 421 that Argos would demand its return. During
the fighting that followed the end of the truce in 421 B.C., the
Spartans captured and destroyed the town of Hysiai, killing all the
Argive citizens they captured there. So Hysiai must have belonged
to Argos at the time of the peace treaty of 451, and her possession of
it was then confirmed. The Thyreatis, on the other hand, would
seem to have remained a Spartan possession, and it was there that
they settled their friends the people of Aigina, expelled from their
own island by the Athenians in 431. It was doubtless this region
that was paramount in the minds of the Argives when they were
demanding the return of Kynouria; but it was to be nearly a
century before they succeeded in recovering their former possession.

Argos was reasonably satisfied by the treaty she had signed with Sparta in 451 B.C.[1] When in 445 Athens in her turn was forced by the Spartans to sign a thirty years' truce (after the loss of central Greece and the rebellion in the island of Euboia, backed by a threat of a Spartan invasion) Argos was treated as a neutral power, being an ally neither of Sparta nor of Athens, though she was allowed to be friendly with Athens. This arrangement held the threat of isolation for Argos, for it would enable Sparta to apply pressure to her without breaking the terms of her treaty with Athens. It seems apparent, however, that Sparta was more anxious to keep Athens and Argos apart, than to prepare for an attack on Argos. She regarded the truce signed with Argos as binding, and in fact the danger did not arise. Argos seems to have tried to secure herself by direct negotiations with Persia in about the year 449 B.C., at which the Persians reassured the Argives that they were regarded still as the friendliest of the Greeks, a reassurance that did not count for much.[2] For her part Argos was in no position to break the terms of her thirty years' truce, however desirous she may have been to regain Thyreatis and Kynouria, and Sparta too was anxious to maintain the situation, both for political reasons, and on the genuine moral ground that it was not right to break truces solemnly entered into with oaths sworn on the names of the gods.

Argos therefore remained at peace, apparently outside the turmoils caused by the rivalry between Athens and Sparta, turmoils that were increasingly of Athens' doing. When the Spartans finally were driven to war in 431, Argos remained aloof from the struggle. The Spartans, doubtless, were grateful. Athenian expeditions ignored Argos. The Spartans made no attempt to coerce her. History, in fact, completely overlooks Argos. She does not feature in Thucydides (after the events in the mid-century already discussed) nor in Diodorus, until the end of the Archidamian war, the first part of the struggle between Athens and Sparta.

From that time onwards, the picture changes. Sparta had fought the war to prevent Athens taking over the Greek mainland. She had been urged into it by her allies who had much more to fear from Athens than did Sparta herself. In 421 B.C. peace had been made by Athens and Sparta, but acting primarily in their own interests. Both were tired of the war, or at least were suffering from it. Sparta had shown no real desire for complete mastery in Greece, and Athens had appeared to have learnt her lesson. There were pro-belligerents on both sides—probably more at Athens than Sparta—but for the moment those in favour of peace prevailed.

Other states were more concerned. Sparta, it appeared, had ignored the interests of her more important allies. She had called a council of the allies, and put the proposed peace terms to them; they were rejected by a number of them, the Boiotians, Corinth, Elis and Megara, the major states. These allies refused to accept the terms. Both Megara and the Boiotian league (or at least, those who controlled these states at this time) feared a return to the situation that had existed in the 450s, when both were controlled by pro-Athenian and democratic governments. Corinth saw that Sparta had achieved nothing that would prevent Athens resuming the pressures on her interests that had led to the outbreak of war in the first place.

Thucydides clearly understood that dissatisfaction with Sparta was growing even before the peace was signed. One of the reasons that induced Sparta to make peace was the fear that a third power group might emerge in Greece; that Argos would seize the opportunity created by the end of her truce with Sparta to bring about a re-alignment in Peloponnesian politics as she had done at the time of Tegea and Dipaia (when she was at last recovering from the disability imposed on her at the battle of Sepeia). Thucydides says that the Spartans suspected that some Peloponnesian states would go over to Argos, though he does not explain what grounds the Spartans had for fearing this, and it may be mere deduction from the actual event—for, says Thucydides, that is what did happen.

The situation was taken one stage further when Athens and Sparta, not content with agreeing to be at peace with each other, formed an alliance, to last for fifty years. The alliance itself was innocuous, being one for mutual defence, an agreement to consider the enemy of one to be the enemy of the other. In addition, the

Athenians undertook to help Sparta in the event of a helot rebellion. Such an alliance is probably no more than a revival of the situation as it had been after the defeat of the Persians, and Kimon and the Athenian hoplites may have gone to aid the Spartans against the helots as the result of a similar clause in an earlier treaty of alliance. The alliance was renewed while some, at least, of Sparta's allies were still at Sparta. It was, however, a consequence of the refusal of Sparta's allies to accept the peace treaty, and of an Argive deputation, consisting of two men called Ampelidas and Lichas, which had refused to renew the Argos-Sparta truce.

It thus appeared that Sparta and Athens had cynically divided the Greek world between them. The ten years' war had proved them equal opponents and manifestly the continuation of hostilities between them would be self-destructive. On the other hand, if they acted together, no Greek state dare oppose them. Nothing could be done in Greece contrary to the wishes of Athens and Sparta. Such an agreement only made the need for a third grouping more desperate and Argos emerged as the leader. Diodorus gives the reasons for this, and though they sound more like the lucubrations of learned scholarship than the exhortations of a political manifesto, they do show the claims to greatness that the Argives still cherished. Argos had a great reputation through her ancient achievements. Before the coming of the Herakleidai, most of the great kings had come from the Argolid (Diodorus carefully avoids saying from Argos). Argos had been at peace for a long time—doubtless a peace of thirty years seemed long in the troubled circumstances of the Greek world in the fifth and fourth centuries B.C. She had great revenues, and large reserves not only of money, but also of manpower. It sounded promising, if in the event it was to prove somewhat optimistic.

After the alliance between Athens and Sparta had been signed, the delegates at Sparta went home, except the Corinthians. They called in first at Argos (which was, after all, on a direct route from Sparta to Corinth). There they negotiated with 'certain of those in authority'—the impression is of private dealings not conducted on an official level, or at least, in the open. They urged that Argos should invite other Greek cities to form an alliance. These 'Argive authorities' in Argos duly persuaded the Argive assembly to pass a decree to this effect, and a commission of twelve was set up, with power to negotiate alliances with any Greek state that was willing to accept the conditions. It is noticeable that the initiative came not from Argos but from Corinth, and those Argives who favoured the proposal had to act circumspectly; though there is never any doubt that the Argives gave their support to the proposals once they were made. The twelve commissioners were given complete authority to sign alliances, this being a more secret method than by open ratification in the assembly. Only in the case of Athens or Sparta wishing to join would the approval of the Argive people be needed.

The first state to join was Mantinea in Arcadia, along with her existing allies, probably consisting of the greater part of Arcadia (that is, except her great rival, Tegea). The Arcadians were afraid that the Spartans would try to dismember this alliance, now that they could turn their attention to Peloponnesian affairs, so presumably it had grown up without Sparta's authority or approval. This was in itself a direct challenge to Sparta's prestige, and indicated that Spartan supremacy in the Peloponnese was in the balance and had been even before she had come to terms with Athens. The Spartan countermove was diplomatic; to prevent Corinth, their loyal ally since the sixth century B.C., from breaking away, they sent envoys there, who tried to convince the Corinthians that to join the Argive alliance would constitute breaking their oath to Sparta. Envoys from Argos urged the Corinthians to join. While they were deciding, an embassy from Elis, another long-standing ally of Sparta, arrived, made an alliance with Corinth, and then went to Argos to make an alliance there. Thus there was a continuous zone of allied states hostile to Sparta across the northern and central parts of the Peloponnese. Argos could now claim an authority as leader of the Peloponnese at least equal to that of Sparta. It was a long time since Argos had reached such a position of strength.

Almost immediately the tide began to turn. Tegea could not be persuaded to desert Sparta, and this at least kept open Sparta's routes to the north. The Corinthians began to waver as soon as they realized that the Argive alliance was losing momentum. The Spartans sent an army against an outlying dependant of Mantinea, which threatened Spartan territory. After entrusting the defence of their own city to an Argive garrison, the Mantineans marched against the Spartans but were defeated.

In the following winter there was much discussion at Sparta between representatives of the leading states and the allies of Sparta, which led to nothing. More secret negotiations were instigated by the Spartans, where new magistrates had been appointed who were anxious to break the peace with Athens. They urged Boiotia to join the Argive alliance, and then bring Argos into alliance with Sparta. This was received enthusiastically by the Boiotian leaders, but it was not put to the Boiotian people, and the whole plan died a natural death.

Thus Argos was still leader of a separate alliance, distinct from and opposed to Sparta. Nevertheless, when the Boiotians failed to join her, she was again threatened with isolation. Now that the terms of her treaty with Sparta had expired it seemed likely that Argos would be faced by Sparta, Tegea and Boiotia with Athens joining in on the Spartan side under the terms of her treaty. Because of this, she tried to get her treaty with Sparta renewed, but on more favourable terms, reiterating her claim to Kynouria and the Thyreatis. Sparta would have none of that, and treated with disdain the Argive suggestion that possession of that region (but nothing else) should be decided by battle, much in the way that an attempt to settle the issue had been made at the battle of the champions, which was of course the precedent for this weird suggestion. The Spartans were inclined to treat the proposal as a joke but finally agreed, in order to avoid a full war that they did not want. The terms for this romantic and preposterous combat were drawn up and referred back to Argos for ratification.

Meanwhile, the Argives had discovered that relations between Athens and Sparta had deteriorated considerably, because certain obligations imposed by the peace treaty had not been fulfilled. Argos' thoughts therefore turned to the possibility of an alliance with Athens, and more envoys were sent there, accompanied by others from Elis and Mantinea, and a counter embassy from Sparta, in order to negotiate this. After a debate in the assembly, the Athenians grew annoyed at the increasing signs of hostility towards them at Sparta. A last minute embassy to Sparta achieved nothing and Athens joined the Argive alliance, or, rather, a new alliance was signed between Athens, Argos, Elis and Mantinea. The older alliance between Athens and Sparta was still in existence, though it cannot have been of much effect. Corinth, on the other hand, did not join in the new alliance, and her allegiance to the anti-Spartan group was obviously doubtful.

These complicated negotiations were followed by an uneasy celebration of the Olympic games. Elis, a member of the anti-Spartan alliance, was responsible for the games, and the declaration of the truce observed by all Greek states during their celebration. She refused to let the Spartans participate, on the grounds that they had broken the truce. The Spartans denied it, but were still refused access to the sanctuary and temple unless they paid a fine. It was an omen of trouble to come.

In the next campaigning season, the first round of the inevitable war was joined. Argos attacked her neighbour Epidauros, partly to gain favour with Corinth, partly to open the direct route to the Saronic gulf and Athens, whose assistance would be of paramount importance should the Spartans intervene. The Spartans, however, merely advanced to their frontier and although they had summoned assistance from allied cities, then withdrew back home. Peace negotiations at Mantinea brought about the withdrawal of the Argive army from Epidauros, but nothing else; the invasion of Epidaurian territory was then renewed. Again the Spartan army advanced to the frontier, presumably hoping that the mere threat of an invasion would cause the Argives to withdraw from Epidauros (though the official reason for Sparta's failure to mount a full invasion was that the omens were unfavourable); again, nothing was achieved. An Athenian contingent of a thousand under Alkibiades (who was the strongest advocate of the pro-Argive policy) had come to help Argos in the event of a Spartan invasion. As it was not needed, it returned home. The impression one gets from the events of this year is of skirmishing and manoeuvring, with neither side anxious to commit itself to a full-scale engagement, and hoping that events would find their own solution. However, the next year, 418, brought heightened activity, which forced a conclusion. The Spartans committed themselves more wholeheartedly to the conflict. A garrison of three hundred was sent to Epidauros during the preceding winter. Then 'about the middle of summer', the full Peloponnesian army marched along with its allies, which included the Tegeates and other Arcadians. The allied army assembled at Phleious, adjacent to the Argolid; the Spartans advanced to join them. The Argives were aware of what was afoot, and moved to catch the Spartans before they joined up with their allies at Phleious. Advancing into Arcadia, the Argives collected contingents from Mantinea and Elis, and prepared to block the Spartan advance. The Spartan king Agis outwitted the Argives by marching at night, and a crucial situation was avoided. The Argives, hastily leaving Arcadia marched first to Argos, and then to the road to Nemea, the obvious route by which a hostile army based at Phleious would attack the Argolid. Agis split his army: Spartans, Arcadians and Epidaurians entered the Argolid by one 'difficult road', the Corinthians, Pellenians and Phleiasians by another, while the Boiotians, Megarians and Sikyonians were to hold the attention of the Argives by advancing down the obvious route to Nemea. As soon as Agis reached the plain he began to lay waste 'Saminthos and other places'. This brought the Argive army from its blocking position on the Nemea road; they fought the Corinthian contingent, suffering more losses than they inflicted in what appears to have been a minor skirmish. The Boiotians and other allies advanced to Nemea as they had been instructed, only to find the Argives had gone. The Argives were now, as Thucydides describes, in a difficult position. The Spartan army was in the Argive plain, between the Argive army and Argos itself (so the difficult route Agis had followed must have been across the mountain from Phleious to the upper valley of the Inachos). The Corinthians and others were 'on the hills above the Argive army'. The Argives, cut off from Argos by the Spartans were in the northern part of the Argive plain, so the Corinthian contingent had presumably crossed by one of the direct passes from Corinthia to the region of Mycenae. The Boiotians and the remaining allies were, of course, still on the direct road from Nemea. The Argives were in fact confident that they had split the Spartan allies, and could attack the Spartan contingent in isolation; but certain pro-Spartan Argives, again acting privately, negotiated a four month truce. They had no right to do this; Thucydides makes clear that they had no authority from the mass of the army, that is, the Argive citizens. Agis, the Spartan king, did have authority to do as he saw fit.

It is a curious episode. Thucydides thinks a Spartan victory would have been inevitable: he considers the army the Spartans led the finest that had ever been assembled, so the nervousness of the Argive notables is understandable, whatever sanguine hopes the rest of the Argives may have had. That the notables could negotiate such a truce without the approval of the people—even more, with the active disapproval of the people, for their leader was stoned, had his property confiscated, and escaped with his life only by taking sanctuary at the altar—is important evidence for the political situation at Argos. It is noticeable that a truce negotiated in this way was binding on the Argives. Agis' behaviour is equally curious. Though he had authority to act as he saw fit while in command in the field, the course of action he followed was regarded as incompetence, at the least, and there were repercussions at Sparta. The Spartans voted that his house should be destroyed, and that he should be fined ten thousand drachmai (that they could contemplate such a fine is an indication of the un-Spartan wealth possessed by Agis). However, he was able to buy himself off. The Spartans did succeed in passing a law restricting the authority of the king in command of the army; henceforward he needed the approval of a committee of ten advisers who supervised his actions.

It is not difficult to see in all this the existence of two political groups both at Argos and Sparta. Each city included those who saw no future in conflicts of this sort and were prepared to negotiate for peace, and another party who sought a solution by war. Whatever the legal authority of the supporters of peace (who clearly included Agis on the Spartan side) the majority in both Argos and Sparta wanted war. Rightly or wrongly they felt cheated by the four month truce, and when it ended they were ready to resume the conflict.

During the time of the truce the Argives were reluctant to break its terms, even when strengthened by the arrival of an Athenian contingent, but they were won over by Mantinea and Elis. The alliance attacked the pro-Spartan city of Orchomenos in Arcadia, and, after a short siege, forced it to join them. The next stage was to be an attack on Tegea. This threat brought the Spartans out; with some difficulty they gathered their allies (many of whom had to march through territory controlled by Argos) at Mantinea, where the Argives and their allies prepared for battle. The position they chose was a strong one. Agis, frightened by the reaction caused by his previous withdrawal from the Argolid, was prepared to risk battle, but discretion prevailed, and the Spartans withdrew to Tegea. Again the Argive army thought they had been let down by their generals who had allowed the Spartans to escape. The Spartans returned to find once more the Argives ready for battle. This time there was no holding back. The Spartans probably had the larger force, though Thucydides is unable to give the exact numbers for either side.

When the battle ended, the Spartans were clearly the victors. The Argive alliance was shattered, the Argive troops in full retreat. The Spartan allies suffered hardly any losses though the Spartans themselves, who had borne the brunt of the fighting were said to have lost three hundred. The Argives (with the men of Orneai and Kleonai) lost seven hundred dead. The Mantineans lost two hundred, the Athenians and Aiginetans a further two hundred.

The situation was now favourable for peace. The pro-Spartan, anti-democratic group at Argos persuaded the people to accept peace proposals. This restored the damage done to Sparta and her allies during the war, and attempted to close the Peloponnese to intervention from outside—that is, of course, from Athens. The dispute with Epidauros was settled, and the Athenians asked to withdraw (which eventually they did). The treaty was to last for fifty years. Sparta and Argos then each contributed a thousand men to a joint expedition, which went round overthrowing democratic governments (suspected of pro-Athenian sympathies) and replacing them with oligarchic regimes. This was done at Sikyon (by the Spartans alone) and afterwards, by the joint expedition at Argos itself.

The next spring brought a reaction at Argos. Waiting till the Spartans were preoccupied with religious observances, the democrats attacked the oligarchs, killing some and driving the others into exile, mostly to Phleious. They then began to build long walls to connect the city with the sea, after the manner of the walls linking Athens with Piraeus; these, together with a fresh alliance with Athens supreme at sea, would render Argos safe from Spartan attack, for it was notorious in fifth century Greece that hoplite armies were helpless against defended walls, and fortified cities normally could be captured only by siege and starvation. If the walls reached the sea, then food could always be brought in under the protection of the Athenian fleet. The Spartans soon found out, and acted quickly, sending an expedition in winter under king Agis. Though the Argives, men, women and slaves, with professional help from Athens had worked hard on the walls they were incomplete, and the Spartans captured them. After they had demolished them, the Spartans took the frontier town of Hysiai and destroyed it, putting to death all free Argives found there. The Argives could only retaliate with an attack on Phleious, where the pro-Spartan Argive exiles had fled. Even so, in the following summer it was felt desirable that three hundred pro-Spartan Argive citizens still in residence should be removed; they were taken away by an Athenian fleet (commanded by Alkibiades) and banished to neighbouring islands under Athenian control. In the winter of 416 B.C. the Spartans, anticipating a policy that they were to use with some success in their later wars, established a group of pro-Spartan Argive dissidents, presumably those at Phleious, along with some soldiers, at Orneai, from which they had access to the Argive plain but which could be reached from outside the Argolid both from Mantinea and from Phleious in particular. The Argives, aided by six hundred Athenians conveyed to Argos in thirty triremes, attacked Orneai with their full army, after the Spartans had withdrawn back home. The people in Orneai slipped away under cover of darkness, and the place was destroyed.

Thereafter Thucydides' account of Argive history is overshadowed by matters more weighty to the history of Athens, particularly the great and calamitous expedition to Syracuse. We hear of a Spartan attack in the Argolid in the spring of 414 B.C. which penetrated as far as Kleonai (where they were stopped by an earthquake) and an Argive counter-raid into the Thyreatis, where Spartan property was plundered. The following summer the Spartans mounted a second invasion, laying waste most of the Argolid. This time the Athenians sent thirty ships to help the Argives by devastating parts of Spartan territory, while the Argives themselves once more attacked Phleious, but none of this activity and counter-activity appears to have been in any way decisive. In the following year, 413 B.C., a small Argive contingent joined the reinforcements which the Athenians had decided to send to Syracuse, where their major contribution seems to have been to throw the Athenians into a panic by their use of the Dorian war chant that the Athenians normally heard from their enemies. Even after the disaster at Syracuse and the first revolution at Athens which put an oligarchic government in power there the Argives continued to support the Athenian democracy, but this had little effect, though it does demonstrate that the Spartans were sufficiently preoccupied with the Athenian situation to ignore Argos. After this, we hear little of the Argives in Xenophon's account of the conclusion to the Peloponnesian war. The final attack on Athens, after her fleet had been destroyed, was made by the entire citizen army of Sparta, and the Peloponnesians, except the Argives.[3] With the surrender of Athens, Argos stood alone.

The events that culminated in the battle of Mantinea and their immediate consequences form but a minor incident in the major history of the Peloponnesian war. Even so their significance for the Peloponnese itself is considerable. During the fifth century the division of the Greek world into the power blocks of Athens and Sparta had led inevitably to the greater exercise of authority by the leading cities. The transformation of Athenian leadership to imperial authority is a theme of Thucydides' introduction to his history of the war between Athens and Sparta, and is therefore a familiar aspect of Greek history in the fifth century B.C. Less obvious is the position of Sparta. Direct interference in the affairs of her allies, where these did not immediately concern her, seems to have been contrary to Spartan policy. Amongst her friends the maintenance of pro-Spartan governments was not excessively difficult. The stability of the Peloponnese resulted from Spartan military supremacy, and governments that profited from that stability would obviously hesitate to disturb it. We know too little about Greek constitutions to describe what these governments were; it is simple to label the supporters of Sparta as 'oligarchs' (as opposed to the democrats of Athens), and leave it at that, but this is misleading, and the reality was probably more complex.

When the Spartans overthrew Athenian imperialism, and reacted against the extremism of the Theban government which wanted Athens destroyed, their policy was to insist on the re-establishment of the ancestral constitution. There was much argument as to what this was, but the dispute resolved itself essentially into a contest between a limited oligarchy, and a broader based government supported by the property-owning class (property, of course, here meaning above all land). The Spartans, perhaps, regarded the 'ancestral' constitution as one in which authority was exercised by a limited number eligible for high magisterial office, having the full approval of the propertied classes. Already in the events following the surrender of Athens, it is apparent that a section of Spartan opinion (associated with the dominant figure of Lysander) favoured the establishment of extreme oligarchies, where the men of power were recognized as the sole authority in the state. This, however, seems a new development, and earlier on it is preferable to consider that Spartans had the support of governments generally far broader than the term 'oligarchy' usually implies. (This, for example, appears to have been the case at Corinth.) Even in enemy states, such as Argos, Sparta seems to have made no sustained effort to maintain the authority of the few, even though she could count on their loyalty; such governments were inherently unstable, and though from time to time it might prove desirable to support their authority, Sparta was loathe to intervene when that authority was overthrown.

The Peloponnesian war had involved Sparta in an effort she could not sustain from her own resources. Compared with Athens, she had no financial organization. She could not attack directly the members of the Athenian alliance, from whom Athens drew a substantial part of her resources, because they were mostly overseas, and Sparta did not have a sufficient fleet to give her access to them, nor the financial resources to organize one. She had to defend her alliance against Athenian attack, the aim of which was to dislodge members piecemeal. She had to protect her vulnerable dominion over Messenia. These factors necessitated the strengthening of Spartan administration. There was less time for elaborate consultation with her allies, or the ponderous gathering of an army, contingents of which came from widely scattered communities. There was greater need for centralized control (such as Athens now exercised over her alliance) and the susceptibilities of allies were more and more trampled underfoot. There was a tendency to regard pro-Spartan oligarchies as more reliable and so to be supported rather than wider based constitutions. Certainly from the Spartan point of view, they would have been easier to deal with.

Thus it appeared that Sparta was going the way of Athens, and when two of them signed the treaty of 421 B.C., it seemed to Sparta's allies that the two great powers were carving up the Greek world between themselves. Only lack of cohesion amongst themselves, and the inclusion of Sparta's enemy Argos, which had no comparable fears of Athens, prevented the effective emergence of a third force in Greek politics (and a credible second force in the Peloponnese) in the years following the peace of Nikias. Sparta was indeed fortunate that the war resumed its old guise of a direct struggle with Athens. Nevertheless, the resumption of that struggle must not be allowed to hide the fact that the Peloponnese continued in a stage of transition. Sparta emerged victorious from the Peloponnesian war, still supported by her allies; but once the old struggle with Athens was over, the new struggle took its place.[2] Argos was of crucial importance in this.

The struggle between Athens and Sparta had frequently taken the form of an ideological struggle between 'oligarchy' and 'democracy' (with the limitations noted above). This passed to the newer struggle. Sparta's blatant establishment of extreme oligarchic regimes sympathetic to her roused the suspicions not only of the extreme democrats, but of more moderate people who might ordinarily have supported her. Thus the struggle to establish a measure of independence from Spartan supremacy usually centred round the supporters of democracy; and though Sparta soon realized her mistake, and reversed Lysander's policy, abolishing the extreme oligarchies he had set up, the damage had already been done. The Thebans, who at the end of the war had been most clamorous for the total destruction of Athens and her democracy, were the first to turn against Spartan policy. Within months they were supporting the Athenian democrats in exile in their successful *coup*, which eventually brought about their return. The causes of this are complex, but the removal of Athenian power had at the same time ended Thebes' dependence on Sparta, and we may suppose that a strongly pro-Spartan minority had been ousted by a majority who preferred Thebes to follow an independent policy of her own. The same change seems to have affected Corinth, where the pro-Spartans found themselves opposed by a majority of the population, who appear to have had some hope of altering Corinthian policy. That Argos continued her hostility to Sparta is in these circumstances not surprising. The danger that faced her in 405 B.C. was that of isolation, that in the face of overwhelming Spartan strength she too would be forced to accept a pro-Spartan minority administration. The removal of Athens had, however, restored the situation as it was in 420 B.C., and brought Argos closer to Corinth and Thebes: the adoption of anti-Spartan sentiments by these cities removed the immediate danger for Argos.

By the end of the fifth century, Greek warfare had become more complicated than in earlier times when citizen armies of hoplites fought each other. Mercenary soldiers with special skills and training were now employed in increasing numbers;[3] Athens had amply demonstrated the importance of sea power. Both required adequate (and considerable) financial expenditure, and even Sparta had been forced to evolve some form of financial organization to cope with the problem. The last years of the Peloponnesian war had demonstrated the easiest solution, and that least harmful to the interests of the mainland Greeks. Persia had vast financial reserves collected as tribute from her empire, and a Persian subvention removed the need for financial oppression of the Greeks by Sparta. That it also involved the surrender of the Asiatic Greeks to Persia had put Sparta in a dilemma; not for the first time (but certainly, alas, for the last) Sparta followed the honourable course and by deciding to give the Asiatic Greeks military support forfeited the Persian subvention.

The Persians naturally turned to the other side in Greece. The historians give the impression that the gold distributed by the Persian agent, Timokrates of Rhodes, was in the form of personal bribes offered to the leaders of the anti-Spartan section in the various Greek cities. This is misleading, and we should perhaps do better to regard it as more general financial support. Certainly, such support gave the anti-Spartan leaders real hope that they would be able to sustain the burden of a war against Sparta; the ending of the subvention once Persian aims in Asia Minor were achieved, may well explain why the resulting war against Sparta eventually fizzled out.

The anti-Spartan coalition involved essentially Athens, Thebes, Corinth and Argos. The Arcadian cities, Tegea and Mantinea, who carried with them the whole of Arcadia, remained aloof, supporting Sparta in battle. Phleious, less directly threatened by Sparta, but much more directly threatened by Argos and Corinth, pleaded religious reasons for keeping out of the conflict. A battle was fought by the river of Nemea, after the alliance had failed to prevent the junction of the Spartans and the armies of her allies. The result was a defeat for the coalition.

After such an event, one would expect the coalition to break up (just as the similar coalition had disappeared after the battle of Mantinea in 418 B.C.). That it did not was due to the reluctance of the allies to accept Sparta's right to leadership, and a preference to continue the struggle; also to the fact that the pro-Spartan sections of the population were politically suspect. So long as the democrats were in control, or at least dominant in the cities, the struggle would continue. Thus the most interesting outcome of this was a political one. Argos had for many years enjoyed some form of democratic government. Corinth had a limited constitution, in which the sympathy of the governing classes and the interests of the state seem generally to have coincided.[4]

This was now at an end, for, although the governing classes remained loyal to Sparta, the others were hostile. They knew that negotiations with Sparta would now inevitably result in a demand that all political power should be entrusted to the pro-Spartan minority. They were therefore bound to continue the war, if at all possible, even after defeat in the field, in order to preserve themselves in the political sense. Unlike Mantinea, therefore, Nemea could never be a decisive battle; the war was bound to continue.

At the same time, it brought repercussions. Argive resistance was assured, but Corinth had wavered before, and was likely to waver again. Support for Sparta at Argos could be deemed unpatriotic; at Corinth it had been accepted policy for over a century. The danger to the democracy was greater at Corinth than at Argos, and it needed to be strengthened. The result, we are told, was that for a brief period in order to achieve this Corinth was incorporated into the Argive state; Corinth 'became' Argos, the territory of Corinth became part of the Argeia. The fullest information on this comes from Xenophon. An ardent supporter of Sparta himself, his sympathies naturally lie with the pro-Spartan element in Corinth. For him as for them, the merger of the two states is a betrayal of Corinthian interests. Corinth ceased to exist as the result of a blatant act of Argive imperialism. When peace terms were eventually negotiated, the great fear of Argos was that under them she would 'lose Corinth' and she was prepared to resist to the bitter end to prevent this. There seems little reason to doubt that this is misrepresentation (though the desire to maintain the union is likely enough). If its purpose was indeed to strengthen the democracy at Corinth, then the democrats there probably accepted it gladly. The opposition of a section at Corinth cannot be taken to prove the opposition of the majority.

The precise date at which the union was organized and the form

it took are more obscure. The weakening of the Corinthian democracy is likely to have been a direct consequence of the defeat at the
Nemea, which was on the very borders of Corinthia. That battle
took place in 394 B.C. During the next year, 393, the Spartans established themselves at Sikyon, and used this as a base from which they
inflicted considerable damage on the surrounding countryside of
Corinth. The wealthier landowners, who were most likely to be
supporters of Sparta anyway, naturally suffered the most from this,
and in that year began to exert strong pressure within Corinth for
the signing of a peace with Sparta. The Corinthian democrats with
the support of the allied states therefore planned a massacre of the
pro-Spartans, which was duly carried out, though not completely.
This is likely to have happened early in 392 B.C. The younger men,
forewarned that the massacre would take place, seized the citadel of
Corinth, where they were attacked by Argive soldiers (whose
presence in the city had undoubtedly boosted the democratic
faction). After being given guarantees of safety, they agreed to
return to their homes. The democracy was now more confident,
and the massacre, perhaps nothing like so serious as Xenophon
implies, had made the lesson clear.

The oligarchs, however, had no loyalty to the democracy. Two
of them, whose names are known to Xenophon, preserved by the
oligarchic tradition to which he owes his information, slipped out
of the city and made contact with the Spartan garrison at Sikyon.
As a result of this act of treachery, the Spartans were able to seize the
long walls that linked Corinth with the harbour of Lechaion.
Xenophon excuses, or rather disguises, the treachery as an act of
patriotism, arguing that the oligarchs were enraged by the merging
of Argos and Corinth, and acted solely to preserve Corinthian
independence. The presence of Argive troops at Corinth, though
easily explained on military grounds, gives some support to this,
for they were prepared to take action against the oligarchs at the
time of the massacre. Nevertheless, it has been pointed out that in
subsequent years Corinth and Argos are still represented separately
at diplomatic negotiations, thus proving that they maintained a
separate identity to some degree. In 390 B.C. the Argives in con-
junction with the Corinthians celebrated the Isthmian games at the
sanctuary of Poseidon in the isthmus of Corinth. This festival,
being held in Corinthian territory, was naturally and normally
under the control of the Corinthians. The Argive involvement here

demonstrates that there must have been by that time some arrangement between the two states, whether or not they still possessed
separate diplomatic existences. Some time after this—perhaps in
the following year—the Athenian general Iphikrates (who had won
renown by his destruction of a Spartan regiment outside the walls of
Corinth in 390) attempted to seize the citadel of Corinth in circumstances that are rather obscure. At this juncture, the people of Argos,
in full expedition, advanced to Corinth, seized the citadel, and, as
Diodorus puts it, 'made the city their own, and made Corinthian
territory Argive'. The people prevented Iphikrates from seizing
the citadel (which he wanted to possess to enhance the Athenian
claim to supremacy). The Athenians were asked to remove him,
and he was replaced by another Athenian general. It has been argued
that Diodorus' account (derived from Ephorus and through him
perhaps from the Oxyrhynchus historian) is more reliable and so
preferable to the special pleading of Xenophon; that the act of
union between Argos and Corinth did not take place until this last
event, and that Xenophon's use of the union as a pretext for excusing
the treachery of the oligarchs in 392 is sheer prevarication. Yet the
joint celebration of the Isthmian games in 390 suggests that a close
unity between the cities already existed in that year.

One of the allies in the anti-Spartan coalition was Thebes, which
had solved a similar problem, the need to merge in an effective
unity neighbouring but independent cities (though the other Boiotian
cities, excepting possibly Orchomenos, were nowhere comparable
in size, status or importance to Corinth). This had been achieved
by the construction of a federal league, in which all Boiotians were
represented; and it may be that the Thebans recommended some
such system as a means of strengthening the other parts of the anti-
Spartan coalition (as they were to do later in the century). The
constitution of the Boiotian league is described in some detail in the
surviving portion of the Oxyrhynchus historian, and it is a great
pity that his text does not survive for the subsequent period. His
interest in constitutional matters would no doubt have led him to
comment on this arrangement between Argos and Corinth. His
account of the Boiotian league is a digression from his main narrative,
and if Diodorus (or rather Ephorus before him) condensed his
text for their purposes, it was the essentials of the narrative that they
preserved, rather than the digressions. Consequently nothing survives in Diodorus of the constitutional investigations into the

Boiotian league, and it might thus appear dangerous to argue that because Diodorus omits all earlier mention of the union between Corinth and Argos, it did not therefore occur in the Oxyrhynchus historian. But the union of Argos and Corinth was a political event which occurred at a moment in time within the period covered by the histories (whereas the formation of the Boiotian league took place long before). Thus the union of Argos and Corinth should have been dealt with in the narrative as an event, not as a digression, and ought therefore to have preserved at least some indication of its occurrence in Diodorus at the earlier date (392 B.C.) rather than the later.

Even so, such argument is incapable of proof; and with a historian as erratic as Diodorus, an omission of this sort is far from being significant. It may well be that he considered the question of the union more relevant to the events of 390 than 392, and so postponed any mention of it until that year.

The form the union took is equally puzzling. That it was a crude assimilation of one city by another, as Xenophon implies, cannot be seriously maintained; the enthusiasm of the Corinthian democrats for the arrangement hardly suggests that they were the victims of imperialistic aggression. It has been argued that there was an arrangement whereby Argive citizens resident at Corinth received the right to vote in the democratic assembly of the Corinthian people, and, conversely, that Corinthians resident at Argos could participate in the affairs of the Argive assembly. Under normal conditions such a concession would have had little effect, for the number of Argive residents at Corinth (and vice versa) can only have been small, and in no ways sufficient to alter voting decisions which depended on the will of the local population. If a full amalgamation of the two cities had been intended, a joint assembly of all suitably qualified Argives and Corinthians would have been more to the point,[5] and could have been arranged without excessive difficulty (perhaps at a midway point between the two cities, such as Kleonai or the Nemean sanctuary). There is absolutely no evidence for such an arrangement, and no reason to suppose that it existed; yet the 'union' of Argos and Corinth caused much concern to the Spartans (who were anxious to demolish it) and was therefore of deeper significance than a mere courtesy exchange of local voting rights.

Spartan concern obviously derived from the influence Argos was now able to exercise over Corinth. Despite the wavering at the time of Mantinea, Corinth had long been one of the most loyal supporters of Sparta, and it was this break in allegiance that hurt. Though the break seems to have come before the constitutional link with Argos, there was obviously a connection between these developments, and it is noticeable that after Sparta was able to break the Argive connection, Corinth reverted to her traditional loyalty; so there is strong reason to suppose that the constitutional arrangements between Argos and Corinth were indeed meaningful, and were intended to keep Corinth in the anti-Spartan camp. The question of Corinthian influence in Argos does not seem to have arisen, and obviously was not an issue. We must therefore suppose that the form of the arrangement was designed for a specific purpose, to strengthen the democratic element in Corinth, rather than the crude aggrandizement of Argos or the symbolic union of the courtesy exchange.

Direct Argive intervention in the internal politics of Corinth can be seen in the part played by Argive troops at the time of the attempted massacre in 392 B.C. The troops were in Corinth primarily for military reasons; with a Spartan force based at Sikyon, Corinth faced serious intrusions into her territory, and needed to defend the long walls that linked the city with Lechaion, its harbour on the gulf of Corinth. These tasks were perhaps made even more difficult by the political attitudes of Corinth's own hoplite soldiers, for some of them, even if we do not know how many, must have sympathized with the Spartans rather than with the Argives. So the military need was also a political one; and the agreement that Argive troops should be stationed at Corinth by itself has political as well as military implications.

In the middle of the fifth century B.C. Argos had been involved in a military and political arrangement with the Cretan cities of Knossos and Tylissos. This is not recorded in any of the literary accounts that survive of fifth century Greek history, but on inscriptions, one set up at Tylissos and the other at Argos itself, both of which are preserved only in part.[6] It seems from the form of the lettering (but nothing else) that they date from around 450 B.C., but this may mean either before or after the signing of the thirty years' truce with Sparta that ended Argos' alliance with Athens. The texts of the inscriptions describe detailed arrangements for religious, political, military and economic co-operation. In the inscription at Tylissos the regulations for the making of treaties are stated: neither party shall make any new treaty, except with the agreement of the assembly, and the Argives shall cast a third part of the votes. Similarly, there are arrangements for the Tylissan representatives to cast a third part of the votes. In the lines that follow, it is clear that the treaty envisages an Argive army present in the territory of Knossos and Tylissos.

These inscriptions have given rise to much discussion, and it is a pity that the exact circumstances which led to the treaty are quite unknown; the treaty itself suggests a clear antecedent for the relations between Argos and Corinth at the beginning of the fourth century. If the earlier treaty belongs to the years just before 451 B.C., it is tempting to see in the arrangements an attempt by Argos to extend her influence over the Dorian cities of Greece, just as Athens extended her influence over the Ionians; and that this was done with the approval and support of Athens who had not included Dorian Crete in her overseas alliance. Otherwise, we must suppose a simple initiative between the Cretan cities and Argos that was concerned primarily with Cretan affairs and quarrels, in isolation from what seem to us the more important affairs of the mainland cities. The latest discussion of the inscriptions inclines to the idea that the political system envisaged is of a federal structure; the most favoured alternative being a less pretentious arrangement in which Argos is called on to intervene in Cretan affairs in consequence of a belief that the Dorian settlements in Crete were originally founded from Argos.[7]

It is probably going too far to think of the arrangement between Argos, Knossos and Tylissos as a fully integrated federal system, in which the individual identity of each constituent city was merged in a unified political structure. Though both the Knossians and the Tylissans have rights at Argos (which are not defined) the important arrangements seem to concern affairs in Crete; it appears that Argos has a significant share in the arrangements there, and that important aspects of foreign policy require a substantial Argive intervention;[8] but it is surely less likely that the Cretan cities were similarly consulted when Argive policy was determined. If the situation at Argos was relatively stable (as it appears to have been by this time) the advantages of Cretan intervention are difficult to determine; but if the relations between Knossos and Tylissos, and Cretan affairs in general were relatively unstable (and this appears

135

to have been the normal situation there) then the advantages of the introduction of Argos, politically and militarily, as a stabilizing factor are clear. This was achieved by the introduction of an Argive military force, and the establishment of a political arrangement which gave Argos an equal share in a joint assembly irrespective of the actual numbers involved.[9] This represents rather an extension of Argive influence than a restriction of Argive sovereignty. The link surely derives from the fact that all the communities involved are Dorian; whether Argos considered the Cretan cities to be her colonies or not, this is an aspect of Argos' claim, so often overshadowed for us by our lopsided knowledge of Greek history, to be the leader of the Dorians in the Peloponnese.

This aspect is, of course, particularly noticeable in her relations with Corinth at the beginning of the fourth century, when the Corinthians' rejection of Spartan leadership (despite her success in the war against Athens) seemed to give Argos once more an opportunity to renew her claim. It seems possible to translate some of the terms in the treaty between Argos, Knossos and Tylissos to the circumstances of Argos and Corinth in the 390s. There are similar religious involvements—joint participation in holding the Isthmian games. There is a merging of political and economic interests, combined with an Argive military intervention at Corinth. It is possible that Argive influence in the voting of the Corinthian assembly was analogous with the one-third voting rights that the Argives exercised at Crete, and had nothing to do with the actual numbers of Argives present in Corinth at any given moment. Such an arrangement could well fall short of the full federated merger which is the more usual interpretation of these developments, and would explain some of the difficulties over the precise dating. To the pro-Spartan Corinthian oligarchs, to the sort of people who gave Xenophon his information about these developments, the acceptance by Corinth of a treaty similar to that between Argos and the Cretan cities might well be tantamount to an abject surrender of independence—Corinth becomes Argos—and from this it would seem to follow that Corinth was henceforth incapable of independent action. But this would be an exaggeration. Even after a treaty of this type Corinth remained an entity, a recognizable city. Indeed, it is probable that the real antecedent for this sort of arrangement is not the treaty with the Cretan cities, but the earlier agreement, whenever it took place, that brought Kleonai, threatened by Corinth, into close alignment with Argos, gave Argos the right to organize (or share the organization) of the Nemean games but left Kleonai in many respects as an independent and recognizable independent city state.[10]

That being so, the ingredients for such an arrangement between Argos and Corinth existed from 394 B.C., as soon as Corinth was directly threatened by the result of the battle at the Nemea. From that moment, the situation in Corinth was politically unstable, as is proved by the attempted massacre and the betrayal by Corinthian oligarchs of the long walls to the Spartans. From that moment (if not before) there were Argive troops in Corinth. The democrats of Corinth must have welcomed (just as the inhabitants of Kleonai welcomed it when threatened by Corinth) a treaty with Argos that would maintain their interests against mounting pressure; and it is logical to suppose that a treaty incorporating arrangements not dissimilar to those of the treaty with the Cretan cities was agreed in 394. The religious implications of such a treaty became most glaringly obvious at the celebrations of the Isthmian games; perhaps a larger number of Corinthians were shocked by the intrusion of Argos into the religious life of Corinth than by the political moves. For this reason historians like Xenophon associated the 'union' of Argos and Corinth more with the celebration of the Isthmian games than the date when the treaty was actually made.

Even so, some strengthening of the 'union' in 390 B.C. seems probable, particularly as the games were normally held at two-yearly intervals, and should therefore have been celebrated in 392. By 390 the Corinthian war had dragged on to a length that was wearying the combatants. Persian support had proved an illusion. The Spartan king Agesilaos in a brilliant campaign had broken through the defences of Peraia, the region north of Corinth and cut off from the isthmus by the western extremity of Mount Geraneia, which the Corinthians were using as a place of refuge for their livestock, all of which with other movable booty, Agesilaos had captured.[11] Even if the achievement had been offset, militarily speaking, by Iphikrates' destruction of a Spartan regiment, the economic loss to Corinth was in all probability considerable. No doubt agitation for peace, for coming to terms with Sparta was once more heard in Corinth. Once peace was signed Sparta could control the citadel of Corinth and the isthmus. Her domination of Greece would be the more assured. The coalition would be at an end, and both Athens and Argos in a most vulnerable position. Hence the race (for such it seems to be) between Argos and Athens to seize the citadel. Hence the realization by the Corinthian democrats that drastic action was necessary. Rather than become subjects of a possibly resurgent Athens, the Corinthian democrats chose a merger with Argos. It was a triumph for Argive political moderation that this should be preferable, though the union was geographically more logical than one with Athens. It is even more startling (and indeed commendable) that the Corinthians were able to put aside the narrow interests of local patriotism to create a politically stronger state—Greek history would have been very different if more states had followed this example. Nevertheless, it is perhaps fairer to remember that the reason for the merger was essentially the maintenance of class interests; increasingly class interests were rising above city patriotism, and though this is more often noticeable amongst the oligarchs than the democrats (for the oligarchs, being fewer in number, usually had greater need of external support) the events of 389 show that this attitude was by no means limited to them.

Argos' success was shortlived. Until 392 B.C., when Agesilaos briefly took an army into the Argolid, that region had been unscathed by war. Corinth, undoubtedly, suffered much more. In 388 the direct attack was resumed, when the other Spartan king, Agesipolis, gathered an army at Phleious, and although religious obstructions (rather than military ones) were put in his way, carried out a successful and destructive invasion, which ravaged the Argolid up to the walls of Argos itself. But by then it was obvious to all that a solution to the war would have to be imposed from outside. The Corinthian war had forced the Spartans to give up their championing of the Eastern Greeks against Persia, and the Persian king could now regard them in a more favourable light. The solution to the Corinthian war rested, ironically, with Persia, for, although Persia had no hope of controlling Greece through her own military endeavours, the provision of a Persian subsidy gave the power that received it mastery in Greece. Persia could make or break Greece states; her relations with Sparta had amply demonstrated this. When the Greeks were weary of the war, it was to Persia they turned for a solution; and when the Persians had to find a solution, it was to the Spartans that they turned themselves for advice and to act as their agents. In 387 B.C. the King's Peace was signed. All

Greek cities (except those subject to Persia) were to be autonomous and free. Thebes lost control of the Boiotian league, which was dissolved; Argos was forced to restore independence to Corinth; and, with the Greek world forcibly divided into individual cities, Sparta emerged clearly as the strongest. For sixteen more years she controlled the Peloponnese and, for much of that time, most of Greece. She became more hated than even Athens had been at the height of her imperial power.

The consequences of this for Argos are not clear. During the whole period, Sparta acted ruthlessly where her interests were concerned. She was ready to intervene, politically as well as militarily, to maintain governments friendly to herself—oligarchies, naturally— or to weaken states which might endanger her security. This policy was extended over the whole of Greece, even into areas which previously had been too remote to concern the Spartans, except at the height of the war with Athens. Naturally, the Peloponnese received special attention. Corinth once more became a loyal ally, and remained so into the 370s. The democrats who had accepted the union with Argos must have been swept from power, and the pro-Spartan minority reinstated. Full military intervention, and a particularly nauseating political purge ensured that the town of Phleious remained loyal. The Arcadian city of Mantinea which from time to time in the past had been an anti-Spartan ally of Argos was dismantled, its inhabitants being scattered into five separate village communities.

Yet we hear of nothing happening at Argos, until the year 370 B.C., when already Sparta had been shattered by her catastrophic defeat in the previous year at the hands of the Boiotians at Leuktra. In 370 Argos experienced a dramatic political upheaval, which Diodorus, our authority for it, describes as the greatest revolution that ever occurred in any Greek city. At that time, he says, Argos was administered as a democracy. The political leaders of the people decided (for reasons that are not clear) to incite them against the wealthy and powerful minority. Fearful because of this, the minority decided to overthrow the democracy, but their intentions leaked out, and the democratic leaders acted first. The conspirators were threatened with torture. Many of them committed suicide, but one saved himself by accusing thirty of his associates, who were put to death. Suspicions then spread more widely, and a larger number of the wealthier citizens were condemned to death. Soon the situation was out of hand: 1,200 were massacred, and when the democratic leaders, alarmed at developments, tried to restrain the mob, they too were seized and put to death. Perhaps they, too, came from the wealthier families, and were suspected of betraying the democratic interest. After this bloodbath, which was known as the 'skytalismos', from the 'skytale', the club with which the unfortunate victims were beaten to death, the trouble subsided.

This does not give us much of a clue to the situation at Argos during Sparta's supremacy. It is possible that the Spartans had engineered an oligarchic minority government in 387 B.C., that this had been overthrown after the battle of Leuktra, democracy restored and then this bloody vengeance taken. If so, it is a little surprising that Diodorus merely states that Argos was a democracy, not that the democracy had been restored; so there is a slight presumption that Argos continued as a democracy even during the years of Spartan supremacy. If this is so, the massacre is even more deplorable, since it is not occasioned by a crucial struggle for political survival, but is rather an act of vengeance taken as soon as the feared supporter of the wealthy minority, Sparta, was known to be powerless to intervene.

It may seem a little surprising that Sparta was prepared to intervene so ruthlessly in Mantinea and Phleious, but to leave her archenemy Argos alone. Spartan policy, however, is sensible and capable of explanation. She limited her intervention (which she must have realized could only earn her criticism and even opprobrium) to areas where it was absolutely essential. As far as Argos was concerned she seems to have been content to keep her in isolation, where she would be too weak of her own resources to threaten Sparta's interest, rather than risk a perpetual source of trouble by interfering in order to maintain a pro-Spartan minority. By controlling Mantinea, and ensuring the traditional friendly governments in Phleious and Corinth Sparta could maintain direct communications with northern Greece, by-passing the Argolid. Moreover, she could threaten Argos with invasion in all directions (we have seen how Phleious was used as a starting point by Agesipolis in his attack on the Argolid in 388 B.C. and by Agis in 418). Sparta did not intervene where it was unnecessary (the seizure of the citadel of Thebes in 382, and an abortive attempt to establish a base at the Piraeus could at least be argued as an expedient for Sparta, although there was strong opposition to both these developments and they were essentially private ventures).[12] Sparta left the Athenians to follow their own choice of government. The earlier attempt to impose or support oligarchy there had been a dismal failure and Sparta was not prepared to repeat the experiment. Presumably the same reservations applied in the case of Argos, and Sparta was again predisposed to leave well alone, just as the democrats at Argos had the sense not to attack the pro-Spartan minority so long as that was likely to provoke a Spartan intervention.

Argos' role after the downfall of Sparta is strangely subdued.[1]
Naturally she took advantage of the new situation to join in the
hostilities against Sparta, but only in what appears to be a half-
hearted fashion. In the Peloponnese the initiative against Sparta
was taken up above all by the Arcadian cities, and shortly after
Leuktra the army of Mantinea was operating against the Spartans,
with a contingent of Argives as allies. Later, the Argives urged the
Thebans to invade Lakonia itself; but they were not themselves
prepared to take the initiative. Argos sent contingents to the allied
armies led by the Thebans, she was associated with Thebes in the
foundation of a free Messenia, but was really more concerned with
her own local advantages, leaving the prosecution of the major war
more to Thebes and Mantinea, which eventually emerged as the
leading Peloponnesian power. The Argive objectives were her
troublesome neighbours, Epidauros (where an invasion got into
difficulties, the line of retreat being cut by Chabrias the Athenian,
with Athenian and Corinthian troops, so that Mantinea had to
come to the rescue) and Phleious, where a prolonged campaign was
mounted to eliminate the city which had been used by the Spartans
as a chief holding base against Argos. The Argives themselves built
fortifications in the mountains that overlook Phleiasian territory
as a base for their own military activity, and this was the principal
event concerning Argos during the troubled 360s, of which we have
record.[2] Even here, though Phleiasian territory was duly ravaged,
the Argives did not have the immediate success one would expect
for a major power attacking one that was small and now essentially
isolated (though at one stage Phleious was saved only by outside
help, again through the intervention of the Athenian Chabrias).
It would appear that Argos had essentially disappeared from the
list of significant Greek cities.

The Argives fought in the alliance against the Spartans at Mantinea in 362 B.C., but achieved nothing memorable in that engagement. After the confusing outcome of the battle, in which the Spartans were defeated, while the Thebans, the chief enemies of Sparta, lost in the battle the one man who was capable of the diplomatic leadership necessary to maintain Theban supremacy, the situation in Greece was chaotic. No single power could hold the Greek world together, and negotiations to establish peace were based on general exhaustion, rather than any reality of power. In this situation Argos entered a period of sad decline. Isocrates, in his *Philippos* written in 346 B.C.,[3] points out that the Argives are 'worse off' than the Spartans (and this must imply despite the losses that the Spartans had suffered in their war against the Thebans). The Argives were so unsuccessful that hardly a year went by in which they did not see their territory ravaged and laid waste by an invading army. Isocrates is perhaps unduly pessimistic, since his purpose is to emphasize the deplorable conditions of the Greek cities and the need for peace; just as it is a little misleading in the same passage to allude to the 'skytalismos' as a sign of Argive political unrest, when that unfortunate event occurred some twenty-five years before Isocrates composed this work.[4] But the general impression is accurate enough.

A sidelight on the chaotic condition that existed in this region at this confused period of Greek history is shown by the circumstances that led to a court case in Athens. One of the speeches made in court survived through being collected with the speeches of Demosthenes.[5] It is not now regarded as a genuine speech of Demosthenes, but it certainly belongs to this period. The case concerns a sum of money deposited with the Athenian banker Pasion by a certain Lykon before making a trading voyage from Piraeus to Libya. Lykon got no further than the gulf of Argos where he was beset by pirates. His ship and his goods were seized, while he himself was wounded. Goods and wounded man alike were taken to Argos by the pirates. That lawlessness of this sort could rage so close to the great cities of Greece (and that apparently the pirates could use Argos as, presumably, a market for the disposal of their plunder) is indicative of the confusion and lack of leadership then prevalent in the Greek world.

However much Argos may have benefited through such activities, in the long run the losses and hardships and the general lack of confidence must have done greater harm. Diodorus speaks[6] of disturbances in the Peloponnese in 351 B.C., caused by a Spartan attack on the newly founded Arcadian city of Megalopolis. Megalopolis called for help from her allies; Argos, Sikyon and the Messenians sent their full forces, and the Thebans, a sizeable contingent. The Spartans, also heavily reinforced, advanced to Mantinea and then over the mountains into the Argolid where they took Orneai by storm and destroyed it before the Argives could get there. In a small, subsequent engagement the Argives were beaten, and lost two hundred men; but then the Thebans turned up, and a more serious but drawn engagement was fought. This, and subsequent engagements were largely indecisive. In the following year the Thebans had to ask the Persian king Artaxerxes for a financial subsidy, while in the same year Artaxerxes himself successfully appealed to the Greeks for troops to help him in his reconquest of Egypt. Thebes sent him a thousand, Argos no fewer than three thousand. These are in effect mercenaries. Argos was not able to maintain her full citizen army to defend herself and despite the possibility of renewed war with Sparta had to allow half her hoplites to serve overseas on behalf of a foreign king; they in their turn, were presumably only too glad to find the rewards such service offered. That Argos was forced to follow the example of the Arcadian cities in becoming a source of mercenary soldiers is a certain indication of the economic hardships that encompassed the Greek world at this time. The Persian king was well enough informed about Argive affairs to name the man he wanted as commander of the Argive contingent. Perhaps this was not the first occasion on which he had used Argive troops. But this marks the last known contact between the Argives and their old friend the king of Persia. Argos, along with other Greek states, was to welcome with enthusiasm the arrival on the Greek political scene of a man who seemed likely to restore order and confidence within the Greek world. It was to this man, Philip, king of Macedon, that Isocrates appealed for a solution to the problems of the Greek cities. He was already rising to power on the Greek mainland and when, as master of Greece, he began the Greek crusade against the Persians, the Argives were already long-standing allies.

It is not certain when the Argives became the friends and allies of Philip. It was already an established fact in 343 B.C. when at Athens Demosthenes accused his political rival Aeschines in the speech on the false embassy. In this speech[7] Demosthenes points out that support for Philip (who had not yet concerned himself with affairs further south than Delphi) had already been manifested in certain parts of the Peloponnese. Support for Philip had caused a massacre in Elis (presumably, though this is not certain, of pro-Spartan oligarchs by the democrats). Statues of Philip had been set up in Arcadia, and decrees passed welcoming Philip if and when he should choose to go there. This, says Demosthenes, had also been done by Argos.

Argos' confidence in the potentialities of Philip as the new leader of Greece were justified after the battle of Chaironeia in 338 B.C. This should not be regarded as a simple matter of taking selfish advantage of the achievements of the man responsible for the destruction of Greek freedom, any more than that the settlement ratified by the Greeks under Philip's leadership at Corinth in 337 B.C. was a cynical sham disguising the reality of Greece's subjection. The traditional leaders of the Greek world had lost all authority. Sparta had never had the support of Argos and was quite incapable of solving the chaotic problems of the Peloponnese. Athens was discredited, and even at her height, never intervened effectively in the Peloponnese, except destructively or for her own advantage. Thebes had exercised no authority since the death of Epaminondas at Mantinea. From the point of view of states like Argos and the Arcadian cities a guarantee of peace and good order was desperately needed, and the terms on which Philip offered that at Corinth were the work of a genuine statesman, and designed to reconcile the divided states of Greece, not only to the existence of a militarily superior Macedon, but also with each other. This was to be the new cornerstone of Argive policy. The existence of the joint organization agreed at Corinth, with its ability to raise military forces to protect the integrity of member states gave the necessary guarantee for peace. Presumably there was also hope that it might do away with acts of piracy, for joint action against the pirates was envisaged in the treaty.

Argos also received more direct benefits. Though Sparta had been invaded in the autumn of 338 B.C. she refused to take part in the peace settlement. Nevertheless she was powerless to resist the loss of certain outlying parts of her territory. Border disputes were settled by the league, and naturally Sparta was at a disadvantage. These disputes were with Messenia, Megalopolis, Tegea and, of course, Argos. The settlements are mentioned in passing on several occasions by Polybius, but he nowhere states precisely what Argos gained.[8] There can be no doubt that from this time the Thyreatis is definitely and permanently Argive. Further south, the remainder of Kynouria had long been claimed by Argos, as part of the erstwhile 'restored lot of Temenos' taken from her by Sparta. One of the Kynourian towns, Zarax (Hieraka) appears as an Argive canton name in an inscription which unfortunately cannot be dated precisely[9] and the same place is attacked by the Spartans (and is therefore an Argive possession) in 219 B.C.[10] However, another small town, Tyros, which is to the north of Zarax, is mentioned in another inscription[11] belonging to the early part of the third century which records the sacrifice of fifty bulls to Apollo at Delphi and there it is described as a village of Lakonia. Thus it appears that Philip did not give Kynouria to Argos after 338. This is a little surprising. It can have been of no advantage to Philip to allow this coastal strip to remain in the hands of Sparta. If Argos already possessed the Thyreatis, then it is difficult to see what else can have been awarded to her at that settlement, and the possibility must remain that in the confused situation at the end of the fourth century Sparta was able to recover at least this possession. But it is more likely that Argos had been unable, by her own efforts, to regain the Thyreatis even from a weakened Sparta, had to wait for Philip to give it back to her and did not regain Kynouria until later. Even if the details elude us, the important fact remains: Philip guaranteed and restored the territorial integrity of the Argolid, satisfying Argive claims to the detriment of Sparta. Argos had every reason to be grateful to the Macedonian king and his successors.

Yet this gratitude did not last. After Philip's murder in 336 B.C. Greek history is more concerned with the spectacular achievements of his son Alexander than the fluctuating policies of one Greek city state—and at that a city which had never dominated the scene in earlier, simpler days.[1] Yet we do know a certain amount about Argos' reaction to events even though it is difficult to see any valid motives or policy behind them. It seems not unlikely that the fluctuations in policy resulted from the existence in Argos of individual politicians who tried to take advantage of changes in public opinion, now for, now against the Macedonian supremacy, to further their own careers. At Athens, the division had been more between those who collaborated with the Macedonians and those who did not; although the distinction between oligarch and democrat can be and has been applied to them, neither the political situation nor the meaning of these terms is the same as at Argos. At times the Argive people must have doubted the efficacy of Macedonian support, and a change of attitude sent them to other leaders. It is the essential anonymity of Argive politics (in contrast to those of contemporary Athens) that makes it impossible to understand the reasons that lie behind these changes.

The rise to power of Philip had been contrary to the usual role of Macedonia in Greek affairs. His own genius was recognized by the Greeks, but this led them to believe that the achievement had been largely a personal one; they therefore anticipated an immediate disintegration of Macedonian superiority after his death, particularly as his successor was merely a twenty-year-old boy, and the Macedonian royal family had been plagued throughout the previous century by assassinations and disputed succession. It is not therefore surprising that Argos, along with most of the Peloponnese, contemplated breaking from the Macedonian alliance at the news of

Philip's death. This moment of disloyalty did not amount to much. In the end Alexander was to demonstrate that he had effectively succeeded to his father's kingdom, and that Macedonian military power and authority were undiminished. The warning was amply demonstrated by his relentless siege of Thebes, and the ruthless destruction of that city after he had captured it. This earned him the fear of the Greeks (not even his much publicized contrition after the event could ever earn him their affection) and Argos, like the other Greek cities, deemed it imprudent to pursue their rebellion further.

The next serious upheaval came when Alexander was miles away, fighting in the heart of the Persian Empire from which, despite his initial success, many Greeks must have considered it unlikely he would return successful. Sparta alone of the Greek states had never acquiesced in Macedonian supremacy, out of stubborn pride rather than any sense of political reality. Now when Alexander was remote and apparently more concerned with his own ambitions than the interests and affairs of Greece a rebellion seemed a more feasible proposition. Under the Spartan King Agis III most of the Peloponnese rebelled. Argos may have been involved, but we have no direct knowledge of this and it is unlikely that the Argives would have joined a rebellion led by Sparta. Alexander's regent in Macedonia, Antipater, was eventually able to muster an army of forty thousand men, Macedonians and allied Greeks, outnumbering Agis' forces two to one. A battle was fought in the Peloponnese, presumably somewhere on the route south from the isthmus to Sparta, in which Agis was killed and the Macedonians were victorious. As long as Alexander lived, the Macedonian grip on the Greek alliance seemed assured; dissatisfied though the Greeks became at the high-handed treatment they now received (unlike the tactful diplomacy of Philip), they knew their weakness and bided their time.

In 323 B.C., unexpectedly, Alexander died. His empire was thrown into an immediate foment, since there was no obvious successor to him—certainly no one of any competence. To the Greeks again it seemed that Macedonian power was about to prove its essentially ephemeral character, and once more there was a rebellion. This time the Athenians took the lead; of the Peloponnesian states Sparta was still licking her wounds, but the rebels were joined by Argos, as well as Sikyon, Elis, Messenia, Troizen and Epidauros.[2] The brunt of the fighting was born by the Athenians and the Aitolians, and took place in northern Greece, chiefly round the city of Lamia (hence its name, the Lamian war). Before it ended, most of the allies had deserted the cause, and only the protagonists were left. The other cities, Diodorus says, each made a separate peace with the regent of Macedonia, Antipater. Events four years later give some idea of the terms that peace imposed on the Argives. By that time Antipater was dead. He had been succeeded in the regency by another Macedonian general, Polyperchon, but the succession was disputed by Antipater's son Cassander, who thought it should be a hereditary office. In order to win the support of the Greeks in the struggle that resulted, Polyperchon renewed the 'freedom of Greece' which had been a term of Philip's settlement, and which had been ended by Antipater after the Lamian war, when he had imposed on the Greek cities garrisons, and oligarchies formed from his supporters. After issuing a general decree to this effect Polyperchon wrote to Argos (named specifically by Diodorus) and the other cities, instructing them to send into exile those politicians put in charge by Antipater, to condemn some of them to death and to confiscate their property. This was followed by the dispatching of envoys to the cities telling them to kill the oligarchic rulers appointed by Antipater and to establish democratic autonomy. Many of the cities obeyed and there was much slaughter. Only Megalopolis in Arcadia remained friendly to Cassander, but when Polyperchon failed to capture it by storm, enthusiasm for him waned. The cities once more reverted to Cassander, and at Athens in particular, a strict regime was imposed, under the care of one of Cassander's supporters, Demetrius of Phaleron. Demetrius' title means 'curator'; in effect he was tyrant, a man exercising unlimited personal power. This form of government was to be used more and more by the rulers of Macedonia, as the most effective instrument for the maintenance of their interests in Greece.

Argos, however, remained loyal to Polyperchon and his son. It was not until 316 B.C. that Cassander, after being checked at the isthmus, was able to ferry his troops across to Epidauros and thence, advancing south, compelled Argos to change allegiance once more. Nevertheless the opposition was still strong; Alexander, the son of Polyperchon, had returned to the Peloponnese backed by an alliance with Antigonos, one of the most powerful of Alexander the Great's former generals who were struggling for control of the empire, together with a substantial subsidy. Argos was kept loyal to Cassander only by the presence of a Macedonian commander, Apollonides, and a garrison. Taking advantage of the return of Alexander and the absence on an expedition to Arcadia of Apollonides, the Argives resolved to changed sides again. Unfortunately for them Alexander did not act quickly enough and Apollonides returned to Argos before anything was achieved. He found the opponents of Cassander, to the number of five hundred, in the town hall[3] of Argos. Quietly closing the doors, he set fire to the building and burnt them all alive. Other members of the opposition he killed or drove into exile. Once more Argive politics had achieved a bloody outcome.

The Greek cities were now pawns in the hands of the Macedonian generals, and the question of their freedom or subjugation was a matter to be decided by Macedonian policies. Antigonos, who by this time had begun the campaign that was intended to give him the supremacy over the whole of Alexander's empire, decided to gain the support of the Greeks by winning for them their freedom; so he sent an expedition, backed by fifty ships, to liberate the Peloponnese. This freed all the cities which had been held by Alexander son of Polyperchon (who in the meantime had been assassinated). Polyperchon, however, succeeded in retaining Sikyon and Corinth. In 311 B.C. the leading Macedonians, including Cassander and Antigonos, made peace with each other; Cassander was recognized as 'general over the Macedonians and Greeks', and Polyperchon ceased to be of any real significance. The freedom of Greece for which Antigonos had fought was officially recognized in the peace treaty, though this was a clause that did not have much significance. In reality, Greece was now controlled by no less than three Macedonian military groups, that of Cassander and others retained, perhaps with dubious loyalty, by Antigonos and Polyperchon.

In 308 B.C., the picture was complicated still further by the arrival in Greece of Ptolemy (who had been ruling Egypt since Alexander's death). His policy, needless to say, involved yet another proclamation of the freedom of the Greek cities—his purpose, to avert the danger of isolation in Egypt, where he might be out-manoeuvred by the other generals, in particular Antigonos. He occupied Corinth and Sikyon, but failed to win over the other Greek cities, or at least, those who controlled them. In disgust, he made peace with Cassander, each to hold the cities he already possessed, and returned to Egypt, leaving garrisons in Corinth and Sikyon. So much for the freedom of Greece.

In 307 B.C. it was Antigonos' turn to resume this insincere crusade. He sent his son Demetrius with a full force and including the siege engines that were to earn him the name of 'the besieger', for the purpose of freeing all the cities of Greece, and in particular Athens. Athens was freed, and, after an interlude when a campaign was staged in Cyprus against Ptolemy, the liberation of other Greek cities continued. In 303 (having failed to capture Rhodes, one of the few Greek cities that actually was free) he at last freed Argos and in addition took Sikyon and Corinth, freed the Achaean cities and captured Orchomenos; the fortunes of Cassander were on the ebb. Then again, there was a startling change of fortune; Demetrius was called from Greece to the east by his father to fight at the battle of Ipsos that marked the culmination of Antigonos' bid for supremacy. In that battle Antigonos was defeated and killed and Demetrius became a king almost without a kingdom, retaining a few cities (in Greece he held Corinth but not Athens) and his magnificent fleet.

From these unpromising resources Demetrius recovered to make himself king of Macedon, after the death of Cassander. His interest in the freedom of the Greeks was no more sincere than that of his predecessors, and a garrison was maintained at Corinth. What happened at Argos is uncertain; but, for the time being, none of the Greek cities was in a position to be overtly hostile to the king. It is unlikely that Argos was garrisoned, since it was not so strategically placed as Corinth. There was little to be gained from supporting the more distant enemies of Demetrius, and a city which had received with some enthusiasm Philip's original league of Corinth had no grounds for dissatisfaction with Demetrius' revival of it.

Argos does not re-emerge in the scantily-recorded history of Greece in the third century until the late 270s. By then Demetrius had been deposed as king of Macedon, had made his last desperate fling to win an empire in the east, and had drunk himself to death. His son Antigonos had clung to the last remnants of his possessions in Greece, particularly Corinth—it is not known whether Argos remained loyal at this juncture—and from this succeeded in restoring himself to Macedon. He had become involved in struggles with the ambitious king of Epirus in north-west Greece, Pyrrhus (whose sister had been one of Demetrius' wives) who had the support of Ptolemy of Egypt; but Pyrrhus had gone to create a new Greek empire in the west. Pyrrhus' western adventure came to nothing and in 374 B.C. he returned to Greece. Antigonos' hold over Macedon was still uncertain;[4] even if Pyrrhus had achieved little in the west, he had won magnificent victories (his lack of success was largely a political one, his failure to win serious support from the Greeks of Italy and Sicily) and his military reputation could still in all seriousness be compared with that of Alexander the Great. Greece wavered in its loyalties, and supporters of Pyrrhus were to be found in the Greek cities, including Sparta and Argos.

In both cities the chief support for Pyrrhus appears to have centred round single individuals, Kleonymos at Sparta and Aristeas at Argos. Kleonymos was younger brother of a Spartan king. On the brother's death the succession had passed to his son, but Kleonymos felt he had been passed over for a kingship that should have been his. He had entered the service of Pyrrhus and doubtless hoped to use Pyrrhus' support to obtain the kingship of Sparta for himself. The Argive situation developed after Pyrrhus had failed to capture Sparta, though probably not so suddenly as Plutarch, anxious to emphasize the sudden shifts of Pyrrhic policy, makes out. Aristeas was in feud with Aristippos. Plutarch does not tell us exactly what the cause of feud was, merely saying that Aristippos appeared to enjoy the friendship of Antigonos. Aristippos was in effect tyrant of Argos, and founder of a dynasty which was to rule Argos until it joined the Achaean league in 229; since Argos, as far as we know, was a supporter of the Antigonids from 303 onwards, this family may well have exercised political authority, with Antigonid support, long before the coming of Pyrrhus in 272.[5] Aristeas presumably hoped to gain the supremacy for himself with the support of Pyrrhus. Baulked in his hopes of occupying Sparta, Pyrrhus suddenly switched his attention to Argos, where Aristeas arranged to admit him to the city. Pyrrhus' change of plan was not so sudden that Antigonos did not get to hear of it, and was thus enabled to dispatch an army to the Argolid. It did not attempt to enter the city, perhaps because Antigonos was uncertain of the reception he would receive, but waited instead on the hills 'overlooking the plain' (probably those above Mycenae and the Heraion, since Antigonos came from Corinth). Pyrrhus brought his army into the plain, past Argos itself and pitched camp near Nauplia (this again indicates that Antigonos was on the eastern side). Antigonos refused to fight. Though he had available garrison troops in Corinth, it is unlikely that he could have mustered a force anything like equal to that of Pyrrhus in fighting ability, at least in open battle. The

Argives were not anxious to be fought over; they sent ambassadors to both kings, asking them to withdraw. Antigonos agreed to do so, leaving, so Plutarch says, his son as hostage for his good behaviour at Argos. Pyrrhus also promised to go away, but left no pledge of his good word. The following night, Pyrrhus advanced to the city walls, where Aristeas had arranged that the Diamperes gate should be opened for him. His soldiers, Gallic mercenaries, entered the city and occupied the agora, unnoticed. The alarm was given when Pyrrhus tried to bring in one of his war elephants, which had caused so much amazement when he had used them against the Romans. This time, they caused only confusion. The elephants carried on their backs, built up for fighting, platforms called towers, which presumably contained soldiers armed with missile weapons. The gates of Argos were large enough to admit the usual wheeled traffic that entered Greek cities; but obviously were not designed to cope with war elephants. Elephant and tower could not pass through the gate. In the darkness the towers had to be removed while the elephants were led through, and then replaced. The delay and the noise were sufficient to warn the Argives and give them time to act, and they occupied the Aspis and other strongholds (not, perhaps, the Larisa, which was too remote to be of use in preventing Pyrrhus' occupation of the lower town). Word was sent to Antigonos, who now brought his armies up to the city, and sent in a relief force. The Spartan king, Areus, who had harassed Pyrrhus on the way north, also brought up Cretan archers and light armed troops.[6]

Pyrrhus was not yet in the city himself. He relied on the advance force he had sent in to open other gates, and eventually entered by way of Kylarabis, at some distance from the agora. By then the Argives and their reinforcement had mounted a successful counter-attack, and Pyrrhus' Gauls were in confusion. The reason for the separate entrance made by Pyrrhus seems to have been that, as befitted a Hellenistic king, and especially a second Alexander, he was mounted, and leading a cavalry force. The road past Kylarabis formed the main route into the city from the southern Argolid, may well have carried more wheeled traffic, and was probably wider and more suitable for cavalry. Even so, there was still confusion; the streets were lined with open water channels, which were deep enough to make difficulties for the horses, particularly in the dark.

When light eventually dawned on this chaotic scene (vividly described by Plutarch, who obviously derives his account ultimately from an eye-witness version) Pyrrhus realized that his hopes of taking the city by surprise had been thwarted, and that he was in a most dangerous situation. He sent orders to his son Helenos, who had the reserve forces outside the city, to demolish a section of the walls to facilitate his retreat, but the message was not carried correctly. Instead Helenos entered the city himself with still more elephants and picked soldiers to help his father. Pyrrhus was a genius in the open field battle, but street fighting, particularly in an irregular and unplanned city like Argos, where many streets were only narrow alleyways, was a completely different matter. Conventional manoeuvring and handling of troops was possible only in the open space of the agora. Once driven from that, Pyrrhus was doomed to defeat. Forced out of the agora, Pyrrhus was driven back towards the gate, only to be hampered by the fresh troops that had poured in to help him. Even those who managed to withdraw found they could not get out of the city, for the largest elephant had fallen sideways on across the gate, and roaring in pain and panic, could not rise. Another elephant inside the city (we are told its name, Nikon) was wandering uncontrolled, looking for its rider, who had fallen wounded from its back. When it found the body it lifted it with its trunk and carried it on its tusks, trampling all that came in its way.

Pyrrhus was trapped. He removed the royal diadem from his helmet, to avoid recognition, and charged on horseback into the thick of the fray, trying to force an escape. He was wounded, and turned on a man who had caught him with his spear. This man's mother, Plutarch says, 'like the rest of the women' was watching the battle from the house roofs. Anxious for her son's safety, she managed to lift a heavy pantile from the roof and threw it down on to the king. Pyrrhus was stunned, fell to the ground and was killed by Macedonian soldiers as he was on the verge of recovery. Thus ended what is certainly the most vivid incident (or at least, the most vividly recorded) in the whole history of Argos.

The presence of a Macedonian garrison at Corinth proved sufficient to ensure the continued maintenance of Aristippos at Argos. Antigonos, however, was king of Macedonia, not merely of Greece, and naturally his chief interest—and, indeed, place of residence—was there. His concern for Greece was largely that it would not be used by an enemy to undermine his authority in Macedonia—and, therefore, he relied more on trusted supporters such as Aristippos to maintain his interests than on unreliable ideals such as the 'freedom of Greece', which would only place Greece in the hands of a rival strong man. The chief concern was stability and peace, and if it required that Argos should be ruled by a man whom the outside world (and his enemies in Argos itself) regarded as a tyrant, that was no concern of Antigonos. So long as Antigonos and his Macedonian kingdom represented the major military power in the Greek mainland, Aristippos' authority was assured. So, also, was the peace and stability of Argos, and there is no reason to doubt that the city was by and large prosperous.[7]

We hear next of Argos at the middle of the century. Antigonos had left a member of his family, Alexander, son of his half-brother Krateros, in charge of the garrison at Corinth, and in effect, viceroy over his Greek interests. Alexander was tempted to declare his independence, and since Corinth and its garrison was the key to control of the Peloponnese, this act crucially undermined Antigonos' authority in Greece. By this time Aristippos was dead and affairs at Argos were controlled by his son Aristomachos. The Macedonian interest was the same, and Aristomachos loyally joined in a war against Alexander, on Antigonos' behalf. In this the Argives were joined by the Athenians, and our knowledge of these events comes from an inscription which the Athenians set up on the acropolis in honour of Aristomachos, who is named only as an important individual, and is given no official title.[8] Apparently Argos and Athens were left to fight Alexander alone, without support from Macedon, and not surprisingly the war did not go too well for them. They were forced to sue for peace, which was granted to them, on condition of payment. Alexander presumably needed cash to pay for his garrison at Corinth, which would have consisted largely of mercenary troops, not native Macedonians. Alexander tried to buy off the Argives separately, at a reduced rate; but Aristomachos was able to secure a joint peace for both Argos and Athens by paying the additional sum of five talents from his own resources. It was in gratitude for this that the Athenians set up the inscription in the acropolis. That Aristomachos could do this is an indication of his family fortune and of the personal advantage to be obtained from controlling a Greek city on behalf of the Macedonian king.

Alexander's rebellion was a sign of weakness on the part of Antigonos and though (after Alexander's death) he was able to regain the possession of the crucial citadel at Corinth, it was only done by a trick. The weakening of Macedonian authority in turn weakened those regimes, like that of Aristomachos, which depended on it, and encouraged not only their rivals but other organizations which hoped to create a Greece freed from Macedonian control. In the Peloponnese the chief of these was the Achaean league. Not only did its importance in the Greek world increase considerably when the pro-Macedonian tyrant of Sikyon was overthrown and that city joined to the league by Aratos (who rapidly rose to prominence in it) but it was now in a position to challenge Macedonian authority and supporters elsewhere and particularly at Corinth and Argos.

Corinth fell first. The capture of Acrocorinth in 243 was Aratos' most famous military exploit, even though it was taken by a trick, in a surprise attack by night, and without the forewarning of a declaration of war. With the capture of Acrocorinth, the city was soon taken. The land link between Macedonia and the Peloponnese was severed. Argos—or at least the pro-Macedonian regime there— was obviously threatened, since its territory now lay immediately adjacent to that of the league.

The account of the inevitable conflict is given in Plutarch's biography of Aratos; this in turn derives from Aratos' memoirs, and can hardly be expected to be favourable to the Argive tyrant. Aratos himself knew Argos and, indeed, the political situation there. At the age of seven Aratos' father Kleinias had been killed in a political assassination at Sikyon. Aratos himself was smuggled out of the city and sent to live with family friends in Argos. Here he received his education and here he remained until he was of age to seize power once more in Sikyon. As the son of a prominent politician Aratos' presence in Argos must have been known to the authorities there and tolerated. Aratos' attacks on Argos was as much an act of treachery as his seizure of the Acrocorinth had been.

His apologia states that he was distressed at the servitude of the Argives, and that he plotted to kill Aristomachos, the tyrant of Argos, being ambitious to restore its freedom to the city as a reward for the rearing it had given him, as well as to attach it to the Achaean league. As Pyrrhus before him, he found supporters in Argos itself, the leaders being one Aischylos and Charmenes the soothsayer. These two fell out, and Charmenes turned informer; the murder was averted, though most of the would-be assassins succeeded in escaping to Corinth. Shortly after this Aristomachos was killed by slaves (we are not told whether or not this was done with Aratos' connivance) and his place as tyrant of Argos taken by Aristippos II, who was presumably son of Aristomachos and grandson of Aristippos I.

Aratos thereupon decided on full military intervention; he called on the Achaean levy and marched against Argos. There he found that the Argives were by this time 'so habituated to slavery and willing to endure it' that not a man came over to his side, so that he had to withdraw. Plutarch's language is ingenuous; but it cannot conceal that, far from being a harsh and oppressive tyrant, the regime of Aristippos and his successors was accepted by many of the Argives, who presumably derived not inconsiderable benefit from it. Certainly they did not see fit to reject local independence (even under a tyrant) in favour of submergence into the broader organization of the Achaean league. Aratos' act had been not only hostile, but treacherous against a city with which the league was officially in a state of peace. The Argives, represented by Aristippos laid complaints against Aratos, and the court case was held (under the rules of international arbitration which had grown up in Hellenistic times) at Mantinea. Aratos was found guilty and fined half a talent.

This had little effect. Aratos continued to harass Aristippos with attacks in Argos openly or in secret, though we are not informed whether or not war had been officially declared. On one occasion Aratos succeeded in scaling the walls and entering the city, only to discover once again that the Argives were not interested in these attempts to win them their freedom. He even attempted a pitched battle at the river Chares, a risky business, since Aratos was no military genius, and turned what might have been a victory into defeat. Even so, by diplomatic means (in which he displayed greater skill) he was able to detach Kleonai from Argos, and bring it into the Achaean league. This gave Aratos control of Nemea, and he was able to celebrate under his own auspices the Nemean games which had been under Argive control and which were by this time normally celebrated at Argos. Shortly afterwards he tricked Aristippos into making an attack on Kleonai in the belief that Aratos was at Kenchreiai, one of the harbours of Corinth. Aristippos was taken by surprise and defeated. Pursued back toward Argos, he was overtaken near Mycenae and put to death.

Even so Aratos did not gain control of Argos and there was no revolution in his favour. The 'younger' Aristomachos (the younger brother of Aristippos), backed by Macedonian troops, took charge of the city and for a while the dynasty continued. Nevertheless, the end was in sight. Since the death of old king Antigonos Macedon had become less involved in the affairs of southern Greece. The prestige of the Achaean league was growing and the support offered by Macedon weakening. One by one the cities of Greece made their terms with Aratos. The first to approach him was Megalopolis, ruled by a tyrant called Lydiades. Lydiades voluntarily surrendered his authority and, in return, was elected general by the league. Obviously the league now offered greater scope for ambitious politicians than absolute control over a single city. There was obvious and open rivalry within the league between Aratos and Lydiades, but there was room for both of them; one of the rules of the league was that no man should be general two years in succession, and so Aratos and Lydiades could hold that office alternately. In the end Aratos prevailed and, after serving as general for the third time Lydiades was put on one side. Perhaps Aratos had other hopes. While Lydiades was still general the Achaeans approached Aristomachos in Argos with the suggestion that he should adopt the same policy, giving up his isolated position as pro-Macedonian tyrant, and join the Achaean league. Aristomachos realized the weakness of his position and agreed, on payment of fifty talents which he needed to pay off his garrison of mercenary soldiers. Plutarch says the initial approach was made by Aratos, but that Lydiades actually made the proposal to the Achaean council that Aristomachos should be accepted. Aratos then spoke against it, and it was rejected. However, Aratos thereupon changed his mind, spoke in favour, and the proposal was successful. Argos and Phleious were admitted to the league and, after a year, Aristomachos himself was elected general. As Plutarch tells it, the story is designed to show Aratos' hold over the league, and is part of Aratos' apologia taken from his memoirs. Aristomachos may not have had any strong feelings about Aratos' part in the death of his brother (which had, after all, put him in a position of power) and he may well have been hard-headed enough to let political realism overcome feelings of sentiment; but on the whole, it seems likely that Lydiades would have been a more suitable go-between for the league with Aristomachos than Aratos. Further, the accession to the league of Argos and Aristomachos would upset the uneasy balance between Aratos and Lydiades. Whom would it favour? If Aratos made the original approach, he presumably saw in Aristomachos a counterbalance to the influence that Lydiades was already wielding. Lydiades may well have realized this, and so, as one ex-tyrant to a would-be ex-tyrant suggested a political alliance of his own with Aristomachos. If his influence was in fact waning, he may even have made the original approach to Aristomachos. Whatever the truth, the final alliance was with Aratos. This tipped the balance. Aratos supported Aristomachos' application and was successful, and Lydiades was eventually supplanted.

It was not without a struggle. While these developments were taking place, Kleomenes III, king of Sparta, had grown suspicious of Achaean ambition. The Spartans had not forgotten their old hostility towards Argos and Megalopolis and anticipated that they might fall the next victim to Aratos' expansionist policies, particularly now that the ex-tyrants of Argos and Megalopolis were prominent in the league. Kleomenes therefore opened an attack, invading the territory of Megalopolis in 227 B.C. Aristomachos had been elected general for that year. Against Aratos' wishes he resolved to fight Kleomenes. Aratos was summoned from Athens to accompany the army and succeeded in preventing Aristomachos from fighting, though the Spartans were outnumbered four to one —it was too dangerous to allow a political rival the prestige of a military victory that Aratos found so difficult to achieve for himself. Megalopolis was put in jeopardy and Lydiades stood against Aratos for election as general for the following year. Lydiades failed, Aratos was elected and in his turn as general was defeated by Kleomenes.

In the same year, the Spartans followed up this success with an attack on Megalopolis itself. In the battle that followed Lydiades taunted Aratos for not making a proper attempt to pursue the Spartans after a skirmish. Lydiades himself pursued the Spartans with his cavalry and was killed in a decisive Spartan counter-attack. The authority of Kleomenes was strengthened by his success and he was able to put into effect social reforms which he had already planned. An essential part of this was the confiscation of large estates and a redistribution of the land to the poor and landless. The new landholders were enabled to serve as soldiers and Kleomenes rapidly recreated a Spartan army of fair proportions. More significantly, this move (which had been foreshadowed in Sparta by an earlier king, Agis IV, and had received the support of political philosophers) roused the hopes in other cities that the

Spartans would extend the social revolution. The support for the Achaean league dwindled, while the strength of Kleomenes' Sparta grew.

A meeting of the Achaean league invited Kleomenes to take over the league, and called him to Argos (where presumably the meeting took place). At Lerna, which he had reached with his army, he was requested by Aratos to come to the city with only a personal escort of three hundred.[9] Kleomenes refused, withdrew his forces and declared war. He made startling gains in the central Peloponnese, in effect splitting the league in two, so that it appeared that it was disintegrating. Taking advantage of the religious truce declared on the occasion of the Nemean games, Kleomenes captured Argos, where he was made welcome by the people. At some stage, possibly before the capture of the city, Aristomachos changed sides once more. The desire to maintain a personal position counted for more than political loyalties and agreements;[10] Aratos himself showed no greater political faith for, with his position undermined by the growing power of Sparta, he was himself forced to come to terms with the Macedonians. Macedonian power proved decisive. Kleomenes had gone on to take Corinth city and to besiege the Acrocorinth itself, but on news of the imminent arrival of the Macedonian king, Antigonos Doson, he had given ground. Argos which had received him with enthusiasm, shut her gates against him; the hoped for revolution had not taken place and fear of the Macedonians was stronger. After Argos had turned against Kleomenes a massacre was carried out, instigated by leading Macedonians, presumably of those Argives who had turned against the Achaeans and had supported Kleomenes as the bringer of social revolution. Aristomachos had changed sides too soon; with Aratos dependent on the old supporter of the Argive tyranny he would assuredly have reached a position of real authority in the league. As it was, even though he had been captured as an enemy, Aratos feared that he would succeed in gaining the support of Antigonos. Aratos therefore had himself elected general by the Argives; as a bribe he persuaded them to hand over the property of Aristomachos and his family to the Macedonians, while Aristomachos himself was tortured at Kenchreiai and thrown into the sea to drown. The blame for this act was fairly put on Aratos himself.

Antigonos soon made it clear that his alliance with Aratos did not involve wholesale approval of the Achaean's previous anti-

Macedonian success. The statues at Argos of Aristippos' dynasty, which had been overthrown (presumably after Aristomachos' death) were reinstated on Antigonos' orders, while those of the Achaeans who had originally taken Acrocorinth from the Macedonians were themselves taken down, a polite exception being made for that of Antigonos' personal friend Aratos. The troubles of Argos were not over. Though Antigonos had set the affairs of Argos in order, the war with Kleomenes continued. In February and March of 222 B.C. Kleomenes staged a daring and successful raid on the Argolid. Though Antigonos himself was wintering in Argos Kleomenes took his army into Argive territory by a difficult route over Mount Parnon. His chief hope seems to have been to provoke a revolution within Argos itself that Antigonos would not be able to contain. The mob were duly indignant with Antigonos, but their indignation was ignored. A sizeable garrison and a fortified position counted for more than political sympathies in the Hellenistic world and later in that same year Antigonos went on to end Kleomenes' hopes for ever at the battle of Sellasia.

Sparta was not harshly treated by Antigonos. The blame for this disorder was attributed to Kleomenes (who had fled to Egypt) and the social revolution. The Spartans were given back 'their ancestral constitution'—power restored into the hands of the few wealthy landowners. Antigonos withdrew by way of Tegea (which also received its ancestral constitution) and Argos, where no political interference was necessary. Having attended the celebration of the Nemean festival (in Argos once more) postponed because of the war, he returned to Macedon, to die shortly after of tuberculosis, leaving the kingdom to his young nephew, Philip the son of Demetrius.

Philip inherited the settlement of Greece created by Antigonos and Aratos; that the major power in the Peloponnese should be the Achaean league, allied to and supported by the Macedonian kingdom, but without direct Macedonian control—a new version of the 'freedom of Greece'. As before, the absence of direct Macedonian control led to political instability, particularly as Achaean supremacy was unlikely to go unchallenged. In central Greece the Aitolian league had successfully maintained its independence from Macedonia since the time of the Lamian war, and, anxious to avoid being isolated by the Achaean-Macedonian alliance, it looked for friends in southern Greece. Any state dissatisfied with Achaea could hope for Aitolian support, and it was not long before Aitolian armies were operating in the Peloponnese. The stability of the Macedonian period was undermined.

Before long full-scale war had broken out in which Achaea and the young Philip of Macedon attempted to coerce the Aitolians. In the course of this a rebellion was started in Sparta, where supporters of Kleomenes sought to challenge the supremacy of Achaea; ironically, this coincided with Kleomenes' death. An alliance was made with the Aitolians and a new king appointed, Lykourgos. His claim to the throne was obscure, and challenged; but he seems to have been a member of the royal family. The awkwardness about the succession makes it likely that he led the revolution; certainly as king he was to play a prominent part in it. In 219 B.C. he took a Spartan army across Parnon to attack Argos. The Argives were not expecting an attack, believing that the events of the previous years and the settlement after Sellasia had made such an occurrence unthinkable. Lykourgos therefore had the benefit of surprise. He captured several of the coastal towns which once had been Spartan— Polichnai, Prasiai, Leukai and Kyphanta, but failed to take Glympeis and Zarax. Nevertheless, Lykourgos' success was short-lived, and his position as king was soon challenged. A certain Cheilon took advantage of dissatisfaction to make a bid for popular support by proclaiming once more Kleomenes' policy of a redistribution of land. He slaughtered the Spartan magistrates, the Ephors, who were Lykourgos' supporters, then tried to take Lykourgos from his house. Lykourgos, however, managed to escape. Thwarted, Cheilon tried to get popular support, and was driven out. The Spartans, in fear of Philip, prepared their defences. Philip was wintering at Megalopolis, but did not attack Sparta; instead he moved north to Argos, spending the rest of the winter there.

In the following year Philip was called on to attack Sparta itself. He had been campaigning in Aitolia, and his arrival at Sparta was sudden and unexpected, by a series of swiftly executed forced marches from Corinth. This time Argos served only as a staging post; in one day Philip had marched from Corinth to Argos; the following day he was in Tegea (this serves to show the importance of Argos on the direct route through the Peloponnese). Again in that year Argos saw the to-ing and fro-ing of the armies; the Messenians passed through Argive territory to the east of Parnon to attack the Spartans. They made an amateurish attempt to capture Glympeis, which was now held by Lykourgos. Philip, too, passed through Argos once more, this time on his way back to Corinth.

In these events, Argos' importance to the alliance seems to have been largely a passive, geographical one. There was little temptation to her to secede, particularly as the Spartans were her old enemies, and the strength of Philip outweighed any minor temporary advantage that might accrue from rebellion. Argos fulfilled her role as a Macedonian base, and there was no significant departure in this from her usual policy in the third century. When the war with Aitolia ended at the peace of 217 B.C. she received her reward. Her borders with Sparta were confirmed by Aratos and the Achaean league, and steps taken to protect the corn supply. Argos' advantage clearly now lay with the Achaean league and the Macedonian alliance.

15 The intervention of Rome

The peace settlement of 217 B.C. was brought about not so much in the interest of the Greeks but in order to free Philip for a fresh adventure.[1] Hannibal had invaded Italy[2] and it appeared that the Roman confederacy, which had already intervened on the eastern side of the Adriatic in areas adjacent to Macedonia, was about to disintegrate. Philip wished to gain what he could by an alliance with Hannibal, and this fatal miscalculation at last involved the Romans in the affairs of Greece. During the first Macedonian war that followed, Rome's chief concern was to neutralize Philip's alliance with Hannibal. This she achieved by stirring up trouble in Greece, and her natural ally in this was the Aitolian league, for the peace of 217 B.C. had not reduced it to submission to Philip. Argos and the Achaean league stood outside this. Aratos had not approved of the Roman adventure, but had died before the Romans intervened directly.

In the following year a definite treaty was made between Rome and the Aitolians and an invitation extended to those Peloponnesian states which were not part of the Achaean league to join in on the Roman side. Elis and Sparta are named by Livy and he later refers to Messenia as an old ally of Rome, so presumably the invitation was extended to her also at that time.[3] The Achaean league, as a friend of Philip, was an obvious target for those Peloponnesian allies and the chief trouble for them was caused by their fellow Greeks, not by Rome. Philip acted effectively on their behalf. Lykourgos of Sparta was now dead and the succession had passed to his infant son, Pelops, but actual power was exercised by Machanidas his guardian (the treaty with Rome had been made nominally by Pelops). Machanidas was regarded as a tyrant; his policy was equally anti-Macedonian.

The involvement of Argos in this was slight and the main contests took place elsewhere. In 208 B.C. Machanidas staged a diversion by bringing up his forces to the borders of Argive territory, presumably the Parnon frontier again, but this did not achieve much. Previously the Achaeans had sought help from Philip against Machanidas[4] with some success, and Philip had also sought to encourage the Achaeans by attending in person the Nemean games held that year in Argos. The grateful Argives had responded by making him president of the games.

None of this changed the essential situation in Greece, though Rome's sale of the island of Aigina to another of her allies, king Attalos of Pergamon, brought another power on to the Greek scene, in a region not too far distant from Argos. But Argos and the Achaean league remained faithful to Philip, and there is no discernible change of policy. When the war with the Romans finally petered out, Philip had forced their Greek allies to a separate treaty. His position in Greece was unchanged.

No sooner was the Hannibalic war concluded than Rome had her attention drawn once more to Greece, and pressure was applied to her to renew the conflict with Philip. It was pointed out that Philip had successfully challenged Rome's authority.[5] Philip was not only securely king in Macedon and much of northern Greece, but controlled 'the whole Peloponnese (an exaggeration) and Argos itself'. When the Romans were eventually persuaded to fight, control of the Peloponnese became once more a vital question. The chief enemy of the Achaean league was again Sparta, now ruled by another 'tyrant', Nabis.

In 200 B.C. a meeting of the Achaean league was held at Argos to decide what measures should be taken against Nabis, who was already threatening Achaean territory and cities. Here the Achaeans were joined by Philip, who promised his help if the Achaeans would help him against the Romans. The request was refused. Philip's hold over the Peloponnese (and Argos) was nowhere as strong as the Roman consul Sulpicius had feared. In 198 the Romans forced the Achaeans, under threat of blockade, to join them. Philip retained a garrison in Corinth, though he was powerless to prevent the remainder of the Achaean league joining Rome. The garrison in Corinth was put under siege, but the siege was broken by Philip's general, Philokles, who crossed by sea from the Perachora promontory with his army. This sign that Philip was still a force to be reckoned with caused a reaction at Argos. Argos had, perhaps, closer ties with the Macedonian royal family than any other city in the Achaean league; and for most of the time that she had been in the league, the league itself had been an ally of the Macedonians. The Argives were resentful at the enforced breach of loyalty. At meetings of the assembly (which continued to function at Argos) the authorities (Livy called them 'praetors') opened proceedings with prayers to Zeus, Apollo and Herakles. To these gods the name of Philip had been added, but this, naturally had been dropped when the treaty with Rome against Philip was signed. The omission of Philip's name met with protest and the people insisted that it should be added. Convinced of considerable popular support in Argos for Philip, the anti-Romans sent for Philokles, who reached the city by night and occupied the Larisa. An Achaean garrison of five hundred was opposed not only by Philokles and his Macedonians, but by the Argive citizens who were arming themselves. The two sides confronted each other in the agora, but, as the Achaean commander Ainesidemos realized that he was completely outnumbered, he sought and obtained permission for his troops to leave. He himself refused to go and was put to death.

At the conference of Lokris in November 198 B.C. the Achaeans had asked Philip for the return to them of Corinth and Argos. Philip promised to restore Argos on reaching a satisfactory settlement with the Romans, but hedged on Corinth. Flamininus, the new Roman commander, outbidding Philip, promised to hand over both Argos and Corinth. In the winter of 198–197 it became apparent to Philip that the Romans were preparing for a major engagement in the following campaigning season, and that it would be necessary for him to gather together as many of his available soldiers as possible for the battle. He could not afford to leave substantial garrisons scattered about Greece to hold down cities. Corinth had to be held; its strategic importance outweighed the number of troops needed to defend it, and the Acrocorinth had such great strength that the size of the garrison need not be that large. Argos was another matter. Though important it was not vital, and the fact that the Achaean garrison of five hundred had been unable to hold it indicated the number of troops likely to be tied down. He therefore decided to make an agreement with Nabis of Sparta, and to entrust the city to him. It was a fatal mistake.

Of Spartan hostility to the Achaean league there was no doubt. The Achaeans had defeated Machanidas, but the hostility continued.

Nabis (whatever his connections with the Eurypontid royal family of Sparta) was a usurper and, as far as external policies were concerned, could justify himself only by the prosecution of that feud. Even so, it was tactless to entrust Argos to a Spartan king, for the hostility between Argos and Sparta was of course of even longer standing and the Spartans still maintained territorial claims against the Argives. It has been suggested[6] that the name Apega, which is given by the MS of Polybius, XIII, 7, 6 as that of Nabis' wife is in fact a corruption of Apia, and that Nabis was therefore married to the daughter of the Argive tyrant Aristippos, who had that name;[7] thus Philip might consider that he was restoring as far as he could the old dynasty which had proved itself to be so loyal to the Macedonian cause. Whether this consideration weighed with him or not, there was little else that he could do in the circumstances; Nabis was the only Peloponnesian ally he possessed.

It was a forlorn hope. No sooner had Nabis taken possession of Argos than he approached the Roman pro-consul, Flamininus for an agreement. Flamininus came to terms, on condition that a truce between Nabis and the Achaeans should be arranged, until the war with Philip was decided, and that Nabis should assist the Romans in that war. Attalos of Pergamon then raised the matter of the occupation of Argos. He claimed that Philip (and so Nabis) had taken Argos by force, and that he himself had been asked in by the Argives to defend them. Doubtless there were factions in Argos which had recognized the growing interests of Attalos in Greece, and the general favour in which that king found himself with the Romans (to say nothing of his consistently anti-Macedonian policy). Attalos demanded a meeting of the Argive assembly to decide and Nabis agreed; but when Attalos also demanded that Nabis' Spartan garrison should be withdrawn to ensure the freedom of the assembly, Nabis prudently refused. The matter went undecided. Nabis strengthened the garrison under the command of Timokrates.

After the final defeat of Philip by the Romans at Kynoskephalai, in 197 B.C., Flamininus proclaimed a return to the old concept of the freedom of Greece, and the league of Greek allies meeting at Corinth. One of the outstanding questions to be settled was Argos, which was still occupied by Nabis' garrison. The Romans intended to interpret the 'freedom of Greece' even more literally than had ever been done by the Macedonians; no Roman garrisons were to be left, even in the crucially important citadels such as the Acrocorinth.[8]

It was unthinkable that Nabis should be allowed to keep his garrison at Argos. Flamininus was careful to point out that this was not a Roman affair; the Romans were prepared to give military assistance, but the decision whether or not Nabis should be removed rested with the Greeks. Even though some Greeks cynically regarded the proposal as an excuse for maintaining a Roman 'presence' in Greece, the Achaeans in particular were grateful for the proposal, and it was approved.

The joint Roman-Achaean army met at Kleonai, and on the following day descended into the Argive plain, making its camp four miles from the city. The Spartan commander Pythagoras (who was at the same time Nabis' son-in-law and the brother of his wife) had strengthened the defences, and put troops in both the Larisa and the Aspis, as well as other strong points. There was also an internal threat, led by a young man called Damokles. With a few supporters he entered the agora, calling on the Argives to follow his lead. None did, and he was killed by the Spartan troops. Others in the conspiracy were put to death, some imprisoned and the remainder let themselves down from the walls and fled to the Romans. These encouraged Flamininus to move his troops closer to the city. An advance force skirmished with the Spartans at the gymnasium of Kylarabis, and drove them back within the fortifications; Flamininus then took up this spot as his base. After waiting a day to see whether this closer presence would provoke a revolution in Argos (it did not, the reason given by Livy being that the Argives were still intimidated by Nabis' garrison), Flamininus called a conference to decide on an attack. Though most of the Greeks favoured such an attack it was pointed out that Sparta, not Argos, was the cause of the hostilities and that it was more sensible to attack there than at Argos. The army therefore moved to Lakonia. The attack concentrated on the harbour town of Gytheion. Pythagoras was recalled from Argos, where the garrison was once more placed under the charge of Timokrates; from Argos came a thousand mercenary soldiers and two thousand Argives.

Nabis entered into negotiations with Flamininus. In the words put into his mouth by Livy he laid stress on his established good relations with the Romans, and then claimed that he was not in occupation of Argos, since the Argives themselves had summoned and invited him in, and the Romans had left Argos to him when he had made the alliance with them against Philip. Flamininus easily refuted the first argument; the summoning of Nabis had not been done by the Argives; the 'long-established good relations' he dismissed with a quibble, that the original alliance had been made with the legitimate king, Pelops, not with the usurper. Whatever the justification for Flamininus' argument, his military strength was insuperable. Nabis promised to evacuate Argos, but asked for time to deliberate. In the end, a six month truce was agreed, on condition that Argos and other places occupied by Nabis were evacuated, during which time the whole matter could be referred to Rome. The garrison was to be withdrawn from Argive territory, and Nabis had to undertake not to take any slaves, public or private with him, and to restore ships already taken from the maritime communities. The terms were too harsh and Nabis resolved on resistance; when this failed, he was forced to submit. While the attack on Sparta was being mounted the Argives, having received false news that the city had fallen and realizing that the greater part of the garrison had been withdrawn by Pythagoras, drove the remainder out. Timokrates, who had behaved with clemency as commander of the garrison, was allowed to depart unharmed. The freeing of Argos was then celebrated at the Nemean festival. Argos once more became part of the Achaean league, and those Argives who had been taken to Sparta by Pythagoras, or earlier by Nabis, restored to their homeland.

Nabis' attitude to Argos is interesting. In Sparta he had renewed the policy of social revolution, confiscating property, exiling wealthy aristocrats, enfranchising the helots and distributing land to them. The hatred the aristocrats felt for him extended to other cities; Kleomenes' successes earlier had shown the danger such a revolution presented to aristocratic privilege, and the aristocratic contemporaries of Nabis were afraid for their own wealth and position. Since our knowledge of Nabis' achievement comes essentially from Polybius (if through the intermediary Livy) and Polybius was himself a member of a leading aristocratic family of the Achaean league, Nabis' opponents in Greece, it is hardly surprising that the account we have of him is venomously hostile. His relations with Argos would appear to have been violent, his policy harsh and oppressive. Argos itself was garrisoned and the population, apparently, plundered. Nabis dealt with the men himself, we are told, and his wife with the women. (This she did even more ruthlessly than her husband, taking money and even clothing from individuals and whole families. It is this activity that suggests that she had some special connection with Argos, that she was taking revenge on her personal enemies and that she was in fact Apia, the daughter of Aristippos.) In the end, when Nabis was forced out of Argos by the Romans, he deported a substantial number of the inhabitants, compelling them to settle in the territory of Sparta, whose population had undoubtedly suffered severe losses in recent years and needed artificial resuscitation of this sort. All this is emphasized in order to prove that Nabis was a relentless, self-centred despot.

On the other hand the town of Mycenae issued a decree[9] favourable to the Spartans, which 'renewed' the rights of Sparta to take part in games organized by the town. Mycenae at this time appears to have had its own civic organization. The decree and the privileges it renews may only represent an attempt by the Mycenaeans to curry favour with Nabis, or even the carrying out of instructions issued to them by their ruthless overlord; but there may be more to Nabis' policy here than is immediately apparent. Nabis was given not merely Argos town by Philip, but the whole of the Argolid. Argos and Sparta had been for a long time bitter enemies; but the enmity was caused by Dorian rivalry for the supremacy in the Peloponnese, and was in essence (however it had grown over the centuries) a quarrel between the Dorian overlords of Lakonia and the Dorian overlords of the Argolid. Nabis had put an end to the supremacy of the old Dorian families of Sparta and had shown himself the supporter of the helots who, it is usually argued, were the descendants of the old, pre-Dorian populations. If Nabis was conscious of the distinction between pre-Dorian, Homeric Sparta and the situation which had arisen after the Dorian settlement, he must surely have been aware that, in earlier times, at the occasion of the Trojan war, for example, the Argolid and Lakonia were friends, not enemies; that, in Homer, Agamemnon king of the Argolid and Menelaos king of Sparta were brothers.

Nabis may therefore have desired to return the Argolid, like Lakonia, to what he conceived to be its pre-Dorian condition. This involved the degradation of the Argive aristocracy, for which we have clear, if abusive, vituperative, and probably unbalanced evidence, and the reinstatement of Mycenae to an important if not a dominant place in Argive affairs. At the least, in passing its own decrees by virtue of its own political organization, Mycenae now possessed a degree of real local independence and the fact that young men from Mycenae were forcibly deported in the end, along with those of Argos, when Nabis withdrew, does not invalidate an earlier, friendly attitude to the surviving shadow of Agamemnon's capital.

The fact that Nabis was still left in power at Sparta was not welcomed by the Greek allies. Nevertheless, in 194 B.C., Flamininus held to his promise, the citadels were evacuated (Acrocorinth being restored to the Achaean league) and the Roman armies returned to Italy. In the following year the Aitolians began to act seditiously against the Roman interest, and encouraged by them, Nabis set about recovering the coastal towns that had been taken from him, and was believed to have ambitions for the recovery of Argos. All this encouraged Antiochos, whose ancestors had inherited the greater part of Alexander the Great's empire in the east, to interfere in the affairs of Greece. Those Greeks who were dissatisfied with Rome regarded him, the most powerful of the Hellenistic kings, as an adequate counterbalance to Roman might. Nabis continued his siege of Gytheion, and raided the territory of the Achaean league. The Achaean league sent a fleet to help Gytheion, but it was defeated by another fleet hastily gathered by Nabis; encouraged by this success Nabis reduced the size of his forces investing Gytheion, and prepared for wider action. The Achaeans used one of the Argive harbours (presumably a Kynourian port such as Zarax) to prepare a new fleet of small ships, with which they were able to surprise Nabis' fleet by night and destroy it by fire. They followed up this success with an invasion of Lakonia. While the Achaean army approached Sparta, Gytheion fell and Nabis hastened to meet it. He was unsuccessful. After further Roman intervention and an unwelcome arrival of the Aitolians, Sparta was brought into the Achaean league. Argos at last had triumphed.

16 Epilogue

Henceforth the future of Argos rested with the Achaean league and Rome. With the declaration of war against the Romans by Perseus, son of Philip V, they became increasingly suspicious of any Greek who was not their wholehearted and uncritical supporter. The third Macedonian war did not involve the Peloponnese directly; but the Romans took the opportunity to increase their hold over the league by deporting as hostages to Rome members of those families which had provided its leading statesmen, particularly those who had shown signs of independence, leaving Rome's supporters in charge. The Roman commander L. Aemilius Paullus visited Argos after the defeat of Perseus.

Even so, resistance was inevitable. The challenge to Rome from within the Achaean league was led by Diaios, who became general in 150 B.C. Rome was involved simultaneously in a war with Carthage and an armed rebellion in Macedon. No such opportunity had occurred before, and the league prepared to take advantage of it. Even the defeat of the rebellion in Macedonia did nothing to deter the Achaeans. At a meeting of the assembly of the league at Corinth a Roman commission led by L. Aurelius Orestes announced Rome's terms. Argos, Corinth, Sparta and Orchomenos were to be taken from the league. The Achaeans were merely incensed the more. The Romans sent L. Mummius as consul with an army of thirty thousand. An Achaean army fighting north of the isthmus in Lokris was defeated. Diaios wrote from Argos to the member cities calling on them to send troops to Corinth. Negotiations with the Romans were broken off, and Diaios offered battle outside the town. He was utterly defeated. The punishment was severe. Ten other Greek cities, including Argos, continued their separate existence under the general supervision of the Roman governor in Macedonia, eventually to be swept into the Roman province of Achaea. The Liberty of Greece had come to its end.

Part Three   The Argive State and
                  its Achievement

17   Military organization

To the Greeks of the fifth and fourth centuries B.C. wars between the city states, however much they deplored them, were normal and expected. The education of citizens was devoted as much, if not more, to developing their physique and skill in the use of arms as to the intellect. It was taken for granted that each city should be able to call on its citizens to fight for it, and that each city possessed the military organization that made this possible. Argos, naturally, was no exception to this. So important to the Greek city was the need to defend itself that the concept of military service as an essential pre-requirement of citizenship was normal and this meant that military organization was inextricably interwoven with the political system. The one should illuminate the other, and, where we have sufficient factual information, it usually does.

So much of this was normal and natural to the Greeks that their historians rarely thought it necessary to comment on it, except in a most general fashion; and in the case of Argos, comment on the military system is made all the more difficult by the discontinuity of the information that we have about it. To attempt an under-standing, it is essential to compare the situation at Argos with that at other similar or dissimilar Greek cities.

Presumably, the original military organization of the Argives was that of the three Dorian tribes, as at Sparta; for the continuing political importance of the tribes (long after they had been divided and scattered) can only have resulted from their continuity in the military and religious life of the communities in which they existed. Each tribe contributed a regiment to the army of the city, recruited from the men of military age belonging by birth to the tribe, and commanded by a general who was also of the tribe.

At Sparta, this simple system had become a thing of the past by the seventh century B.C. when the poet of the second Messenian war, Tyrtaios, probably referred to it as the method of former times, in apparent contrast to that used by the Spartans of his own time.[1] In Argos the tribal system would at first sight appear to have been retained until the fifth century B.C., the chief modification being the addition of the fourth non-Dorian tribe, for an inscription commemorating the Argives who fell alongside the Athenians at the battle of Tanagra in 458 B.C. names them according to the tribe to which they belonged; and even as late as 370 B.C., on the occasion of civil disturbances in Argos itself, the citizens gathered in arms, standing 'each in his own tribe'.[2] But this is misleading; there is other evidence for a different military system and the listing of the dead at Tanagra by their tribes probably results from the continuation of the tribe as the basis of citizenship; while the incident in 370 is clearly political, rather than military, in character.[3]

The most detailed account of the Argive army is that given by Thucydides in his description of the battle of Mantinea in 418 B.C.,[4] though, unfortunately, it is by no means as full as his description of the Spartan organization. Significantly, there are once again close resemblances between the Argive and Spartan systems. The Argive army consisted of two parts, a select brigade ('lochos') numbering a thousand, and 'the other Argives', organized in five 'lochoi'.[5] The select brigade, says Thucydides, were provided with the necessary practice and training in military matters by the city, at public expense. At the same battle the Spartans were also divided into 'lochoi', seven in all. Thucydides also describes the sub-divisions of the Spartan, but not the Argive lochos; it comprised four units known as 'pentecostyes', while each pentecostys was made up of four 'enomotiai'. Each enomotia contributed four soldiers to the front rank. The number of ranks varied, in accordance with the wishes of the lochos-commander (not the commander in chief of the Spartan army, who at this battle was the king, Agis), but 'for the most part' was eight. There were therefore thirty-two soldiers in each enomotia, one hundred and twenty-eight in each pentecostys, and five hundred and twelve in each lochos. From an inscription of the third century B.C. we learn that the pentecostys was also a unit of the Argive army.[6] A certain Alexander from Sikyon was granted citizenship of Argos, as an honour, and it was required of him that he should be enrolled into an Argive tribe, brotherhood (phratry) and pentecostys. At that date, the Argive citizen army was no longer a significant force:[7] the tyrants who ruled Argos in the third century relied on mercenary troops hired from other regions so the significance of the pentecostys is as a survival from earlier times. It is not improbable that at Mantinea in 418 the Argive army, like the Spartan, consisted of lochoi sub-divided into pentecostyes. The reason Thucydides give so much more detail about the Spartan forces than those of Argos and the other allies is twofold; firstly, he was writing primarily for Athenians, who knew their own military system, and must have had a fair idea of that used by the cities who fought on their side at Mantinea; while the Spartans were the enemy and were notoriously secretive about such details. Thus the details of the Spartan army were of much greater interest to Thucydides' readers. Secondly, Thucydides is obviously interested in the numbers of the Spartan army, and particularly the length of the front rank. The Argive lochos of a thousand was the expected size for such a unit; the Spartan lochos of about five hundred was therefore significantly reduced in size.

At Sparta, the lochos system came into existence when the old tribal system became obsolete, that is, in the seventh century B.C., at the time of the second Messenian war and the poems of Tyrtaios. The sub-divisions into pentecostyes may be a later refinement, though there can have been no great advantage (in Spartan circumstances, at least) of a five lochos system, the original Spartan form, over the traditional three tribal regiments unless it facilitated further sub-division and organization. It is simpler to assume, both at Argos and Sparta, that the lochos and pentecostys were both parts of the same rearrangement. The interpretation of the term 'pentecostys' has caused some confusion. Like other similarly formed terms used in other Greek cities[8] its basic significance is numerical, the number in this example being fifty. But it is not certain whether it has a collective significance ('group of fifty') or a divisive one ('a fiftieth part'). At the battle of Mantinea, as we have seen, the Spartan pentecostys apparently comprises one hundred and twenty-eight men, and is a twenty-eighth part of the total Spartan force. Here it appears that we are concerned with a unit which, whatever its original size, had altered in composition over the years as a result of Sparta's changing resources of manpower, without altering the name by which it was known. By themselves, these figures tell us nothing about the origins of the term. More significant is the obvious relationship between the meaning fifty in pentecostys, and the five lochoi employed in the earlier Spartan arrangement and the main section of the Argive army at Mantinea (as well as the board of five generals who commanded it). This appears to imply two stages in the division of the total citizen force, firstly into five units, and then a sub-division of each unit into ten. It is easier to see how pentecostyes formed in this way became twenty-eight employed by the Spartans at Mantinea, than to calculate how contingents originally of fifty men grew to contain one hundred and twenty-eight, a reduction in the number of pentecostyes in each lochos, first by a half, from ten to five (by combining them in pairs) and then by a fifth from five to four (either by distributing one pentecostys amongst the others or leaving it elsewhere as a reserve) making a total of twenty pentecostyes instead of fifty; but the increase in the number of lochoi to seven, perhaps desirable on geographical grounds, or to make the army more flexible would bring the total number of pentecostyes up to twenty-eight (it is possible that the reduction of the number of pentecostyes per lochos from five to four, and the increase in the number of lochoi were part of one and the same reorganization). The major reduction of the original number of pentecostyes by a half suggests that the Spartans were having difficulty in keeping the size of the unit at the required standard; and this in turn suggests a sudden and cata-strophic drop in manpower resources, presumably the consequence of the earthquake. The incompatibility of the numbers in the Spar-tan pentecostyes at Mantinea and the numerical significance of the term suggests that the system had been in existence for a considerable period of time. It also seems more likely that the term originally signified 'a fiftieth part' of the army than 'a group of fifty men'.

During the eighth, and particularly the seventh century B.C. the style of fighting employed in the armies of the more developed Greek states seems to have changed, and more complex armour introduced.[9] Armour of a transitional type was found in the late eighth century grave of a warrior at Argos;[10] and there is no reason to doubt that Argos was in the forefront of the innovation. The outcome of this development was the classic, bronze armoured infantryman, the hoplite, and the highly organized phalanx forma-tion in which he fought. Since this development is taking place at about the time when the rearrangement of the Spartan army took place (and this is what Tyrtaios' poem implies in pointing the contrast between contemporary styles of fighting and those of the Spartans' forefathers) it seems logical to connect this with the lochos-pentecostys organization. In other words the classical hoplite is evolved as a result of two parallel developments in the armies of the Greek cities, the improvement of armour and the introduction of improved, more detailed, military organization. The famous Chigi vase,[11] painted at Corinth shortly after the middle of the seventh century B.C. (that is, not long after the battle of Hysiai) shows that at the time, hoplite equipment and more particularly hoplite discipline and organization, were familiar features in that part of the Greek world. It is therefore more than likely that the essential organization of a hoplite army into lochoi and pentecostyes was already practised by the Argives in the seventh century.[12]

The reasons behind the development are complex. That they are closely connected with the development of the city states, and the renewal of contacts with the overseas world can hardly be doubted. That the improvements in armour, and the closer cohesion now possible in the battle line gave distinct advantages to the army that employed them over one whose equipment and tactics were more old fashioned, is equally obvious. The improved system required greater training and practice and since hoplites fought as part of extended units, rather than as individuals, it was essential that members of the unit trained together. Ideally, the hoplite fought with the same fellow-soldiers to either side of him, for the phalanx formation created a system of overlapping defence, in which each soldier was partly protected by the shield of his right-hand neighbour and in his turn protected his neighbour on the left. Thus each soldier needed to know and trust his neighbours. For this it was an obvious advantage that members of the same unit should live in the same neighbourhood. The random gathering of members of the same tribe from different localities was no longer a practical proposition, particularly after the expansion of the city states over wider territories; the hoplite armies were made possible only by the institution of a system which was based on the sub-division of the army into local units, and this meant the lochos-pentecostys system.

A second advantage of the lochos system (or something similar to it) was that it enabled recruitment and training to take place on a wider basis than that of the Dorian population, in those areas where a significant section of the population was not Dorian by descent. So long as a community was exclusively Dorian, or if it controlled non-Dorians like the helots, it could afford to disregard them for military purposes, then the Dorian tribes could remain the essential basis of the military system. In other communities the alternatives were either to organize the non-Dorians into a comparable tribal system (and thereby put them also on an equal footing politically) or devise a new system.

Such a development is as likely to have taken place at Argos as at Sparta. There seems to be no reason for crediting the one rather than the other with priority in the development of hoplite armour, for the bronze equipment in the warrior tomb at Argos can be paralleled by the metal corselet used by Timomachos the Aigeid, who captured Amyklai for the Spartans in the mid-eighth century B.C.[13] On the other hand, it is clear that by the time of Hysiai the Argives had gained an advantage, and if this did not result from the equipment, it must have resulted from new methods of fighting and military organization which enabled Argos to take full advantage of the increased resources of manpower that the enlarged city state now possessed. This appears to be the work of Pheidon. The public arming of 'the slaves' after the battle of Sepeia indicates that at that time the hoplite army of Argos was formed from the political élite, equal in numbers to the Spartan army, but definitely not its superior. If Pheidon had extended the basis of recruitment, not only would the Argive army have been larger and stronger than the Spartan, but it would inevitably have included numbers of soldiers drawn from outside the political élite. It could well have been this action that earned him, from his political opponents, the title of tyrant. If so, we must suppose that it provoked a stormy political reaction, which in turn helps to explain Argos' subsequent decline. If the lochos system was retained it was because it was inextricably part of the hoplite organization; but, as at Sparta, it now served for the recruitment of an élite, of people with a certain level of wealth who could afford to provide themselves with the necessary armour.

That the system changed in detail over the centuries at Argos and elsewhere is more than likely. Changing circumstances could well make practices that were relevant in the seventh century less relevant in the fifth; what was unusual about the Spartans was the effort they made and the lengths to which they were prepared to go in order to maintain and strengthen their system.[14] At Argos, the impression obtained from the occasional reports that survive of military action is that internal privilege and status were more important to the Argives than overall military efficiency; and that, unlike the Spartans, they neglected the latter to the detriment of the former. Under this arrangement, the army formed a homogenous unit; all those qualified for recruitment (however this was done) were armed, equipped and trained in the same manner. All fought alike as heavily armoured infantrymen, and cavalry played no significant part at all. After Sepeia, certainly, a change can be discerned, at least in the organization of the Argive army. It is seen most clearly at Mantinea in 418, when Thucydides shows that the Argive army was in two parts; a select brigade of one thousand who were specially trained at the expense of the city, and 'the other Argives', the normal hoplite citizen army. There are other instances of a brigade of one thousand employed by the Argives in the fifth century. When the city officially refused help to the Aiginetans, a body of one thousand Argive 'volunteers' came to their aid. At Tanagra in 458, the Athenians were aided in the battle against the Spartans by a lochos of one thousand Argives. After Mantinea a lochos of one thousand Argives was used by the Spartans to help enforce oligarchic rule in the city.[15]

It is possible that this represents the appearance at different points of time in the fifth century of a body of soldiers recruited, organized and trained in the same way. The thousand used by the Spartans to establish oligarchy after Mantinea are often assumed to be the same unit as the select lochos that fought in the battle, though Thucydides does not say so (and one would have expected him to say so if it had been).

The distinction is one of training and organization, not method of fighting, for the select units still fought as hoplites. Basically, the difference is between the part-time soldiers, the farmers who spent most of their days working in the fields, and put on hoplite armour when called out to defend the city, and individuals who were enabled to devote all their time to the practice of the hoplite art. In most Greek cities, this was class distinction. It was most noticeable at Sparta, where the Spartan citizens owned lands worked for them by helots; they did not need to till their own fields and so were completely free to submit themselves to a military discipline which, notoriously, monopolized their lives. Because of the Spartan social system, or rather the extreme way in which it had been developed, the Spartan army included a very high proportion of these full-time citizen soldiers (though it also—increasingly after the earthquake —included a proportion of part-time hoplites, recruited from the outlying communities which did not have full citizen rights, the perioikoi). In other cities the possessors of landed estates which were large enough to free them from the need to toil in the fields were fewer in proportion, but it was these people who were able to frequent the gymnasium, where they exercised to improve their military skill beyond the period of compulsory training in youth.

Men of this social class inevitably favoured a political system which was restricted rather than open, one in which they formed a dominant élite. They were predisposed to support oligarchies, or at least constitutions in which full political rights were limited to those who served in the hoplite armies. In democracies, such men were politically undesirable, and it was dangerous to rely on them in any way in military matters; yet against the existence of a large army of this type at Sparta, some form of military élite was obviously desirable. At Athens, the solution appears to have been that the élite class was merged into the ten ordinary regiments of hoplites. Whether or not this was the cause, after the Persian invasion the Athenian hoplite army was never of first-rate quality.

In Argos, the situation undoubtedly fluctuated. At the beginning and end of the period, we seem to be dealing with members of a social élite. At the time that Aigina approached Argos for help, the members of the lower social orders had taken over control of the city as a consequence of Sepeia (as Herodotus makes clear) and the thousand volunteers who went to Aigina did so despite the refusal of the government to send aid. It appears therefore that they were politically opposed to the existing government of Argos, and were themselves supporters of the former oligarchy. Similarly, after Mantinea, the Argives who support the Spartans are clearly oligarchic in their political outlook, and therefore in their social origins,[16] but between these extremes of time, the situation was probably different. At the time of Tanagra and Mantinea, Argos had a democratic constitution and fought in both battles as an ally of democratic Athens against Sparta. The select unit that fought at Mantinea was enabled to carry out the full-time professional training necessary for a crack hoplite unit, not because of the personal wealth and landed estates that its members possessed but, as Thucydides specifically makes clear (implying that this was unusual) because they received the necessary support from the state.[17] The Argives who fought at Tanagra may well have been trained in a similar way. True, the inscription which records the names of those who were killed heads the list with the name of the Dorian tribe, the Hylleis, to which those first named belonged: but the inscription is not sufficiently well preserved for us to know how many of the dead were members of the Dorian tribes (and so probably members of a Dorian élite) and how many (if any) were from the non-Dorian Hyrnathioi.[18] No conclusion is possible on this evidence and the names of the traditional tribes probably appear for religious and traditional reasons, rather than because they were the basis of the military organization of the unit sent to help the Athenians. After their victory at Tanagra the Spartans and their allies made dedications at the sanctuary of Zeus at Olympia and Pausanias records the commemorative epigram that he saw there (which has also survived in part on the fragments of a marble slab found there). The sanctuary had received a tithe of the spoils which had been taken 'from the Argives and the Athenians and the Ionians'. This precise order, putting the Argives first although they formed only a small part of the army (since the Athenians sent out their full citizen force[19]) may result merely from the needs of the verse form used in the epigram; but an alternative possibility is raised by the inscription from Athens which lists the names of the Argive dead. Although this is preserved only in part, it has been calculated that there was originally room on it for four hundred names. Out of a total Argive force of one thousand, this would mean that fully forty per cent were killed. The actual number of dead may be smaller, since it cannot be proved that all the available space was filled; but the absolute minimum figure is still one hundred and twenty-nine dead and even this represents a significantly high proportion of the total force. This demonstrates that the Argives bore the brunt of the fighting, since Athenian losses on the same scale would have amounted to a major catastrophe, and nobody ever suggested that Tanagra was that.[20] If the Argives suffered heavier losses than the Athenians, there is more justification for their name coming first in the Spartan dedication. At all events, the Argive losses were proportionately severe. There are several possible reasons for this; the Spartans may have singled them out, in an attempt to weaken the alliance between Athens and Argos; the Athenians knowing the Argive hatred of Sparta may have put them in a particularly exposed position; it may have been due simply to chance and the fortunes of war, but above all, the severe losses suggest that these soldiers, like those at Mantinea, were the unit specially trained at the expense of the state. One thing is absolutely certain; of their loyalty to Argos and the Argive democracy and their opposition to the Spartans, there is no doubt.

It seems therefore that this picked lochos was developed by Argos not solely for military reasons, but to avoid the equation of a military élite with a political one. It would be interesting to know (but we do not) how the special lochos was selected.

The military purpose has more aspects than the need to confront the Spartans with troops similar in skill and training. A citizen hoplite force, in which the majority are 'part-time' soldiers is necessarily less flexible than a professional army. Though it may have formed the basis for Pheidon's successful aggressive policy, its function is primarily defensive, to ward off aggressors from Argive territory. If it came into being in the early part of the seventh century B.C. it is significant that the first recorded success for this citizen army is Hysiai, which was manifestly a defensive battle fought against Spartan aggressors. The other major engagements in which we meet the full citizen force are also defensive; the battle that followed the clash of the three hundred champions and Sepeia, both fought inside Argive territory, while the battle of Mantinea, though beyond the frontiers of Argos was fought shortly after the Argolid had felt the presence of a Spartan army and when, if the Spartans were successful (as it eventually transpired) there was the immediate danger of renewed interference in the Argolid itself. An élite force freed from the more mundane economic ties was obviously an advantage to a state that wanted to involve itself in the struggle for leadership over a wider area of Greece. To achieve this leadership (as the Spartans had discovered) the old idea of territorial and political domination was ineffective; it could only be done by a series of alliances, involving the would-be leading state in obligations to send a military force to help defend the ally. The Spartan social system made this possible. For Argos, once she had become a democracy, the pattern had changed; there was still the need to possess a force capable of being sent away from home under treaty of obligation and the select force was used for this purpose. Unlike the citizen army, we hear of it invariably outside Argive territory; at Aigina, at Tanagra. Even at Mantinea, though the presence of the full citizen force implies a defensive engagement, the cause of the engagement was originally aggressive, an attempt by the other Arcadians, with Argos, to detach Tegea from her alliance with Sparta.

It is noticeable that Argos did not become a naval power. The Athenians avoided some of the problems of depending on a hoplite élite for service outside Attica by relying, in part at least, on her triremes and the crews that manned them, who were drawn from the least privileged ranks of Athenian society and supported when on active service by the state. When hoplites were sent outside Attica they were recruited from the tribal regiments and again received state support. Argos' treaty obligations and ambitions were directed particularly towards the inland cities of Arcadia and for this a fleet was useless; but she also wanted to recover the territories along the east coast of the Peloponnese, Thyreatis and Kynouria, which the Spartans had taken from her and here, as the Athenians were to demonstrate in the course of the Peloponnesian war, possession of a fleet would have conferred an immense advantage on the Argives militarily and as well would have avoided the political disadvantages for a democracy of dependence on hoplites. That Argos also had overseas commitments is proved by the treaty with Knossos and Tylissos, and it is possible that under the guidance of democratic Athens the Argive democracy in the 450s was moving towards a similar naval policy. If so, this was ended by the Spartan treaty of 451; but the implications behind this are political, rather than military.

After Mantinea, the picture once more becomes obscure. During the fourth century B.C. and following developments that took place in the Peloponnesian war at the end of the fifth century, many Greek cities came to appreciate the advantages of professional soldiers, with their greater skill, specialized training and freedom from the more mundane commitments of the peasant soldier. Nevertheless, the citizen armies were kept in being, probably with very little change in their organizations. The citizen levy fought to defend Argos from the consequences of a Spartan invasion in 352 just as it had done in the previous century; and inscriptions of the third century (as we have seen) make it clear that membership of a pentecostys division of the army was still an essential requirement for citizenship. Argive troops were employed to help allied forces outside the Argolid. A contingent was sent at the request of Athens to join the expedition to Sicily; at the siege of Syracuse they frightened their Athenian allies by their use of a Dorian war chant. It is unlikely that these were members of the crack lochos; Thucydides does not say that they are and Argos might well be wary of sending her best troops so far away from home. During the Corinthian war, there was an Argive garrison in Corinth. Again, we are not told who these soldiers were (this is not the sort of detail that

Xenophon would bother himself with); but in view of the political arrangement between Argos and Corinth and the part the Argive soldiers played in the suppression of the Corinthian oligarchs, political reliability must have been as important a criterion for their selection as military skill.

Thereafter, the tradition appears to disintegrate. Argos is unable to support her citizen troops, let alone the select lochos. The peasant soldiers would seem to have experienced increasing difficulty in maintaining the property requirements for admission to the hoplite ranks and the dispatch of Argive soldiers as mercenaries to help the Persian kings put Argos on the same level as other Greek communities (the Arcadian cities in particular) who were experiencing the same pressures and problems. As supporters of the Macedonian kings, Argives would have joined in the campaigns of Alexander. In Hellenistic times we find them settled in Ptolemaic Egypt[21] (though their Hellenistic loyalty was rather with the Antigonids of Macedonia, the enemies of the Ptolemies). As the population dwindled as a result of economic and other pressures, so the size of the citizen force became more and more restricted. When he was forced to evacuate the Argolid, Nabis took with him to Sparta two thousand Argives of military age. How great a proportion of the available population this represents is unknown; the Argives were unwilling to go to Sparta and no doubt many eluded the enforced deportation, but even so a decline of fifty per cent from the figures of six thousand for the fifth century is not impossible. Nominally, at least, the young men were trained for military service, but the impression is of a largely ineffective force, a show-piece relic of former days, insignificant and obsolete in the face of armies recruited from mercenaries and Macedonians.

18 Political development to the fifth century

During its early history, the political organization of Argos would seem to have been typically Dorian, the settlers coming to form an ascendancy that kept to itself the more important privileges of citizenship.[1] At the beginning, if we are to trust the traditional accounts that have come down to us, this ascendancy was itself ruled over by hereditary kings, the Temenid line who claimed descent from Herakles himself. That such a royal family actually existed is certain, but its position in the Argive state was by no means simple or straightforward. The Dorian king was above all else a war-lord, the leader of his people on the field of battle, and in primitive Dorian society this function was doubtless of paramount importance. He would seem also to have functioned as priest, that is, to have acted as a go-between for his followers with the gods who controlled all the events and destinies of mortal life, and, presumably, he would have acted as arbiter in disputes between his followers. All this must have been at the most primitive level, for there is little reason to doubt that on arrival in the Argolid the Dorians were a backward people. Whether these functions were transported directly with the migration of the Dorians, or whether they grew up on a traditional pattern, once the Dorians had settled in the Argolid, can never be known.

The primitive situation was changed first by the enlargement of the Argive state to include the other communities of the Argolid at a politically subservient level. The Dorian ascendancy now became wealthy and began to taste real political power. It is conceivable that in these circumstances their ability to tolerate the authority of an individual and the hereditary transmission of that authority declined. Certainly, the powers of the king were attacked, but how and in what direction we do not know and there are other possible explanations. In the eighth century we still hear of kings leading the Argive army into battle, but there are growing signs of discontent with the traditional Dorian monarchy as a system of government. In the seventh century Pheidon, descendant of Temenos and hereditary king of Argos, emerges as a powerful ruler and commander of the Argive army, but Aristotle was aware that his power was based on more than that of hereditary kingship, that his position was analogous to that of the completely unconstitutional autocrat, the 'tyrant', even though here the 'tyranny' grew out of traditional monarchy.

Aristotle does not explain precisely what he meant by this, or the historical facts on which he based his argument; perhaps he assumed that these were universally known, or had been made clear by contemporary historians. So we can only speculate on the meaning of this. In Corinth at the same time the ruling ascendancy of the Bacchiadai (who had earlier removed their kings from a position of authority, if they ever possessed it) was under attack and successfully destroyed by the tyrant Kypselos. Similar tyrannies occur elsewhere in the same region, for example at Sikyon, and it is tempting to associate these as parts of a general development. These areas, along with other parts of Greece where the strain was perhaps less intense (or delayed to the following century) were affected by the development of trade, or wealth and the changes of society that this created—particularly the development of a Dorian aristocracy politically capable of exploiting a subservient population to its own ends and anxious to do so because of the selfish advantages they gained from this. The subservient population sought to ameliorate its lot by the overthrow of the political ascendancy, but often, where this was a matter of internal strife (rather than the rebellion of a suppressed nation, as in the case of the Messenians against the Spartans) the subservient people looked to a member of the ascendancy as their leader, or even, where monarchy still persisted, the king. Thus Pheidon is likely to have become more than a constitutional king by championing the inhabitants of the Argolid who were outside the ascendancy; and if this meant their integration into the armed forces of Argos, the reason for Argive military success becomes more apparent.[2] Membership of the ascendancy was restricted to the three Dorian tribes. The tyrants of Sikyon tried to break the ascendancy by renaming the Dorian tribes (with derogatory versions of the original names, so this may be a joke that has been reported as serious history) but more seriously, elevating to an apparently equal political position a fourth tribe in which the non-Dorian population was gathered.[3] There is a similar non-Dorian tribe at Troizen,[4] like Sikyon a neighbour of Argos and, eventually, at Argos itself.

The name of the fourth Argive tribe, the Hyrnathioi, first appears in inscriptions of the fifth century B.C.[5] and it is possible that it was not fully integrated into the Argive constitution until that date. There is some evidence that in the first half of the sixth century B.C. a board of magistrates comprised nine members, a number easily divisible among the three Dorian tribes, but not if the Hyrnathioi are added. Nevertheless, it is tempting to attribute the first introduction of this non-Dorian tribe into the political life of Argos, if not its first creation as a tribe, to Pheidon and to date it to the seventh century B.C. Such a political rearrangement does not amount to the establishment of democracy—Pheidon's actions suggest very much that he was a completely authoritarian ruler—but his acceptance of the fourth tribe seriously undermined the Dorian ascendancy and gave the subservient peoples a status of equality with them.

Quite clearly, if Pheidon achieved this, his revolution was short-lived. By the sixth century the monarchy was at an end and the descendants of Temenos were in exile in Kleonai. The existence of a college of nine magistrates, the damiorgoi, in the first half of the sixth century, reduced later in the century to six, suggests not only the exclusion of the Hyrnathioi, but the substitution for monarchy of a closely controlled oligarchic system.[6] This suggests a reaction against Pheidon and the system he represents. The ascendancy had restored itself and remained essentially in control of Argive affairs until Sepeia, that is for a period of a hundred years or so. Whether this renewed ascendancy went unchallenged from within, we cannot tell; it has been suggested that Perilaos (or Perillos) who is described by Pausanias as a tyrant may belong to the sixth century B.C.[7] Certainly Argos at one stage was sympathetic to the Athenian tyrant Peisistratos, though this does not necessarily mean that Argos was herself under a tyrant's rule at that time.

A period of political confusion and perhaps the exclusion of the non-Dorians not only from the political organization of the city but from the military as well might explain the decline in the fortunes of Argos which quite clearly set in after the death of Pheidon. The gradual rise to supremacy of Sparta, the intrusion into Argive territory and the occupation of the Thyreatis provide such a contrast to Argos' success in the previous century that some such internal weakness, an inability to use the full resources which Argos possessed in the previous century (and still possessed in essentials) is the most likely explanation.

Kleomenes' invasion marks the complete failure of the ascendancy. Its numbers decimated, it could no longer hold on to political control, or, indeed, justify its conduct of Argive affairs. In these circumstances, the development of a broader based constitution was inevitable; but the rapidity and smoothness with which the development took place suggests that it was not something totally new, that there was a precedent for the extension of citizen rights to the Hyrnathioi. The situation at Argos in Pheidon's time is as likely as anything to be the reason for this.

However, there were now significant differences. Quite apart from the fact that under Pheidon Argos had been strong while now after Sepeia she was at her weakest, her constitution had changed. There was no longer an Argive king, so the integration of the Hyrnathioi with the active political body meant not their acquisition of a new subject-status but the transformation of Argos into a democracy. The non-Dorians were now entitled not only to membership of the assembly, but to the various magistracies and executive offices of the state; as Herodotus puts it, they now ruled and managed everything.

How long this arrangement continued is uncertain. Herodotus implies a complete reversal of the situation, when the sons of those killed at Sepeia came of age. But there are different ways of interpreting this. The young men in Greek city states came of military age at twenty and it must be presumed that a large number of twenty- to thirty-year-olds were killed in the battle. A higher age was a normal qualification for magisterial office, invariably thirty; and thus a gap of at least eleven years must have occurred before the first of the Dorian generation too young to fight at Sepeia were eligible for office. If the annihilation of the Argive army was not quite so complete as the Argive apologists who told Herodotus their version of what happened would have him believe, there could still have been enough individuals surviving of Dorian origin to hold the necessary offices. What is important is the voting power of the Dorians in the assembly which elected them and here one would suppose a gradual increase over the years as the losses of Sepeia were made good from the rising generation. Certainly by the 470s

Argos was able to resume a dominant role in the Argolid and then reduce Mycenae and Tiryns once more to submission; but the restoration of the ascendancy at best was partial and the Argos which had existed after the Persian wars was reckoned a democracy.

19 The Argive democracy

Democratic Argos was the ally of Athens in the 450s, at the time of Mantinea and after, at the time of the Corinthian war. She withstood attempts in 418 and 370, if not on other occasions, to overthrow her system of government and replace it by an oligarchy. She opposed Sparta on these ideological grounds; she actively promoted, in the 390s, the cause of democracy at Corinth.[1] Nevertheless, it is not supposed that her democratic form of government was similar to that at Athens; there were different degrees of democracy in the Greek cities, just as oligarchy could be different in the ways in which it restricted political power.

The democratic principle, as it evolved in Athens, was to vest all real authority in the popular assembly, in which all adult male citizens were entitled to vote. The power of the individual was denied or restricted as far as possible. Executive authority was vested in committees, rather than individuals; appointment was by sortition, making it impossible for an ambitious individual to be sure of achieving any particular post; the holding of office was restricted to a period of one year, with severe restrictions on re-election (when this was permitted, a considerable period of time had first to elapse). Direct election was permitted only in the case of the generals of the ten tribal regiments and they, in addition, could be re-elected without any restrictions; but even the generals, who became the most powerful men of the state because of this, had to submit their actions to the scrutiny of the people and had to act as a committee (or, on active service, in groups), not receiving individual command.

Comparison between the Athenian system and the Argive is difficult, because the information about the working of the Argive constitution is deficient. There are certainly points of similarity between them. Like the Athenians, the Argives possessed a popular assembly, which was attended by all citizens (the demos or people).

The name of the assembly was the 'aliaia', a term which was also used for the assembly at Athens (normally the 'ekklesia') when it functioned as a court of law. The assembly was the source of authority for legislation; the decisions of government were the decrees of the assembly. Whether or not the assembly was democratic in character depended on the people who were admitted to membership of it. Originally, no doubt, it was restricted to members of the three Dorian tribes, but in the period of the democracy the non-Dorian Hyrnathioi were also admitted (since we find members of the Hyrnathioi in more important political positions in equality with the representatives of the Dorian tribes).[2] Membership may have been restricted to those who possessed landed estate above a fixed minimum level. In Athens, at the time of political upheaval that followed the disastrous defeat at Syracuse, membership of the assembly was restricted to those who could afford to equip themselves with hoplite armour (and so excluded the now large number of citizens who did not possess that degree of wealth and served the city by rowing in the fleet). Such a restriction was not necessarily regarded as incompatible with democracy. At Argos, there was a distinction between 'the rich' and 'the people', which is particularly noticeable at the time of the skytalismos (assuming that it was to that occasion that Aeneas Tacticus referred); the implication is that the 'people' were not wealthy and were, at best, of the peasant class. On the other hand, it is noticeable that Argos never tried to equip herself with a fleet in the way that Athens had done although, as we have seen, this would have been advantageous to her in her ambitions to recover the Thyreatis and Kynouria and in her overseas commitments in Crete. Her amphibious operations against the Thyreatis in the Peloponnesian war were achieved with the help of the Athenian fleet. In view of this, there is a strong probability that the 'demos' of Argos, the citizens entitled to vote in the assembly, were those who possessed property to an extent sufficient to enable them to own hoplite armour; that, even if the poorest, labouring classes were admitted to the assembly, they were in a strict minority;[3] and that the Argive constitution was that of a moderate rather than an extreme democracy, of the sort that existed at Athens before the reform of 462 B.C. and, more particularly, at the time after the fall of Syracuse when the Athenian assembly was restricted to the five thousand of hoplite rank.

The roles of the other organs of government and administration which occur in the ancient literature and on the inscriptions are even more uncertain, though it is clear that the true character of the Argive constitution depends on them. There was a council (the bola, the Dorian Greek equivalent of the Athenian boule) which is mentioned in the preambles to decrees inscribed in stone; but it is not there recorded in the same way as the Athenian boule, where decrees represent 'the decisions of the people (i.e. assembly) and the boule'. In Argos, the decisions are attributed to the assembly alone and the bola is mentioned almost incidentally, by reference to its president and secretary, more as a means of identifying the occasion on which the decree was passed and its place in public records.[4] The bola almost certainly prepared business for decision by the assembly; this was normal in democratic constitutions and Argos could hardly have been described as a democracy if the council did not have this function. It also had direct administrative and judicial functions (for example, it dealt with cases involving the confiscation of property and dedication of the proceeds to Athena).[5] The council at Athens also had legal responsibilities. All in all, a comparison should be made not so much with the Athenian council as it functioned after the reforms of 462 (and it is about this council that we have the most detailed information) but rather with the council that existed before the establishment in Athens of the more extreme form of democracy.

Unfortunately, we do not know how the bola was appointed. At Athens, the council consisted of fifty representatives from each of the ten tribes, appointed by lot, and serving for a period of one year (each group of fifty taking it in turn to act as a full-time sub-committee of the council). It is probable that the Argive council also served for a period of one year, since the president and secretary (that is, the individuals whose names serve to identify a particular council) are named in the inscriptions, after the day and month have been specified, with the obvious purpose of identifying the particular year in which the decree recorded was passed. It is not known if it was appointed by lot (like the Athenian) or elected; nor whether there were any restrictions on re-election. It is these matters which would determine the character of the council. Councils that were elected, perhaps from the more wealthy citizens only and where re-election was possible, would be oligarchic in character; the mere existence of a council is in itself no guarantee that the character of the constitution did not change.

If the square building in the agora at Argos is to be identified as a bouleuterion (the meeting hall of the council) the fact of its construction in the later part of the fifth century may indicate a connection with the definitive establishment of a democratic constitution at that date. But Herodotus, VII, 148 proves the existence of a bouleuterion in Argos as early as 481 (unless he is here guilty of an anachronism) and the later construction of a new meeting hall need have no political significance. Five hundred people were holding a meeting (apparently political in character) in the 'prytaneion' of Argos in 315, when they were trapped in it by Apollonides, general of Cassander and burned alive. This may indicate the size of the council, if this is, in fact, what the body of five hundred was and assuming that the 'prytaneion' is in fact the building in which the council met. Neither of these assumptions can be proved.[6]

In Thucydides, the Argive council is mentioned in the treaty arrangements made by Athens, Argos, Mantinea and Elis.[7] These arrangements afford a useful comparison between the government bodies of the different cities. They refer particularly to the administration of an oath, by which the terms of the treaty and the alliance it created were secured by invoking the wrath of the gods on a transgressor. The oath, and the administration of it, were as much religious as political matters and were undertaken by the appropriate officials and groups of officials, not by the people as a whole. At Athens, the oath was taken by the council and the magistrates and administered to them by the prytaneis (the tribal sub-committee of the council). At Mantinea the oath was taken by (and they are named in this order) the magistrates called the 'demiourgoi', the council and 'the other magistrates' and administered by the 'theoroi' and the commanders (polemarchoi); at Elis by (again in order) the demiourgoi and those holding authority and the six hundred, and administered by the demiourgoi and the 'custodians of the law'. At Argos, the oath was taken by the council, the 'eighty' and the 'artynai' and administered by the 'eighty'.

In all four cities, the responsibility for the acceptance of the oath is placed on the council (for the six hundred at Elis are comparable in number, if not in formation and method of election, with the five hundred of the Athenian council) together with the chief magistrates. The administration of the oath at Athens is entrusted to the effective sub-division of the council, but at Mantinea to two separate groups, the theoroi and the polemarchoi (who, if they also took the oath, would have done so among 'the other magistrates'), at Elis by the demiourgoi (who also took the oath) and the thesmophylakes (who, if they took the oath, did so among 'those holding authority'). In Argos, the administration is entrusted to the eighty. This body occurs once again in the epigraphic record in an inscription of the third century B.C., a decree honouring the Rhodians[8] where the treasurer and the eighty are responsible for seeing that an inscription of the decree is set up in the sanctuary of Apollo Lykeios. It is more likely that the eighty at Argos refers to a separate group than a sub-division of the council as at Athens. The figure eighty is strange as a mathematical sub-division of a council in which (to judge from its importance in the assembly and on the magisterial boards) the fourfold tribal division is likely to have existed. Eighty is more likely to represent four tribal groups of twenty than a quarter of a council totalling three hundred and twenty. If so, the eighty constitutes a sizeable body in its own right and is equivalent in size to admin-istrative councils found in other cities, where they are formed from suitably qualified persons appointed for life—the traditional oli-garchic council, such as the gerousia at Sparta (and, indeed, the Areopagus at Athens) as opposed to the elected democratic council where membership is limited to a single-year tenure. If this is so, then it is probable that in Argos, as in Athens, the old council survived even under a more democratic system; and if the function it performed at the signing of the alliance with Athens, Elis and Mantinea is anything to go by, then, like the Areopagus, the functions it retained after the establishment of the more democratic council were religious; for the administration of the oath binding the alliance is essentially a religious, not a political, act. Nevertheless the extreme scantiness of the evidence concerning this body makes any comment about it most speculative.

By the sixth century B.C., the hereditary monarchy had ceased to be of political significance in Argos and the family of Pheidon was in semi-exile at Kleonai. Nevertheless Argos, like Athens, continued to have kings. They existed, apparently, at the time of the Persian wars when, according to Herodotus, the Spartans asserted they had a better right to command of the Greek alliance against the Persians than the Argives because they had two kings, against the Argives' one (but this is hardly serious history and might refer rather to the traditional pattern). More significantly, the treaty between Argos, Knossos and Tylissos was set up 'when Melantas was king at Argos'.

It appears that a king was appointed each year to carry out the religious duties of the former hereditary monarchs, and that, in the fifth century at least, his name could be used like the name of the president and secretary of the council (and the archon in Athens) to identify the year in which he served. He was politically unimportant.

The generals were the commanders of the five lochoi into which, as we have seen, the Argive army was organized. In early times, the king commanded the army (as, on important occasions at least, the Spartan kings continued to do to the end of Spartan independence), but with the end of the hereditary monarchy, all trace of a single overall military commander disappears. As in democratic Athens, the generals of the five lochoi acted as board of command. When the 'select lochos' existed, it must surely have had its own commander, for at Mantinea certainly it acted as an independent unit. Similarly, the contingents sent separately to help other cities (even if these are not identified with the select lochos) required their own commanders and, indeed, Herodotus mentions that the thousand 'volunteers' who went to help Aigina had a general in charge—Eurybates (though whether he was a city official rather than an *ad hoc* commander may be doubted). There is no sign at all that the commander of the select lochos, whatever he was called, ever acted as supreme commander. The board of generals continued to exist in the third century B.C.; the decree giving Argive citizenship to Alexander of Sikyon is dated by reference to the secretary of the council and to the secretary of the board of generals. The relevance of the military commander here, undoubtedly, is that the new citizen has to be admitted (as we have seen) to tribe, brotherhood and pentecostys: that is, to the political and military systems of the city; the generals appear here as administrators of the army, not merely the commanders in the field. By this time the generals may have become the chief civil officials of Argos. Livy[9] refers to the opening of meetings of the assembly at Argos, when the appropriate prayers were offered to the gods by the 'praetors', the Roman magistrates normally used by Latin authors to translate the Greek 'strategoi', the generals.

In Athens, under the extreme democracy, the generals, as the only officials to be directly elected, formed the most prestigious of the administrative boards. In understanding the Argive democracy and comparing it with the Athenian, it would be an advantage to know whether or not the Argive generals had similar authority. The other boards of officials to be considered here are the artynai and the demiourgoi.

The artynai appear as Argive representatives in the alliance with Athens, Elis and Mantinea, in which they take the oath. Though demiourgoi are mentioned among the representatives of Mantinea and Elis in the same treaty, they do not appear as Argive officials in that context. On the other hand, they are the oldest group of officials for which evidence survives at Argos, for they are named in an inscription belonging to the first half of the sixth century B.C. and on two others of about the middle of the century.[10] They are never mentioned again, though in Hellenistic times, a board of demiourgoi existed in Hellenistic Mycenae.[11] The artynai are mentioned only in this passage of Thucydides, though in a fifth century inscription there is a reference to the 'joint-artynoi' who are presumably the same.[12] It is tempting to speculate that the one board replaces the other; the demiourgoi are oligarchic in character, the artynai democratic. In the dearth of factual information, it is impossible to be dogmatic: 'artynai' in the treaty corresponds to the general word for 'magistrate' used in the case of the Athenians and it may have a similar significance (in which case it might include the demiourgoi, as well as other officials such as the tamias or treasurer).

Nevertheless, on the rare occasions when we learn something more detailed about the working of the Argive constitution, it appears to be the generals who have the initiative. During Agis' invasion of the Argolid, before Mantinea, it appeared to one of the generals, Thrasylos, that the Argive army was in a dangerous position and he therefore decided to negotiate with the Spartan king. In this, he had the support of one other Argive, Alkiphron, who was 'proxenos' of Sparta at Argos (that is, the Argive who represented Spartan diplomatic interests in Argos and who would be strongly pro-Spartan); but neither had the support of the Argive citizen army. Nevertheless, they came to terms with Agis and a four month truce was agreed. Agis withdrew to Sparta and the Argives returned to the city. Before he entered the city, the army began to stone Thrasylos at the gorge of the Charadros, which Thucydides explains was the place where 'they judge cases concerned with a military expedition before it enters the city'. Thrasylos escaped with his life by taking sanctuary, but his property was confiscated. Nevertheless, the unpopular truce which he had arranged was observed and the Athenian Alkibiades was at first refused permission to address the

Argive assembly when he wanted to persuade it to break the agreement. At the insistence of the Mantineans and Eleans, he was eventually allowed to do so, but the truce was maintained nevertheless.

No doubt the generals had complete authority concerning the conduct of a campaign; but the arranging of a truce, if only a temporary one, is also a political act and Thrasylos had gone beyond the limits of his authority in arranging it. Nevertheless, two significant points emerge from these events. Firstly, the army appears as an autonomous unit, free from interference by the authorities or the assembly in Argos. All disputes that arose in the course of a campaign (presumably, matters of discipline and cowardice, for the most part) are tried in the presence of the army and, it would seem, require the approval of the army, in a place outside the city. It would appear that the generals lost this authority when the campaign ended (much in the way that the authority of Roman generals ended when they entered the city). This hardly puts them in a position of permanent political authority. Secondly, even though the army and the people of Argos, in what appears to be the majority, disapproved of Thrasylos' action and punished him severely, the action itself was not countermanded. Perhaps the religious obligations of the truce were too strong, even if they had been entered into in an unauthorized fashion.

Here again, it is dangerous to construct a whole principle of government on the basis of a single action. Nevertheless, it appears that the officials of the Argive state, while they had considerable scope for personal initiative in the conduct of their administration, had to submit their action at the end of their period of office to the approval of the Argive people or at least to that section which constituted the citizen assembly. In an oligarchy, the officials of state are freed from this responsibility and are judged only by each other; the fate of Thrasylos is a clear indication that the Argive constitution was indeed democratic. Yet, in the negotiations that led to the establishment of the anti-Spartan alliance in the Peloponnese before Mantinea, the Argives were prepared to entrust their affairs to a commission who had *carte blanche* to make whatever arrangements they saw fit. Such an action implies a willingness on the part of the assembly to delegate its authority that is atypical of an extreme democracy such as that at Athens. The Argive democracy is one in which the citizens of hoplite rank appear paramount, and the continuation of the 'trial by the army' concept again indicates a moderate democracy, not the radical form evolved in Athens.

20 Religious cults of the Argolid

Introduction

When Pausanias visited the Argolid, at many places which had been
flourishing and even famous communities in earlier times he found
only the local temple surviving, the cult continuing long after the
population which had originally created it had left. This pheno-
menon (which is by no means confined to the Argolid) demonstrates
the longevity and the capacity for survival of the Greek cults.
Through the upheavals and wars, and the migrations and the
turmoil that they caused, the religious practices and beliefs tena-
ciously remain. At the basis of the religion of the Argolid in
classical times are the practices and beliefs of the Bronze Age. The
newcomers who settled in the Argolid at the end of the Bronze Age
could not but be aware of the deities that presided over and protected the region into which they had come and accepted the need
to propitiate them. On the other hand, they were not without beliefs
in the gods before they arrived and may be assumed to have introduced something of these into the Argolid. Contacts with other
regions, in Greece and beyond, may also have led to the introduction
of new cults and beliefs. To disentangle the various threads of
classical religion in the Argolid with any hope of accuracy is an act
of optimism; but it is possible to detect some of the connections and
influences that created it. This is of historical and antiquarian
interest and it is fascinating to consider the various facets of Argive
religion and the complex movements of history that brought them
together; but at the same time it must be remembered that this
religion and its practices were a vital, living part of Argive society;
that the Argives of the fifth century were aware only of the immediate
importance in their daily lives that the gods exercised, not their
historical origins. As in many Greek societies, the original simple
piety becomes changed in the course of time. New superstitions

flourish, minor deities become more important. It is possible to detect a certain cynicism in the manipulation of festivals and taboos for a completely non-religious political purpose—the blatant rearranging of the calendar to produce a religious truce is a device employed more than once when the Argolid was threatened by an invading army.[1] But overall, the number of shrines, the offerings made at them and the way their significance persists through to the time of Pausanias and beyond, all this testifies to the importance of the cults to Argive society.

By far the fullest account of the temples and sanctuaries in the Argolid and information about the cults practised in them comes from Pausanias.[2] It is noticeable that he knows much more about the cults practised in Argos itself than in the outlying areas and it is obvious that he is recording the situation as it existed in his own day, in the second century A.D. At that time, the chief sanctuaries of the abandoned towns were, for the most part, still functioning; but the minor sanctuaries, for which he gives abundant evidence in Argos itself, would seem to have become defunct.

Passing references in other authors give some information about the cults and archaeological discoveries help considerably, by revealing the actual remains of the sanctuaries mentioned by Pausanias and adding others unknown to him. Particularly helpful, whether they are chance discoveries or the result of archaeological work, are the inscriptions which record dedications and other evidence for various cults.

There was not, of course, any systematic organization of religion in the Argolid, any more than in other cities of ancient Greece. There was no fixed hierarchy of the gods; some had greater importance than others and different significance to the people who worshipped them. They were concerned with different aspects of human life and society, or with different regions; the cults should not be regarded as being in competition or any form of rivalry, though doubtless, because of the regional significance which a particular cult might attain, it could come to have a political significance. Where a cult was of special significance to the state, a certain amount of official organization is to be expected. Boards of officials, comparable to the more secular officers of state, were elected from among the Argives, the hiaromnamones and the agonothetes who arranged the contests at the sacred festivals.[3] Greek society was dominated by fear of the gods or, at least, an awareness of the way in which they controlled human affairs. It was the responsibility of the government, whether king, oligarchs or democrats, to see that the affairs of the gods were attended to in a fitting and proper manner; and though it was from this obligation to regulate religious matters that the government of Argos was enabled to manipulate them for purely secular purpose, in general this was operated in the belief that the welfare of the community depended on the welfare of the gods. Of particular importance was the calendar, though we know little of how this was organized at Argos, except that it was the basis of the manipulations that led to the declaration of a religious truce at the moment of invasion. The calendar in Greek cities was based on the phases of the moon and their observation, with a system of intercalation to keep lunar and solar years in harmony. On the calendar depended the sequence of religious festivals; for though it was always open for individuals to make offerings to any deity whose support and interest were required, it was the occasion on which particular attention to the deity was paid on behalf of the city that counted for most. The chief festivals were undoubtedly holidays in the fullest sense; there was a truce from arms and from everyday labour. The inhabitants flocked to the sanctuary, offerings were made and, if appropriate, animals were slaughtered at the altar, the meat roasted and distributed among the pilgrims. Such festivals were very much the concern of the state.

Apart from the state officials, each cult had its own priest, or college of priests. At Argos, we hear most about the priestess of Hera, who presided over the Heraion. These priestesses were appointed young, though how, and from what section of the community is uncertain. The mother of Kleobis and Biton (if she was a real person) did not possess great wealth; her sons had to drag the cart to the Heraion because their oxen were still on the field and though possession of even a single yoke of oxen lifts them above the very lowest stratum of society, it does not imply that the family belonged to the Dorian ascendancy.[4] Personal names ending in -bis are unusual in Greek; it may be significant that the most famous holder of such a name was the Spartan tyrant Nabis whose claim to membership of the Dorian royal family is dubious at the least and who was notorious for his championship of the non-Dorian members of Spartan (and, perhaps, Argive) society. The succession of priestesses was used by the fifth century author Hellanicus as the basis of a chronological system; their names certainly were recorded and the number of years that each priestess served. As each priestess held office for life, the number of names recorded was not excessive, perhaps as few as two per century, if a priestess took office in her teens and lived to be seventy. Though the names were doubtless recorded in writing in later years, it would not have been impossible to commit the full list to memory. Hellanicus apparently drew up a list of names that extended back in time to the middle of the second millennium B.C. How accurate such a list was cannot be shown and it is more than likely that the remoter names were inventions; but at least the list indicates that some people in the Argolid in the fifth century B.C. were aware that their religious history was of remote origin and that there was an essential continuity between the religions of pre-Dorian and Dorian Argos.

It seems best to treat each god, or group of gods separately. It is difficult to devise an altogether appropriate order for them. Hera comes first for she was in a special sense the protecting deity for the whole of the Argolid. She was, indeed, Argive Hera, Hera Argeia. Then the gods of the important localities, Apollo of Argos, Athena of Mycenae, though their sanctuaries in other localities (which might involve what was in origin a distinct cult) will be discussed. The remaining major gods will follow in alphabetical order, even though this means banishing Zeus to the end of the list; after that, again in alphabetical order, the less important cults.

Hera

The cult most particularly associated with the Argolid was undoubtedly that of the goddess Hera. Her chief sanctuary, on the eastern side of the Argolid, an hour's walk south-east of Mycenae, attracted worshippers from all over the Argolid.[5] At the time of her festival, a sacred procession went across the Argive plain from Argos itself, on foot or in ox-carts. We have seen how Hellanicus recorded the names of her priestesses back into what we term the second millennium B.C. There is ample evidence for an all-important goddess (whatever her name) in Bronze Age Greece and in the Argolid in particular,[6] and there is no reason to doubt that the protecting influence which she exercised over the land continued beyond the 'dark age' into the classical communities. It is significant that her chief sanctuary was situated not in the city of Argos, politically dominant in the classical period, but on the other side of the Argolid; that is, in the region which was more important during the Bronze Age and in a place that had then formed a settlement. In a sense, the Heraion is neutral ground, not too closely associated with any one of the communities that made up the Argolid in archaic times (when the sanctuary began to flourish particularly and to develop in the architectural sense), though it is not far distant from Mycenae. Hera had other sanctuaries elsewhere; there was one on the slopes of the Larisa at Argos and another in the lower town. There was a sanctuary on the acropolis at Tiryns, from which the Argives took the old wooden cult statue (to the great Heraion, not to Argos) when they destroyed the town. There was a ritual of Hera at Nauplia where she was supposed to recover her virginity by bathing in the spring of Kanathos, a ritual that was apparently still continued in Pausanias' day (presumably by immersing a cult statue in the water) although Nauplia was then uninhabited.

Hera was thus much more than the goddess of one particular community, or group of people, in the Argolid. She was identified with the whole region. The Argolid 'belonged' to her, as it had done from time immemorial. On one occasion, like Athena at Athens, she had had to dispute her possession of the Argolid with Poseidon, the god of the sea. The waves had come inland as far as the town of Argos, where a sanctuary to Poseidon Proklystios marked the point from which they had retreated. If this has a rational explanation, it can only refer to a substantial tidal wave which swept over the lower lying regions of the Argolid and which was presumably one of the consequences of the now notorious eruption of the volcano on the Aegean island of Santorini, about the middle of the second millennium B.C. Even at this early date the Argolid belonged to Hera.

Hera also had a sanctuary at Mycenae, though she was not apparently the chief goddess there. An inscription on a marker stone denoted the boundary of the Heraion;[7] to judge from the form of lettering, it was set up about 500 B.C., and subsequently re-used in the Perseia fountain.

Apollo

Although the Argolid belonged to Hera, Apollo was the chief god of Argos itself. The most famous building in Argos, says Pausanias, was the temple of Apollo Lykeios—the epithet means either Wolf Apollo or Apollo from Lycia. It was situated in the agora at Argos and would seem to have been the only religious building in Argos large enough to bear comparison with the major temples of the other Greek cities. It was very much the chief temple of the city. Numerous inscriptions have survived recording decrees of the Argive people, which end with the instruction that they should be set up 'in the sanctuary of Apollo Lykeios', just as Athenian decrees were set up on the Acropolis, in the sanctuary of Athena who was chief protecting deity of the city that took her name. The treaty between Argos, Elis and Mantinea, which Thucydides records,[8] was set up both in the sanctuary of Apollo Lykeios and the Acropolis at Athens. So Apollo was the special protector of Argos as distinct from the Argolid. The significance of this distinction can perhaps be deduced from the position of the temple within the city. The agora was in the region that developed as the centre of the Protogeometric and Geometric town, that is, the Argos of the Dorian settlers. Apollo Lykeios ought therefore to be the god of the newcomers, brought with them when they descended into the Argolid from the north and established as the god of the ascendancy in a region where the chief goddess of the older population still held wider sway; on this argument, Apollo is more likely to be a wolf god from the northern mountains than a Lycian deity. Though he established his importance as the god of Dorian Argos, it is noticeable and significant that he did not replace or drive out Argive Hera. The local Bronze Age tradition was too firmly rooted and survived even the most catastrophic material upheavals that are represented by the destruction of the Bronze Age sites and the arrival of the new settlers.

The other cult of Apollo established in Argos was that under the epithet Pythaieus, situated on the flanks of the Aspis, overlooking the Deiras col, where its poorly preserved remains have been excavated.[9] It is thus in the area of the community that survived the major destruction of the Argolid at the end of the Bronze Age and might for that reason be associated with the pre-Dorian population; but the construction of the sanctuary would seem to belong to a comparatively late period, probably the fifth century B.C. and there is no archaeological trace of a Bronze Age connection, except in the locality chosen. There was also a sanctuary of Apollo Pythaieus at Asine and at Hermione, at the eastern end of Akte. In the summer of 419 B.C. a war broke out between the people of Epidauros and the Argives because the Epidaurians had not sent the compulsory sacrifice to Apollo Pythaieus.[10] Thucydides appears to think of one specific sanctuary over which the Argives had the chief authority but which obviously was not exclusively Argive. Since the Epidaurians were involved, this would seem rather to be the temple at Asine, though according to Pausanias the Argives (or, to be more precise, their poetess Telesilla) claimed priority for the establishment of this cult. But if the cult was also at Asine, there appears to have been a more direct link with Delphi, which was its centre, for the people of Asine had claimed to be the descendants of Dryopes (a tribe that had lived in the region of Mount Parnassus, behind Delphi) who had migrated into the Peloponnese towards the end of the Bronze Age. The cult was clearly of importance beyond the areas controlled by Argos; and this suggests, not that it was a late introduction at the time when the Bronze Age organization was disintegrating and migrations were bringing sporadic groups of settlers into the Peloponnese, but that, like the cult of Hera, it derives from the religious practices of the Bronze Age proper. That it was centred on Asine, which is closer to Epidauros than Argos, is likely enough. The cult may have been brought to Argos in the Bronze Age, at the time of the disturbance, or at the growth of Argive power and the incorporation of Asine into Argive territory. Telesilla's poem, written presumably around the time of Sepeia, may have been intended as propaganda for Argos' religious, as well as political, supremacy, but since we have only Pausanias' passing reference to it, we cannot really tell what was involved.

Athena

Athena was the warrior goddess, protectress of cities; and in this guise she is the chief divinity of several Greek cities besides, of course, Athens. They include cities of the Greek migration to the east Aegean, such as Priene, so that it is reasonable to see here a cult well established in the second millennium B.C., and which was continued in the Argolid after the arrival of the Dorians.

In Argos, the chief sanctuaries of Athena were away from the area of the lower town, though the agora contained a sanctuary of Athena of the trumpet. There was a temple in the defensive ring on the summit of the Larisa, the remains of which (going back to the archaic period) have been excavated. Pausanias describes this as 'worth seeing' for the votive offerings it contained, though the one that interests him most is the wooden image of Zeus with three eyes, which he believed was taken by the Greeks from Troy after its fall. There was evidently also a wooden (and so certainly archaic) cult statue of Athena here for when Pausanias visited the small town of Lessa on the border between Argos and Epidauros he found there a temple of Athena with a wooden cult image 'like the one in the Larisa'. A temple to Athena situated on the top of the protecting acropolis, looking out to watch over the town must be that of Athena Polias, Athena who protects the city. Inscriptions have been found in Argos (e.g. *SEG*, XI, 314) which refer to the temple of Athena Polias.

The other sanctuary of Athena Oxyderkous—sharp-eyed Athena —was on the slopes of the Aspis, overlooking the Deiras pass and adjacent to the temple of Apollo Pythaieus. This, too, has been excavated;[11] or at least an area containing a circular building (a 'tholos') has been found by the sanctuary of Apollo, and identified with the sanctuary of Athena on the analogy of the sanctuary of Athena at Delphi, also adjacent to the sanctuary of Apollo and also containing a 'tholos'.

But Athena was also the protecting goddess of Mycenae.[12] Her temple was on top of the acropolis, close by the remains of the Bronze Age palace and its 'megaron'. The temple appears to have been built at the time when Mycenae was already under Argive control, but the cult presumably had continued on the acropolis from the Bronze Age. This element of continuity has been vividly illuminated by the recent discovery, on the lower slopes of the citadel, of a Bronze Age shrine, with fresco paintings and terracotta images of a goddess.[13] In the terracotta figures are small holes, the purpose of which may have been to enable them to wear armour; if this is so, this could well be a Bronze Age shrine of Athena, the warrior goddess.

In addition, besides the temple at Lessa with the wooden image, there was also a temple of Athena on Mount Pontinus at Lerna, ruined in Pausanias' time; but this belonged to a completely different goddess, Athena Saitis.[14] She was the Egyptian goddess Neith, of the delta town of Sais, whose cult had been introduced to the Argolid and identified with that of Athena, for she also seems to have been a warrior goddess. The date of the introduction is not known, though it is more likely to have been in the Hellenistic age than at the time of the Bronze Age connections between Greece and Egypt (at a time when Sais had not yet achieved prominence in Egyptian affairs). The possibility that the cult was introduced at the time of the Egyptian independence in the seventh and sixth centuries B.C. cannot be completely ruled out.

Other Gods

Aphrodite Aphrodite, normally goddess of love, was worshipped at several sanctuaries in and around Argos, and also possessed a shrine at the harbour town of Temenion. Her temple in Argos near the theatre has been excavated.[15] The building itself was small, about thirteen and a half metres long by some six metres in width, and comprised a porch with a sacred 'cella' behind. Only the foundation and bottom-most courses of the superstructure were preserved, even in part. The use of the site for the cult of Aphrodite seems to have begun about the end of the seventh century B.C.; previously the site had been unoccupied since the end of the Bronze Age. The earliest structure must have been very small and simple; the temple building to which the foundations belong was constructed in the period of peace between Argos and Sparta, probably in the decade 430–420 B.C. The sanctuary in which the temple stood was in part formed from artificial terracing. It continued to flourish into the Roman period.

Besides this, there was a sanctuary in Argos of Aphrodite Ourania —heavenly Aphrodite—near the temple of Cretan Dionysus, the locality of both being unknown.

But at Argos, Aphrodite appears rather as a goddess of war, her cult being connected with that of the war god, Ares. This is an old connection, and is reflected in the famous story in the *Odyssey* of the love of Aphrodite and Ares. There was a joint sanctuary of Aphrodite and Ares, just outside Argos, on the road that leads to Mantinea, between the Deiras gate and the Charadros river. It was an old sanctuary, for it contained wooden cult-images, and it is presumably to be connected with the place at the Charadros where the Argives passed judgment on matters arising from military campaigns before they returned to the city. There was also a wooden image of Aphrodite Nikephoros—Aphrodite, bringer of victory— in the sanctuary of Apollo Lykeios. Pausanias says that this was an offering made by Hypermnestra, in return for her victory after being brought to trial; but this is unlikely—it sounds like a guide's tale that Pausanias heard when he visited the sanctuary—and it may be that this image also reflects Aphrodite as a goddess of war.

Even the temple near the theatre was not unconnected with this aspect of Aphrodite. It was here, says Pausanias, in front of the cult statue that there was a relief representing Telesilla the poetess, her books at her feet, and looking at a helmet which she was about to put on her head. He then goes on to tell the story of Telesilla arming the slaves and the women to save Argos from the Spartans after Sepeia. Whatever the truth that lies behind this story, whether there is a historical reality, or an 'explanation' that derives perhaps from a poem by Telesilla on Aphrodite in which the warrior aspect of her cult was described, or whether, indeed, the relief in fact depicted Telesilla herself, the helmet alone is enough to show that this sanctuary has a reference to military matters.

Enyalios Another name for the war god was Enyalios. His sanctuary was not among those visited and described by Pausanias, either because it was out of his way, or because it had ceased to function by the time he visited the Argolid. It is situated a little to the north of Mycenae and has been excavated recently by the Americans.[16] It was completely unpretentious; the temple proper was a small room, some eight metres long by a little under five metres wide, facing south, and with a secondary doorway in the east wall. An altar stood in front of the temple. The remains of various offerings were discovered in the excavation, suggesting that the sanctuary originated at about the beginning of the seventh century B.C., that is at a time when Mycenae was already part of the enlarged Argive state; but the most interesting object unearthed was a fragment of a metal shield, carrying an inscription which states that the Argives dedicated it to the gods, having taken it from king Pyrrhus. The dedication of the sanctuary is known from an inscription on the cheek piece of a helmet, 'to Enyalios'. Another inscription, found earlier in the same region[17] records the dedication of armour and weapons, in sets consisting of a shield, a helmet and a javelin. The dedication was made by members of a priestly college (hiaromnam-ones). The inscription is not fully preserved, and the title of the priestly college is missing. They may be the hieromnamones of Perseus from Mycenae rather than those of Argos.

According to Plutarch[18] the women who helped Telesilla to organize the repulsion of the Spartans after the disaster of Sepeia were in consequence allowed to build a temple of Enyalios. Lucian believed that because of the victory Ares (the more usual name for the war god) was considered to be a god of women.[19] It is not clear whether in this context the cult of Enyalios has been assimilated to that of Ares, so that the two names are regarded as alternatives for one and the same god. That Enyalios was worshipped under that name at Argos is proved by an early inscription on a bronze plaque from Argos, recording a dedication.[20]

Aiolos An inscription from Argos (SEG, XI, 332) records a dedication to Aiolos, presumably the god of the winds and father of Pheraia, who was worshipped in Argos as Artemis.

Artemis Artemis was sister of Apollo; but her cult, unlike that of her brother, was distributed in several places on the western side of the Argolid, as well as in Argos itself. She is associated with wild animals and hunting and in this guise certainly represents the continuation of a prehistoric cult. It is therefore not surprising that her influence seems stronger in the hillier, wilder country of the western Argolid, where she was more important than Hera.

At Argos she is associated with Apollo; there was a wooden image of her in the temple of Apollo Lykeios. Its antiquity can hardly have been as great as Pausanias imagined when he attributed dedication to Danaos. There was an image of Artemis (with others of Zeus and Athena, but not, this time, Apollo) near the grave of Pelasgos, also in the agora. As Artemis Peitho—Artemis of persuasion—she had a sanctuary in the agora, and as Artemis of Pherai (in Thessaly) she was worshipped somewhere in the city—Pausanias mentions this cult after he has described the equally unlocated 'most famous' sanctuary of Asklepios, so the cult probably had its place in the lower town. A statue base of the third century B.C. records a dedication to Artemis by a Demetrios and his wife (SEG, XI, 331).

Outside Argos there was a sanctuary of Artemis Orthia on the top of Mount Lykone. The most famous sanctuary of Orthia is now that at Sparta, since it was excavated by the British School at Athens, though there it is on low-lying ground. A structure believed to be the Argive temple was excavated at the end of the last century. It was not fully published but, like so many of the outlying religious sites of the Argolid, seems to have been small and insignificant.[21] Beyond Mount Lykone, and further along the road to Tegea was a temple of Artemis. Associated with the western valleys was a sanctuary on top of Mount Artemision (to which, of course, the goddess gave her name) and further north, a sanctuary at Orneai.

Asklepios The healing cult of Asklepios as a god developed quite late on in Greek history. In the fifth century B.C., it was comparatively insignificant, but gained rapidly in importance, and in the support it received from the people of Greece, in the troubled times at the end of the century. In the succeeding fourth century his sanctuary in the territory of Epidauros, adjacent to the Argolid, achieved international importance, and came to outshine the nearby sanctuaries under Argive control. The Argives were deeply interested in the development of the Epidaurian sanctuary. Many of them worked there, as architects of the several substantial buildings that were put up there, and also as craftsmen and entrepreneurs, and the Argives visited the sanctuary in numbers to participate in the ritual; but it was controlled by citizens of Epidauros, and so essentially outside the Argive sphere of influence.

Asklepios at Epidauros was able to call on financial contributions from all over the Greek world for the development of his sanctuary. In Argos and in other adjacent areas of the Greek mainland less money was available, and the shrines achieved far less magnificence (though several of them, such as those at Corinth and at Athens were not negligible) at least by the usual standards of the early fourth century. Such shrines essentially served local needs; it is significant that they were required at Argos, in addition to the neighbouring major sanctuary.

Pausanias lists three of them, all in Argos town. There was a temple in the area of the agora, which he visited immediately after descending from the theatre. There was a precinct on the Hollow street, the road through the lower ground between the two hills of Argos; but the most famous sanctuary was visited by Pausanias when he was returning from this Hollow street—returning where, and in what direction is uncertain, so we cannot tell exactly where the sanctuary was; presumably somewhere in the lower town. It contained a seated statue of the god, in marble, and another of Hygieia, the personification of Health, whose worship is linked with that of Asklepios.

Demeter   Demeter and her daughter (Kore) were propitiated for the sake of the crops and a fair harvest, so vital to communities which normally depended on the food they could grow for themselves. There was a sanctuary near the agora, with a pit, into which flaming torches were thrown at the ceremony in honour of Kore. This was the sanctuary of Pelasgian Demeter; the name probably signifies its antiquity, for the Pelasgians were supposedly the early inhabitants of Greece; but to Pausanias the name merely meant that the sanctuary was founded by Pelasgos son of Triopas, who had received the goddess in his house when she came to Argos. The Argives had their own legends about this cult, which Pausanias mentions briefly when he is talking about the sanctuary of Demeter in Athens;[22] he implies that there was a dispute over the priority in the institution of the cult between Argos and Athens, but such disputes are caused by later rivalry (and differences in the legends attached to the cults) not by any significant difference in the institution of the ritual.

There seems to have been another sanctuary of Demeter actually in the agora. Here were buried the remains of Pyrrhus king of Epirus, for it was by this sanctuary that he was killed. His shield was hung as a trophy over the door.

Outside Argos, Pausanias refers to a sanctuary of Mysian Demeter, at Mysia on the road from Mycenae. More significant was the sanctuary at Lerna of Demeter Lernaia, where the secret ritual, the mysteries open only to people who had been initiated into the cult, was celebrated. It was situated in a grove of plane trees. This was a cult which had connections beyond the political boundaries of classical Argos; the fire used in the ritual had to be especially fetched from the temple of Pyronian Artemis on Mount Krathis in Arcadia. These connections suggest that the cult was established long before the Dorians settled in Argos, and developed the classical state.

Dionysus   Dionysus had two sanctuaries in the city. One was by the road from Kylarabis (and the Kylarabis gate) through to the Deiras col. The locality of the other is less certain; it is listed by Pausanias with other miscellaneous places and objects 'worth seeing', presumably in the lower town. This second temple belongs to Cretan Dionysus, a Minoan god whom the Greeks identified with Dionysus. It would be interesting to know whether this cult was a survival of second millennium B.C. contacts between Crete and the Argolid, or whether it was introduced as a result of the relations which undoubtedly existed between Argos and the Cretan cities in the classical era.

Dionysus' festival included drama; though there is no trace at Argos (as there is at Athens) of a sanctuary and temple in the vicinity of the theatre. In Hellenistic times Argos was the centre of the local guild of the 'craftsmen of Dionysus', the organization of actors whose headquarters was the sanctuary of Dionysus at Teos in Ionia.[23]

Dionysus was worshipped in other places of the Argolid. To the south of Argos sacrifices were made to him, and to Pan, at the springs of the Erasinos, where that considerable underground river gushes to the surface. Such a sanctuary, in a cool, well-watered, rural locality undoubtedly provided (as the spot, now duly Christianized and sacred to the Panagia, still does provide at the present day) a pleasant place for excursions from the heat of the city. The annual festival, says Pausanias, was called Turbe. Rites sacred to Dionysus were also performed at the Alcyonian lake by Lerna.[24]

There was also a festival of Dionysus at Mycenae attested in Hellenistic times by inscriptions (SEG, iii, 312) and from the construction of the Hellenistic theatre.

The Dioskouroi In Argos, the sanctuary of the Dioskouroi, Kastor and Polydeukes (Pollux) seems to have been situated on the eastern side of the city, not far from the sanctuary of Eileithuia and, consequently, the Eileithuian gate. There was another sanctuary, with similar cult statues, about eight stades to the east of the road from Argos to Lerna, before the crossing of the river Erasinos. Plutarch states that the Argives called Kastor 'mixarchagetas'—joint founding hero—and believed that his tomb was in the city; Polydeukes, on the other hand, was a full god. As at Sparta (and in the western colony of Sparta at Taras) the cult of the Dioskouroi seems to have achieved considerable popularity. There are several inscriptions that record dedications to them; on these they are referred to by a title 'anakes', the lords, and there is no hint of any distinction between the two of them. The title would seem to be that of the Bronze Age kings; and here, too, it would appear that a Peloponnesian Bronze Age cult has survived, particularly at a popular level, into the classical state.

Eileithuia The sanctuary of Eileithuia was on the eastern side of Argos, possibly just inside the city.[25] It gave its name to the nearby city gate, which was on the road by which Pausanias entered the city from Mycenae.

Eileithuia was the goddess who protected women in childbirth. The name appears to be Cretan in origin, and her cult is important there. Her sanctuary at Argos (which would appear to have been ancient and important to give her name to one of the city gates) was said to have been founded by Helen, who, while on her way to Sparta, gave birth at Argos to Klytaimnestra, who was to marry and murder Agamemnon of Mycenae. It seems more than probable that the cult was introduced to the Argolid in prehistoric times.

Hekate Hekate, goddess of the moon and magic, possessed a temple in Argos, by the sanctuary of Eileithuia. The cult was important; the stone cult statue was by Skopas, and there were bronze statues apparently by Polykleitos the younger and his brother Naukydes.

Helios Helios, the sun god, had an altar which Pausanias noticed at the crossing of the Inachos river, on the road to Argos from Mycenae.

Hermes Pausanias does not describe any sanctuaries to this god. As the inventor of the lyre he appropriately possessed a statue (which depicted him with the tortoise from whose shell the first lyre was made) in the temple of Apollo Lykeios. In the same temple there was also a wooden statue to him. Outside Argos, as the god of boundaries, he had a stone image on Mount Parnon, at the spot where the territories of Argos, Sparta and Tegea met.

Leto (Latona) Leto was the mother of Apollo and her cult origin-ated with his, presumably in the eastern Aegean (she gave birth to Apollo on the sacred island of Delos) and Asia Minor. The cult was particularly prominent in Crete[26] (more so than on the Greek mainland) and her presence at Argos may be yet another indication of the close connections between Crete and the Argolid. The sanctuary was in the agora, and so, appropriately, not far distant from the temple of Apollo Lykeios. The cult statue in Pausanias' day was by Praxiteles and is depicted on a series of Argive coins.

Pan Pan was worshipped, with Dionysus, at the springs of the Erasinos. In view of the close connection of Pan with the district of Arcadia, it was appropriate that his cult was associated with a spring that was believed to draw its water from the Arcadian lake of Stymphalos, and which was situated by one of the routes from the Argolid to Arcadia.

Poseidon   Apart from his sanctuary at Argos which marked the spot where the waves receded after his dispute with Hera, Poseidon was worshipped particularly at the coastal communities, as befits the god of the sea. He had a sanctuary at Nauplia, which apparently survived the abandonment of the town in Pausanias' day; another at Temenion; and a small sanctuary at Genesion near Lerna.

Tyche (*Fortune*)   The personification of Fortune had her temple by the agora, near the temple of Nemean Zeus. Fortune was a favourite goddess of Hellenistic times, when she frequently represents the good fortune of a particular city. Pausanias believed that her cult in Argos was an old one, if only because Palamedes was supposed to have invented dice, the favourite Greek game of chance, in the sanctuary there.

Zeus   In the standard mythology of Classical Greece Hera was married to Zeus. That Argive Hera had a consort is proved by the ritual at Nauplia. There was an altar to Zeus alongside one to Hera on the top of Mount Arachnaion (the mountain between the Argolid and Epidauros), but Zeus was of secondary status to Hera in the Argolid, a situation that reflects the attitude of the Bronze Age and Crete.

There were several shrines or sanctuaries of Zeus in Argos itself. In the area of the agora there was a sanctuary not far from the temple of Apollo Lykeios, which contained a famous bronze statue of the god, the work of the fourth century sculptor Lysippos; but this was a sanctuary to Zeus of Nemea. Nemea was not an integral part of the Argolid, however closely associated the two regions became; it was a separate region whose local protector was Zeus, not Hera. There would appear to have been a deliberate transferring of the cult from Nemea (where, of course, it continued as one of the major international festivals of the classical world) to Argos, which in a sense symbolized the political links between the two regions. Argos assumed the right to the presidency of the Nemean festival, and at those times when she had lost control of the Nemean region, transferred the games, like the cult, to Argos.

Zeus was a sky and weather god. He possessed hilltop sanctuaries, on the Larisa (where he was Zeus Larisaios) and, as we have seen, an altar on the top of Mount Arachnaion, where the Argives made sacrifice to him when they were in need of rain. In the agora he was Zeus the Saviour. There was also a marble statue of him as Zeus Meilichios, carved by Polykleitos and set up, Pausanias says, to atone for the massacre of the thousand picked troops who had set up the pro-Spartan oligarchy in Argos in 418 B.C. after the defeat at Mantinea. The occasion may or may not be correct. Pausanias' version of the massacre is a fanciful one, presumably derived from Ephorus, and in contrast to the more sober narrative of Thucydides, who merely says that the democrats killed some of their enemies (and, one would have thought, were not very likely to put up a statue to atone for it, though that may belong to a later period, when the oligarchs were once more in power). In other regions of Greece the cult of Zeus is found under this epithet (which means the gracious or kindly one) and is perhaps intended as one of propitiation. At Argos the cult probably existed before the execution of this particular statue, and the circumstances, whatever they were, that caused it to be made.

Also in Argos, by the grave of Pelasgos, was a bronze vessel of great size that supported images of Artemis, Athena and Zeus Machaneus, Zeus the Contriver. This, again, is a cult found in other parts of Greece, on the islands of Kos and Corcyra (both of them Dorian), at Chalcedon, a colony of Dorian Megara and (a non-Dorian context) at Tanagra. Machaneus appears in the mid-fifth century agreement between Argos, Knossos and Tylissos, in which he receives a sacrifice of sixty full-grown rams, from each of which Hera receives a leg; for once, the part of Hera is inferior to that of Zeus.[27] Perhaps Machaneus (like Meilichios) was originally a deity in his own right, who later came to be identified with Zeus. Vollgraff, in his commentary on the treaty with the Cretan cities, identifies him with Kastor.

Finally, Pausanias mentions in the agora at Argos an altar of Zeus Phyxios—Zeus who puts to flight (in Apollodorus, Deukalion sacrifices to Zeus Phyxios on Mount Parnassos when the floods began to ease). The Argive context remains unclear; perhaps this aspect of Zeus is similar to that of him as Alexikakos—averter of evil—that is, Zeus who puts to flight misfortunes, as well as enemies.

Divine Groups

'*All the gods*' Joint sanctuaries of this form are nowhere so numerous as individual sanctuaries, however economical (to the cynical commentator) such an arrangement must have been. There was a temple, dedicated, Pausanias says, to all the gods in common, at Orneai.

The Epitelides This name appears to be a euphemism for the Erinyes or Furies and similar to other euphemisms for them, Eumenides, Semnai, Potniai. Two reliefs showing a triad of divinities (one relief depicting them in profile, seated on thrones, the other showing them in a frontal pose) occur on the wall of the terrace at Argos, near the theatre, on the lower slopes of the Larisa, which is usually identified as the 'Kriterion' or judgment place.[28] If these are the Epitelides, the existence of whose cult is attested for this part of Argos by an inscription, and if the terrace is indeed the Kriterion, then the comparison with the Eumenides who are closely associated with the court of the Areopagus at Athens is most persuasive.

The Dryads An inscription found at Mycenae (SEG, XVIII, 140) and dated to the first century B.C. or the first century A.D. has been restored to record a dedication to the Dryads, the wood-nymphs.

The Horai (*The Seasons*) The Seasons had a sanctuary near the agora at Argos.

Foreign Cults, probably of late introduction

Adonis The cult of Adonis was eastern in origin, and became popular with the Greeks particularly after Alexander's conquests. His was a women's cult. The ritual was observed in a building in the agora at Argos, where space had been found for what was presumably a late addition to the list of cults observed there.

Kybele A statuette found at Argos by the late S. Charitonides in excavations in the east part of the city was identified by him as Rhea

Kybele.[29] Charitonides suggested that there was a sanctuary to this goddess in this region, which was near the Eileithuian gate. It would have been completely unpretentious.

The Egyptian gods W. Vollgraff excavated in Argos a partly preserved terrace some seventy metres south of the larger platform identified as the Kriterion, and not far from the theatre.[30] He found an inscription of Roman date, recording a dedication to Isis and Sarapis. Another inscription of earlier date (first century B.C.—first century A.D.) had been found by Vollgraff in his excavations at the agora. The cult is also attested on Argive coins of the Roman period.

The Hellenized cult of Isis was particularly popular in Roman times; but its initial propagation in the Greek world belongs to the time of the Ptolemies, and reached Greece through Ptolemaic military and political interests in the third century B.C. Vollgraff suggests two periods, when Argos' allegiance to Macedon, the enemy of the Ptolemies, was broken, and when this Egyptian influence could have entered the city; these were brief periods, sometime between 278 and 272 (the time of Pyrrhus) and between 249 and 244. He prefers the earlier period for the establishment of the cult. It is a little surprising, since there is good evidence for the continuation of the cult in Roman times, that Pausanias does not mention it.

See also under Athena for the cult of Athena Saitis.

Heroes

Heroes hold a lower rank than full divinities. They may either be human beings, perhaps from the remote past, who have achieved a special claim to veneration (usually the kings of the Bronze Age, or their supposed successors); or they are divinities of such minor or local importance that they have become downgraded, as it were, to a lesser rank. Many heroes were supposedly the offspring of the gods by mortal women, an origin which serves to explain their lower status.

Agamemnon Agamemnon was regarded as a hero at Mycenae and an area was set aside for his cult. His place of burial was known to Pausanias, in the area now called the 'grave circle', just inside the walls by the Lion Gate.[31]

Amphiaraos Amphiaraos, one of the *Seven against Thebes* had a sanctuary in Argos, not far from the temple of Dionysus. Amphiaraos' most important sanctuary was at Oropos, at the border of Attica and Boiotia. He was a divinity of healing at Argos, as at Oropos. Significantly, Asklepios established his cult in the immediate vicinity of Amphiaraos' shrine. In the same area was a sanctuary of Baton, who was Amphiaraos' charioteer.

Argos There was a grove sacred to the hero Argos outside the city.[32] The cult seems to have had no great importance; we know of it primarily because the grove was the place where the Argives who had survived the battle of Sepeia were trapped by the Spartans and slaughtered, and where Kleomenes, told by the oracle that he would capture Argos, realized that he had been cheated in his hopes that this meant he would take the city.

Herakles The name Herakles occurs (by itself, in the genitive case, 'of Herakles') on an inscription at Asine (SEG, XI, 372).

Hyrnetho Hyrnetho was a daughter of Temenos, and married to Deiphontes of Epidauros. She was being taken back to Argos, against her will, by her brothers when Deiphontes and the Epidaurians came to rescue her. In the ensuing struggle Hyrnetho, who was pregnant, died, and her baby was taken back to Epidauros, where it was buried at the place subsequently called Hyrnethion.

Nevertheless the Argives also claimed that they possessed the grave of Hyrnetho, which Pausanias saw when he was returning from the Hollow street in Argos. He did not believe that it was the grave, for he preferred the Epidaurian story. Such cults of heroes who were of some particular importance for a town, often centred on their graves; and though many such cults were concerned with actual burial places, the idea that a cult centre was a burial place could develop without a corresponding basis in reality. The quarrel over Hyrnetho is connected with the struggle between Dorian and non-Dorian; Hyrnetho, of course, gave her name to the fourth, non-Dorian tribe at Argos, the Hyrnathioi (which is why she is important to the Argives) and served to link, as a daughter of the Dorian king Temenos, the non-Dorians with the Dorian political organization.

Linos   Linos, the son of Apollo by Psamathe daughter of Krotopes, had his grave in the sanctuary of Apollo Lykeios.

Perseus   The hero Perseus belongs essentially to the earlier Argolid. His sanctuary was passed by Pausanias soon after he had left Mycenae, on the road to Argos. A statue of Perseus, holding the gorgon Medusa's head, is represented on Roman coins from Argos.[33]

There was a college of priests at Mycenae responsible for the cult of Perseus.

Temenos   The founder of Dorian Argos was buried at the place named after him, the coastal town of Temenion, which he was supposed to have used as the base for his conquests. At that tomb he received the appropriate cult from the Dorians in Argos.

Personifications of Rivers

Kephisos   The river Kephisos had a sanctuary by the shrine of Adonis near the agora at Argos, because it was believed that here the sound of water running underground could be heard. Vollgraff identifies this with a small terrace east of the Kriterion.

Inachos   The river god Inachos was the father of Phoroneus, who in Argive legend was the first man, and who acted as judge in the dispute between Hera and Poseidon for possession of the Argolid. Because Phoroneus awarded the Argolid to Hera, the Inachos was punished by Poseidon, who made it run dry.

Erasinos   The name of the Erasinos occurs on the lip of a bronze vessel, a dedicatory offering of about 475 B.C.[34]

The political history of Argos gives the impression of a stodgy unimaginative people, content for the most part to hold their restricted territory and unable to devise the means for themselves of achieving their ambition, the recovery of the lost regions of Thyreatis and Kynouria. Though they succeeded in establishing a democracy, it did not attain the brilliance of that at Athens. It was more a middle of the road affair, a peasant democracy rather than a democracy of city-dwellers (as was the Athenian to an abnormal degree in Classical Greece).

It is impossible to assess the Argive contribution to Greek literature and learning. Argos produced no important philosophers, no great historians; as we have seen, it was left to others to fill the gaps in the recorded history of Argos, as best they could, and not with any great success. It was many years before a local historian—Sokrates of Argos—wrote. The most probable date for Sokrates is the Hellenistic age.[1] He seems to have specialized in religious matters rather than conventional history, and he wrote a description of the Argolid, in all probability similar to that which Pausanias compiled several centuries later. It is not unlikely that Pausanias owed something to him for his section on the Argolid, but how much it is difficult to say. The name of the Argive poetess Telesilla is mentioned several times by other authors from Herodotus onwards, and she was a writer of some importance. Pausanias obviously knew her work, which was therefore preserved at least until the second century A.D. but her significance is essentially local. From the way in which Pausanias refers to her it would appear that the themes of her poetry, like those of Sokrates' history, were mythological, religious and local. Again, it is impossible to assess her quality as an author. Two lines only of her poems survive, quoted by Hephaistion as examples of a particular metre used by her, and called the 'Telesil-leion' after her. They are about the goddess Artemis. She seems to have lived during the first part of the fifth century B.C.

Thus Argos is of little importance in the literary classical tradition, and this in turn helps to explain why, in comparison with other Greek cities, Argos has been neglected by classical scholarship, which over the years, depended on the survival of literature, and was concerned so deeply with literary studies. Yet Argos was not negligible in the fine arts, in painting, sculpture and architecture; and in sculpture in particular, the ghosts of her achievement survived in the reputation of her greatest sculptors, the respect paid to them by the encyclopaedists who recorded something of the art history of Classical Greece, and in the copies of their most famous works which were produced for the Roman market. Even here, it is obvious, much has been lost; and architecture as well has to be judged by fragments and foundations rather than the complete buildings. Again, Argos has been unfortunate in comparison with Athens, and it is easier to assess the importance of Argive work rather than form an aesthetic judgment of its quality.

Only the greatest artists are named, so that we can appreciate them and their work as individuals. Most are anonymous; some are recorded as names but we know nothing of them as persons. Thus it is difficult to find out the status of the artist in Argive society. In Athens some, at least, were not merely citizens, but people who held the respect of their fellow citizens, who were admitted to the circle, and, indeed, the affection of the leading men of the state. Many of the important Athenian authors were men of political standing, who came themselves from families which provided Athens with her leading politicians and soldiers—Thucydides and Plato are examples. In the Dorian society of cities such as Argos (and to an even greater extent, Sparta) the significance of the social divisions carried into the arts, and it would be valuable to know if the artists came from the ranks of the politically dominant Dorians, or from the subservient, non-Dorian population. In a society where the proper activities for a gentleman were politics and war, craft and mechanical skills belonged to a lower level of society, and it was here, one suspects, that even the greatest of the artists belonged. Thus we may suspect a dichotomy of achievement; the political and military history that we have considered depended largely on one section of the community, the artistic achievement on another. For all its democratic constitution, the social divisions in Argos surely continued.[2]

Argive Art

The Argolid had been a most flourishing centre for the fine arts in Late Bronze Age Greece. Fresco painting, sculpture, architecture had reached a high level of achievement, even though much was derivative in form, and the minor arts of metalwork, ivory carving and vase painting reflect the prosperity and connections of the political organization under which they were produced. Who the artists and craftsmen were will never be known, but it may be surmised that many of them were not of local origin, though local schools must have been developed. Much was achieved particularly in the context of royal authority: architecture in the palaces and royal tombs, sculpture to decorate tombs and the gateways to the citadels, frescoes on the walls of the palaces. The homes of the craftsmen sheltered under the walls of the citadels, and no doubt many of the products of their craft also served an essentially royal purpose, whether used in the palaces themselves (or buried with the royal dead) or sent overseas as objects of trade to increase the wealth at the disposal of the king. Of these crafts, only that of the potter can be regarded as serving essential needs of the ordinary people, though the palace must have been the most important consumer still, and discoveries of Mycenaean pottery outside the Argolid show that it was exported extensively.[3]

This form of patronage ceased when the palaces were destroyed. The splendid buildings were replaced only by hovels, and though, as we shall see, it is unlikely that all real knowledge of Mycenaean architecture was lost in the Argolid, there were no buildings of architectural merit for another five hundred years or more. There were no more palace walls to be decorated with fresco paintings, no more stone sculptures. The precious materials, gold and ivory, used in the minor arts were no longer available, and even workaday bronze in all probability was very scarce. Greece was thrown on its own resources, and the only craft to survive the shock of the destruction was the essential one of the potter (and, perhaps, that of the woodcarver).

Though in quality and quantity the work produced by the potters of the Argolid declined considerably there is sufficient of both to prove a continuity. The best evidence comes from Argos itself.[4] The pottery comes from the tombs, both those of the old Bronze Age community on the Deiras ridge, and those of the newer settlement in the area of the later agora. A chamber tomb on the Deiras ridge contained a vase in the Protogeometric style of the eleventh century B.C., comparable with vases produced in a similar style in Athens. In the same cemetery, in other chamber tombs, other vases were found of an even earlier style, closer to that of the last Late Bronze Age wares, from which it had clearly degenerated. The style is therefore called sub-Mycenaean.[5] Though the material remains are scanty, they demonstrate that the community on the Aspis of Argos which buried its dead in the Deiras cemetery continued the manufacture and decoration of pots in a tradition handed down from the more flourishing days of the Late Bronze Age.

The other burials are in the area of the agora. Here the style is essentially Protogeometric, and apparently influenced by the styles of Athens. It has been argued above that the settlement in the area which later became the agora represents the Dorian foundation, while that on the Aspis was inhabited by the descendants of the Achaeans who had lived in the Argolid during the Bronze Age. Presumably the newcomers, without a tradition of pot-making of their own, were anxious to secure the services of the Achaean potters, and certainly pottery workshops were established in the lower area.[6]

Similarly, Protogeometric pottery is also found, though not in any considerable quantity, at Mycenae and Tiryns as well as at Argos implying, but not proving, the continuity of potters' workshops in those areas. None of this pottery is impressive, and its importance is more for the early history of the Argolid in the first millennium B.C., than for the history of art.

The tradition continued; the recent French excavations in Argos have now produced a considerable quantity of pottery in the Geometric styles, [Figs 3–8] and these have been fully published and studied.[7] The mass of material is from graves in Argos itself (in the lower area exclusively; the Deiras cemetery had been abandoned) and the evidence for potters' workshops in the same region proves conclusively that this pottery was manufactured and decorated in Argos.[8] Vessels in essentially similar styles occur elsewhere in the Argolid, at Tiryns and Mycenae, which may well have continued to produce their own, though it might be expected that the

Figure 3 Early Geometric amphora

Figure 4 Middle Geometric amphora

Figure 5 Middle Geometric amphora

Figure 6 Late Geometric amphora

Figure 7 Wrestlers under the handle of the Argos krater

Figure 8 Man leading a horse, from another late Geometric krater

large-scale production in Argos would lead to this pottery being used in the other centres of the Argolid. At Asine differences of style and in the character of the clay used in the pots prove the existence of a separate centre of production, emphasizing Asine's political separation from the Argolid at this early period. This ends at the moment of Asine's destruction and her incorporation into Argos.

In its earlier phases, Argive Geometric vase painting is conventional enough. The types of pattern, their evolution, developments of technique and even changes in taste do not vary significantly from those produced at Athens. The reasons for this are probably more complex than the simple assumption that the Argive pot-painters copied Athenian ideas. Very few examples of pots made in Athens have been discovered in the Argolid;[9] perhaps the transmission of ideas was more important than the actual movement of the pots themselves, while the designs may have been influenced in part by other methods of transmission which are not obvious in the purely material, archaeological remains. Most attractive of the pots from these early phases are the amphorae with well-shaped, rounded bodies and restrained decoration that emphasizes their form. Tall necks flaring gracefully outwards from the rim merge, almost but not quite imperceptibly, into the curving shoulder of the body. Two vertical handles rise from the shoulder to a point more than half way up the neck, turning sharply to meet it. The pots are widest at about the middle of their full height, including the neck, and about two-thirds of the way up the body; from here the sides curve in gently towards the flat base. The base itself is marked off by a low ring foot. The decoration acknowledges the different parts that make up the pot. The overall effect is dark; the fabric is mostly covered by paint which turns black when the pot is fired. The darkness is relieved by restrained decoration. On either side of the neck, between the handles, a rectangular panel is left in the natural colour of the clay. On this is painted a simple pattern, a hatched maeander, or a series of lozenges, with perhaps subordinate decoration to form a frame or part frame, lines, dots or a series of zig-zags. On the body the decoration is even more restrained, and the dark paint is relieved only by a series of thin horizontal lines grouped together in twos or threes, in which the natural clay colour appears reserved; these lines are, of course, separated by equally thin painted black lines. As the Geometric style develops there is a tendency for the number of these lines to increase, though for a brief moment, perhaps in the early part of the eighth century B.C. some painters return in a conservative fashion to even simpler decoration with only a single band. Other decoration, in dark paint on reserved sections of the natural clay, still essentially simple, occurs at the rims, and on the outside of the vertical handles.

In the course of the eighth century the style of vase painting underwent a series of sudden and startling developments. These were simultaneous with the equally sudden and startling development of the Argive city state, and probably reflect the same ultimate cause: the redevelopment of trade contacts between Greece and the eastern Mediterranean, and the influx into Greece of oriental works of art. The influence on Argive vase painting comes in two stages, and possibly from two directions, and it is noticeable now that the close parallelism between the development of Geometric styles in Argos and Athens ends.

The first new development concerns the decoration on the body of the amphorae. The old, predominantly dark, scheme goes, except for the subordinate area near the base. For the rest, the body is completely covered with a series of dark and light parallel lines. This form of decoration is also found on vases made at Corinth at the same time. Otherwise, the decoration on the pots keeps to the old restraint.

In the second development, the restraint is ended. The pots—large bowls ('kraters') in which wine and water were mixed for drinking parties now seem more important than the simple wine jars—are essentially treated as areas left in the natural clay colour to be covered in patterns and drawing in thin painted lines. Though much of the drawing still consists of abstract geometric designs the use of figure decoration is now common and important. It is found on the necks of the amphorae, in the place of the older abstract pattern. It is also found on the bodies of the pots, again in panels, and surrounded with abstract designs.

In many of the more exuberantly decorated pots, the design no longer seems relevant to the shape of the vessel it adorns. This is particularly noticeable in a great krater from Argos, now in the museum there. The shape of the pot itself is unattractive; a low, wide, collar-like neck with a poorly proportioned bead rim, a balloon-like body, whose maximum diameter is placed too high, and at the bottom, three insecure looking strap feet that descend vertically from the side of the body, and then curve inwards and up to meet it again. The body is covered with a complexity of small panels with a bewildering variety of design. A close and careful inspection does reveal the ghost, as it were, of the old articulation, for there is a separate band of decoration for the neck, and there are still distinct bands of horizontal lines running all round the body, and a subordinate area of solid black at the foot; but these are completely swamped by the other patterning, and seem to function more as parts of the complex framing that divides it up into groups and panels. Such an overall pattern detracts from the still formal and varied geometry of the pot itself.

It is commonplace to argue that such designs did not originate with vase decoration, but in other forms of art to which they were more suited. The vase painter has been carried away by his enthusiasm for the new motifs, and he has not yet properly assimilated them to the true discipline of vase decoration. If we are to look for external influence it should perhaps be sought in the designs on textiles and embroidery; since none of this has survived we cannot be sure, and a direct copying of textiles is perhaps unlikely; the vase painter has been influenced, perhaps, but the precise form of the elaboration is his own work.

More important is the introduction of figure decoration. The vase painters of the Argolid are amongst the earliest to develop this style, beginning, perhaps, in the years not long after 800 B.C. Gradually a full repertoire of animals is developed; birds first of all, followed by horses, fishes, and eventually men and women. Heraldic-style groups are particularly favoured, such as confronting horses. Another common favourite is the group of a man leading a horse on a rein. Animals—horses and birds—and human beings appear in lines or processions; groups of women joining hands in the dance. Often it seems that the figures are used merely as decorative elements to form patterns that differ little, if at all, in purpose from the purely abstract designs; but not infrequently isolated groups appear more as self-contained pictures, or, at least, vignettes. There are examples on the Argos krater. Under the loop handles, on either side of the body are pairs of naked men, wrestling. Another scene shows a long-beaked bird, together with two recognizable fish, and a fish-like object in the bird's beak; such a scene might have been observed by the artist in the marshes of the Argive coast. Indeed, all these figure scenes seem to reflect the Greek world. The horses appear at a time when society in the Greek city states was essentially organized on an aristocratic basis, when the possession and breeding of horses marked out the relatively wealthy landowner. The wild life may well have been observed in the Argolid itself. Yet the idea of this type of decoration, and in certain respects its form—the heraldic group, the processions—occurs also in Near Eastern art, and this would seem to be the ultimate inspiration. These new ideas affect several parts of the Greek world: Corinth and Athens, for example, and though there is no longer a close parallel between the art of Argos and Athens, certain similarities in the ways in which both cities develop their art suggest that they are both reacting to the same stimulus. It was left to Corinth to chart the way out of the still dominant geometric conception.

Argive vase painting died in the succeeding seventh century. There were two kinds of development. One was a simple continuation of the linear tradition, still using outworn geometric patterns and ideas. More ambitious were vases where the body was decorated with larger figures scenes. The most famous of these is on a vase from a tomb in Argos[10] depicting a scene from the *Odyssey*, Odysseus and his followers blinding the Cyclops Polyphemos. It is interesting that this, one of the earliest recognizable representations of a scene from the essentially pre-Dorian epic cycle of the Trojan War should have come from Dorian Argos. It may well indicate the continued importance of earlier traditions in a region which was regarded as being at their centre; but the whole scene is more interesting as a historical document than as a work of art, and the style was not developed.

Architecture

Of all the important regions of Classical Greece the Argolid has been the most thoroughly devastated and the architectural remains of this period visually speaking are unimpressive. Nevertheless what does survive is important and from the fragments something can be discerned of the part played by the Argolid in the early development of Greek architecture.

As we have seen, little survives from Argos itself, and the more important remains are those in the sanctuary of the Argive Heraion (Fig. 9).[11] From the point of view of its architecture the importance of the Heraion rests largely with the earliest structures. It contained one of the earliest peripteral temples in Greece (that is a temple in which columns extended along the sides as well as across the façade) and possibly the earliest with stone columns; it contained one of the earliest stoas (porticoes) with stone columns; and an early courtyard building, apparently used as a place for cult meals, and one of the earliest buildings in a Greek sanctuary devoted to that purpose.

In the strictest sense the architectural history of the Heraion began with the seventh century peripteral temple. No traces of an

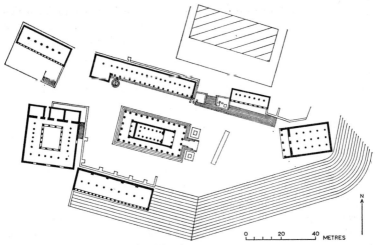

Figure 9 Plan of the Argive Heraion

earlier building have been found, but it is reasonable to postulate an earlier and simpler structure on the same site. Among the objects found during the excavations was a terracotta model of a building, apparently given as an offering to Hera, along with the more ordinary pots and other more precious gifts which it was normal to deposit in a sanctuary. Similar models were later found at a sanctuary of Hera at Perachora in Corinthia.[12] The Heraion example is decorated with an oriental lotus pattern and belongs therefore to the seventh century B.C.; the Perachora examples have geometric designs on them and are somewhat older. The Heraion model shows a simple, one-roomed building with a steeply pitched roof and a plain roofed porch added at one end, in front of the door. The wall at the back of the porch, in which the door is situated, continues up above the level of the porch roof, to form the gable under the main pitched roof. Here there is a rectangular window-like opening, directly over the door. The model almost certainly represents a temple; the alternative, that it is a model of a seventh century house is not so likely, since it is reasonable to suppose that by that time the better houses (and no one would want to offer a god an inferior house as a gift) were more complex in plan. The model appears to reproduce faithfully important features of the full-scale buildings. There are obvious reminiscences, conscious or unconscious, of the architecture of the Late Bronze Age. The plan of

231

the building—a rectangular room with a porch at one end—is that of the megaron which forms the heart of the Bronze Age palaces. The steeply pitched roof, much steeper than that of the later temples, suggests that terracotta tiles were not employed in the original; in fact, their use was not developed in Greek architecture until almost the middle of the seventh century B.C. The model, like those at Perachora, represents an older tradition. Also found in Mycenaean architecture—it survives, for example, in the treasury of Atreus at Mycenae—is the idea of an opening above the lintel of a door, to relieve the unsupported section of as much as possible of the weight imposed by the superstructure. These features seem to be traditional, handed down from the days of the Late Bronze Age, and certainly executed in humbler materials, but forming, like the early pottery, part of the link with the prosperous past. The importance of this evidence for the understanding of one of the formative influences in later Greek architecture extends beyond the limits of the Argolid.

From the middle of the seventh century B.C. Greek architecture underwent considerable development, and the Argolid, along with the adjacent region of Corinth, is in the forefront of this. First came the development of terracotta tiles; Corinth certainly played a leading role in this, and Corinthian influence must have spread rapidly to the nearby Argolid.[13] Such tiles made possible a more durable, and certainly more watertight roof, at a distinctly lower pitch than that in the Heraion model, but they also increased considerably the weight of the roof to be supported by walls and columns, which until the seventh century were invariably of unbaked mud brick and timber respectively.

The Argive Heraion covers a series of terraces built on the hillside as it rises from the lower level of the Argive plain. The remains of the early temple survive on the highest terrace, which consists in part of an artificial fill of earth held in place by a massive wall of rough boulders. The character of this wall led the original excavators to suppose that it dated back to the Late Bronze Age, but the earth fill which contains pottery fragments in the geometric and proto-Corinthian styles proves that it was not built until the end of the eighth century. Further support walls at the south-east of the terrace were probably for an access ramp, up which processions could reach the temple. The surface of the terrace platform is paved with irregular slabs of stone at least over the part that is artificially built up. The remains of the temple lie partly on this paving, partly on the natural earth and rock.

Not much of the temple survives. The best preserved section consists of the west part of the southern outer step, on which the external colonnade was placed; inside this line there are odd scraps that belonged to the inner structure (the cella) but quite insufficient to permit the accurate restoration of the plan. The excavators found what they took to be 'the foundation of the cella walls' but these were obviously extremely slight. The slightness of the foundations belonging to the walls is in itself an indication that the superstructure was not particularly heavy and the walls must have been still of unbaked brick. The colonnade, on the other hand, was more substantial. The surviving part, the step or 'stylobate' consists of sizeable limestone blocks, cut to shape. The width of the step, and therefore of the individual blocks, is just over a metre, and they were just under half a metre in height. The blocks are not rectangular, as they would be in later temples; their sides are trimmed diagonally, to fit the next block. On the upper surface are the traces left by the columns, circles lightly cut into the stone. They are 0·80m in diameter and are at a distance of 3·5m from each other, measured from centre to centre. The fact that the columns were set in hollows (which might be expected to accumulate rain water and so rot the columns if they were of wood) has led to the suggestion that they were in fact of stone. Their relatively wide spacing nevertheless implies that the entablature they supported was wooden.

These scrappy remains raise several tantalizing problems. The original excavators restored a long, narrow temple extending over the greater part of the terrace. If the temple is basically of the seventh century B.C. there can be little doubt that such proportions are likely and reasonable. An early date for the temple, perhaps in the first part of the seventh century has received some support. The most recent study of the temple has led to the suggestion that a much later date is more likely, close to the middle of the sixth century;[14] if this was so, it must be supposed that the real length of the temple was not so great, and that the eastern part of the terrace was occupied by the altar. The arguments are that a peripteral temple with stone columns is unthinkable as early as the first part of the seventh century, while the fact that the stylobate was constructed in part over the paving of the terrace suggests that it did not belong to the original temple. Finally, there is evidence that the terrace was cleared of the offerings it contained at about the middle of the sixth century. These were dumped outside the sanctuary, and it is suggested that the cause of this was the rebuilding of the temple.

None of these arguments is conclusive. There is no proof one way or the other of the original length of the temple; there is no need for the dumping of the votive offerings outside the sanctuary to be connected with the rebuilding, since such clearings-out were periodical, made necessary when the sanctuary had accumulated too much broken rubbish from the offerings of earlier years. Finally, the wide spacing of the columns and their relatively narrow diameters makes a date in the middle of the sixth century, when stone columns were normally thick, massive and more closely spaced unthinkable for a temple situated not in a remote and primitive region of Greece, but in the major sanctuary of one of the most powerful city states.[15] An earlier date is preferable.

The architectural history of the Heraion in the seventh and sixth century is obviously complex yet its importance makes necessary an attempt to disentangle it. In the sixth century, as we shall see, there were several improvements made to the sanctuary, and ancillary buildings, substantial for their date were provided. This makes it all the more likely that an impressive temple already existed; since the remains of the temple appear to be essentially more primitive than those of the sixth century buildings, a date in the seventh century should be preferred. If so we must surely and not unreasonably suppose the Heraion to be indeed a pioneering structure.

On the other hand, we need not go so far as to believe that it was already a peripteral temple with stone columns at the beginning of the seventh century B.C. The criticism, that this is far too early a date for stone columns is essentially correct. Two alternatives are possible. Amandry points out that, even if it is unlikely that wooden shafts were placed directly in the hollows cut in the stylobate, it is possible that these merely held low circular stone bases, on which wooden shafts were then placed. Bases of this sort occur at the Heraion of Samos, from the earliest peripteral temple there, and closer to Argos, at an archaic temple at Orchomenos.[16] So, if the peripteral temple is as early as the beginning of the seventh century, it must be supposed that the columns were in fact wood on stone bases. On the other hand there is a marked contrast between the relatively solid stylobate under the colonnade, and the negligible foundations of the cella. It is by no means improbable that the difference in construction technique signifies a difference in date; and that the Heraion provides an example of the modernizing of an older structure in accordance with developing tastes. This seems likely; if so, the architectural history of the temple taking into account the political history of Argos might well be as follows:

At first a simple primitive shrine was constructed of the type derived ultimately from the Late Bronze Age, existing on the site of the Bronze Age settlement of Prosymna. Such a shrine might have been renewed several times, without any fundamental development.

The second stage came with the definitive absorption of the Argolid into the city state of Argos. The Heraion thereby obtained more than a local significance, or, at least, its wider significance was recognized in Argos itself. The story of Kleobis and Biton, who themselves hauled the cart in which their mother the priestess rode from Argos to the Heraion proves Argive involvement in the sanctuary, and the dedication of the early stone statues of the two men at Delphi indicates an early interest in the story.[17] In this stage came the construction of the massive temple terrace and its access ramp (which perhaps destroyed the remains of an earlier structure) at the turn of the eighth century B.C. Despite the massive terracing works, the temple itself was probably still of the simple type reflected in the near contemporary model, for structural methods and techniques of building had not yet begun to develop. So this temple had mud-brick walls on a simple and insubstantial stone footing, and a steeply raked roof of thatch, supported by wooden beams spanning the width of the structure and resting on a wooden wall-plate along the top of the mud-brick walls. Such a temple cannot have been very wide, or it would have been impossible to roof in this fashion; if it at all matched the imposing character of the terrace on which it stood, that could have been achieved only by extending its length.

The third stage belongs to the crucial period of technical innovation which began with the development of terracotta tiles, and culminated with the creation of a stone architecture, modelled on that which the Greeks were now seeing for the first time (or at least for the first time since the Bronze Age) in Egypt. This period begins at about the middle of the seventh century, and it does not seem possible for the stylobate of the early Heraion to be earlier than this. The development of stone architecture was gradual, but the essentials were probably established by the end of the century. The Heraion seems to belong to the beginning, rather than the end, of this process, particularly if the columns were of wood over stone bases. At the middle of the seventh century Argos was prosperous and successful. Her soldiers had high repute. She had just shattered the Spartans at the battle of Hysiai and while they were involved in the protracted Messenian rebellion that resulted, the Argives formed the major power in the Peloponnese. There were anti-Dorian rumblings in Corinth and Sikyon, but, though the latter directed its hostility against Argos, the Argives seem to have solved or at least overcome the problem. The redevelopment of the principal temple in the Argolid seems a fitting way to celebrate contemporary Argive success. The heart of the temple was not altered to any great extent. The cult statue probably remained in the same position, on the base discovered during the excavations; and the mud-brick walls of the cella surrounding it were either left unaltered or, at the most, renewed to the same plan and probably the same dimensions. Outside and, to the south at least, placed directly on top of the paving that covered the original terrace, was constructed the new, up-to-date stone stylobate with its colonnade. The addition of these columns not only beautified (or rather made more spectacular) the existing temple, but also made possible the reconstruction of the roof. The old roof timbers and the thatch which had needed constant renewing to keep it watertight were swept away, and new more massive timbers partly supported on the new outer colonnades and their entablatures placed across the greatly increased total width. Over this came a terracotta tiled roof; with only the minimum attention, this would remain watertight as long as the temple stood.

In fact the temple stood, as an increasingly antique example of Greek architecture, until the end of the fifth century B.C. when it was accidentally destroyed by fire. Its old-fashioned character should not be allowed to disguise the fact that in its day it had been a pioneering structure; whatever other uncertainties still shroud it in mystery, it is certainly one of the earliest peripteral temples known in mainland Greece. Argos was in the forefront of seventh century architecture.

The development of the sanctuary continued in the sixth century. South of the temple terrace, and on a lower level, a precinct wall enclosing a substantial area was built at a date subsequent to the original construction of the temple terrace and before the redevelopment of the area enclosed by it as the site of the fifth century temple. This area contains several structures apart from the later temple. These include a long stoa, or colonnade, with an internal line of columns behind those of the façade, and a walled section at its eastern end (the north stoa); a smaller colonnade, also with an inner line of columns (the north-east building); and on the east side, a large building whose single room (divided internally by three rows of columns) is preceded by a temple-like porch with three columns, with two doors in the dividing wall.[18] To the west, beyond the area marked off by the precinct wall, are two more buildings, another portico (the north-west building) and a building in which three rooms face on to an enclosed courtyard (the west building). In addition another portico was constructed to the south of the precinct area.

Of these buildings, Amandry argues that the north stoa is of the seventh century B.C., the north-east building of either the seventh century or the first part of the sixth century, the west building of the last quarter of the sixth century; the north-west building, also, he suggests is archaic in date. The others are later, belonging to the fifth century redevelopment. Miss Bergquist denies an early date to all of them except the west building, on the grounds that there are no recognizably archaic features in them, apart from the Doric capitals, and that the proportions of the porticoes suggest a more developed period of Greek architecture, in the fifth century B.C. She also points out that the north portico and north-east building with the platform between them block the access to the old temple, which was therefore presumably already out of use when they were constructed. Against this it must be objected that the undoubtedly archaic Doric capitals must have belonged to buildings in the Heraion and it is difficult to see that these have otherwise totally disappeared; that the annexe to the sanctuary would be surprisingly empty if the early buildings did not exist, and it is more than surprising that the building she accepts as sixth century was constructed outside this empty area; the north portico and the north-east building do not block completely the access to the old temple, while the north portico in particular is in precisely the same relationship to the old temple as the south stoa to the new temple, suggesting that the later development is a deliberate attempt to reproduce the earlier situation.

If we accept the early date for at least the north, north-east and west buildings, the Argive Heraion again appears in the forefront of architectural development; though the function of each building cannot be determined with certainty (indeed it is more than probable that they fulfilled more than one function) their relationship to the area of the sanctuary and its position seems meaningful. Since the Heraion was not in or adjacent to a major town it had to provide more amenities than were at that time normal in an urban sanctuary.[19] A certain degree of shelter, both for worshippers and the gifts that they might offer to the goddess was provided in the north and north-east buildings. It is significant also that these buildings turn their back on the sanctuary and look out over the Argive plain towards Argos itself. The story of Kleobis and Biton suggests that a sacred procession made its way to the sanctuary across the plain, and the north portico in particular provides an excellent place from which to view its arrival. The function of the west building seems more certain; in the three rooms on the north side are the remains of couches, stone uprights which once supported wooden mattress-bases, indications that in this building the Argives reclined at the sacred feasts, which were part of the religious festival observed in such sanctuaries. It is not unlikely that the feasting was not restricted to the three rooms, each of which held eleven couches; around the courtyard on to which the rooms opened, on the three other sides the surrounding colonnade was doubled, leaving ample space for a larger number of couches, perhaps less durable in form, to be laid out at the time of the festival. Similar buildings are found in other sanctuaries in regions close to the Argive plain; in the sanctuaries of Asklepios at Epidauros and at Troizen, for example, with the same distinction between rooms with a limited number of couches and larger rooms, but these are all later in date.[20] The Heraion west building again is one of the earliest examples of this type. In all these buildings, substantial use of stone was made. The walls, if not completely of stone, had high footings on which a mud-brick superstructure was kept well clear of the ground. Well-fitted stone steps are normal, even though the individual blocks may not be perfectly square as yet. Moreover, even these subordinate buildings employed stone columns in the Doric order and the Heraion has provided a relatively full sequence of Doric capitals, which show how the early form developed.

By the fifth century, the old temple of Hera was a venerable antique. It was unlikely that it would be deliberately destroyed for the sake of modernization, for it seems to have been the usual rule that the older buildings in sanctuaries were carefully preserved and totally replaced only in the event of accidental or hostile destruction or when they had decayed beyond repair.[21] Thus the great fire which destroyed the temple in 423 B.C., though apparently giving an opportunity for a complete modernization of the sanctuary, was not necessarily welcomed for that reason, while the loss of the venerable temple was undoubtedly deplored.

The new temple was not constructed on the same site, but on the lower terrace to the south. This is a little surprising, since elsewhere, where a temple suffered accidental destruction (for example, the sixth century temple of Artemis at Ephesos burnt to the ground in 356 B.C.) it was usual to rebuild on the same hallowed site. There seems no good reason why the site of the old Heraion should not have been re-used, and it would appear from the fact that very little of it now survives that the terrace on which it stood was left virtually clear.

Amandry, in his recent study of the Heraion, has suggested the probable explanation of this, that it had already been decided to build a new temple to Hera before the accidental destruction of the old. This seems very likely; the old, venerable temple would be preserved, but a more up-to-date and impressive temple would be constructed by it, more in accordance with the status of the fifth century city. (The same attitude perhaps, had already appeared at Athens, where, in the period between the two Persian invasions, a new, up-to-date temple of Athena was begun on a site adjacent to the existing sixth century building.) The south terrace was therefore prepared to receive the new building. Here again, we can see a possible reflection of political conditions. At the end of the sixth and beginning of the fifth century Argive affairs, as we have seen, suffered severely at the hands of Sparta. Since then, Argos had steadily recovered. With the destruction of Mycenae and Tiryns her hold over the eastern Argolid had been restored, and with it, possession of the Heraion, which may even have been lost to her at the time of Mycenae's independence. A policy of alliance with Athens, and the continued observation of the peace treaty by Sparta left her in peace, and Thucydides shows that she had prospered. It cannot have been long before the renewal of Argive fortunes made the reconstruction of the sanctuary possible and desirable.

The first step was to prepare the terrace. On the western side a massive support wall, of which a substantial part still remains, was constructed as close as was practicable to the west building, which was to be left outside the new temple terrace, as it had been outside that of the old temple. This wall has an outer face of hard limestone, of ashlar blocks with drafted margins; behind these, and originally concealed, the bulk of the wall was built of poorer, more friable rock, locally quarried. Little of the outer face is preserved, and the exposed inner core had weathered badly, giving the remains of the wall a more primitive appearance than it originally possessed. This section is a little over thirty-six metres in length. It then turns to the east, at an angle of about 95° and forms the southern boundary of the new terrace, corresponding to the arrangement of the north stoa and the old terrace. The west wall of the stoa formed a continuation of the west terrace wall, but at a changed angle. It projected forward beyond the front of the stoa where it formed the western support to a flight of steps that ascend to the stoa from the probable line of the road leading into the sanctuary. Beyond the stoa, the southern and eastern boundaries of the new terrace present serious problems. When the sanctuary was first excavated it appeared that the area immediately to the east of the stoa was occupied by a substantial flight of steps, terminating in another support wall. Further investigations showed that the substructure of the steps continued beyond the line of this wall, and extended as far as the eastern part of the terrace. It was therefore suggested that, as a monumental flight of steps on this scale is unheard of in Greek architecture at this date, the 'steps' in fact belong to a special form of support in which, rather than build vertically the massive structure necessary to hold up the quantity of soil and rubble represented by the terrace fill, the courses are placed each a little behind the course below. The wall therefore forms rather a stepped stone cover to the natural angle of the hill, and need not be so substantial.

The only difficulty about this argument is the apparent ease with which the wall becomes the undoubted steps in front of the stoa; and it does seem more likely that, even if this is the correct interpretation of the structural form of the wall, it also functioned, at least in the section immediately east of the stoa, as a flight of steps; not to give access to the sanctuary (for the height of the blocks, as about 0·75m, is too great for that) but as a stepped platform from which pilgrims to the sanctuary could watch a procession as it made its way towards the temple. Such flights of steps, undoubtedly for purposes of viewing rather than access, exist in other Peloponnesian sanctuaries, particularly in Arcadia—e.g. the sanctuary of Despoina at Lykosoura.[22] It may even be that this is a much older feature (perhaps deriving ultimately from the 'stepped theatral areas' of the Minoan palaces) surviving in regions where connections with the pre-Dorian peoples of the Peloponnese and their religion were still strong.

The interlocking of the rear wall of the south stoa and the terrace wall shows that these two structures were built at the same time, and that the stoa is an integral part of the planning for the new terrace. A detailed investigation of the forms of the Doric capitals of the stoa has proved a closer relationship with the Peloponnesian Doric than that of Athens: on the other hand the Doric order of the new temple of Hera built on the terrace above shows a close relationship with the Athenian form. This suggests (but does not prove) that the stoa was planned and built before the great construction programme at Athens got under way in 449/7 B.C.; at least, at a time before Athenian architecture was well known. On the other hand, the temple was influenced strongly by Athenian proportions, and this is what we would expect from what we are told about the circumstances of its construction, after the burning of the old temple in 423 B.C. It therefore seems certain that the rebuilding of the sanctuary was planned long before the accidental destruction of the old temple, and that the essential work of preparing the terrace was completed by about the middle of the century, or a little later; that it was the consequence of the firm re-establishment of Argive control over the Argolid and the conclusion of a satisfactory peace treaty with Sparta seems equally certain.

However, the construction of the temple itself was delayed. The place of its capitals in the sequence of architectural forms demonstrates that it was not built until about the time that the old temple was destroyed. Since we have a direct statement that the rebuilding was the consequence of the fire, the archaeological evidence should not present any problems. Yet, if the replanning of the sanctuary does indeed belong to the middle of the century it is necessary to explain the delay (since the Argive architects could hardly be expected to predict the eventual destruction of the old temple). Between the reconstruction of the new terrace, and the building of the south stoa, at one extreme, and the building of the new temple at the other came the great Athenian building programme, beginning with the virtual end of the war with Persia in 449 B.C. and interrupted by the outbreak of the Peloponnesian war. No other Greek city ever undertook such an ambitious programme, which was made possible only by the fact that Athens had at her disposal the economic resources of an empire. It is most unlikely that Athens, creating this programme almost out of nothing, possessed among her own population the skilled masons and other craftsmen in the numbers required for the new work. Many of them must have flocked to Athens from other regions. It is not impossible that a shortage of skilled workmen resulted in other parts of mainland Greece and this may have interrupted work on the Heraion. On the other hand, the cessation of work in Athens demonstrated by the unfinished state in which the later Doric buildings, the Propylaea and the temple of Nemesis at Rhamnous still remain to the present day, suggests that on the outbreak of war the group of skilled workmen, experienced in the construction of Doric buildings, was dismissed, and that many of them left Attica.

What is certain is that the new temple to Hera shows a complete familiarity with Athenian Doric design. The architect, Eupolemos, was an Argive; we know nothing about him besides his name. He may personally have been responsible for the introduction of Attic elements into the design; at any rate, he obviously did not object if his craftsmen, working in accordance with tradition and training rather than precise instruction, introduced features that belong to Athenian influence. Of the temple itself only the foundations remain *in situ*. The superstructure has been totally demolished, though enough fragments remain to give us a reasonable idea of its design and quality. During the excavation of the sanctuary, the area within the foundation was cleared, so that at present what is left of the temple looks like a crude and inelegant stone built tank; the temple should not be judged by its present unfortunate condition.

The dimensions of the foundations are about 39·5 metres in length by a little over 20 metres in width. These dimensions are comparatively modest, a little over half the size of major temples such as the Parthenon, and comparable with Athenian temples such as that of Hephaistos or Poseidon at Sounion. The exact dimensions of the temple platform over these foundations cannot be recovered. A variety of different stones was employed; the foundations, and much of the superstructure were of poros stone; the steps, the paving, the footing of the walls and the ceiling behind the exterior colonnade were of local limestone, more hardwearing in character. The tiles and most of the carved decoration were in white marble, presumably Pentelic from Attica. There were six columns across the façade, twelve along the side, the proportions already established for the latest temple in Attica, that of Nemesis at Rhamnous. The principal end of the temple, the east, was approached by a ramp; otherwise the temple possessed the three steps normal in Doric architecture. One block of the top step survives with the markings showing the position of the column that stood on it. The front surface is decorated with a raised panel on its upper part, and a double undercutting at the bottom; similar decoration was intended for the steps of the temple of Nemesis at Rhamnous. There is no evidence to prove that similar decoration was carried out on the lower two steps of the Heraion.

Several column drums and capitals of the colonnade survive. The height of the drums is reasonably constant, and though not all the drums of any one column survive, the dimensions of those missing must have fallen within fairly strict limits. The total height of column and capital was approximately 7·4m or about six times as great as the lower diameter, proportions which are similar to those of the late fifth century temples at Athens, as are the proportions of the capitals. On the column were found traces of the stucco with which they had originally been coated. Only fragments of the entablature were found,[23] and the full measurements are not assured (the excavators calculated them on the basis of the proportions current at the end of the fifth century: they add nothing to our argument). The fragments of the metope panels, excellently carved, tell us more about the sculpture of the Argolid, and will therefore be discussed under that heading. The other marble parts of the architecture (as opposed to the added sculptural decoration) are sufficiently preserved to give us some details. The tiles were about 0·54m wide; this measurement should be one sixth of the normal axial spacing of the columns, which is therefore about 3·24m— perhaps 3·26m, or ten of the 'foot' units. A continuous gutter (sima) ran along the bottom of the roof, also in marble. The profile of this is similar to Athenian examples and it is decorated in relief, with a lotus and palmette pattern linked by acanthus scrolls, on which are perched birds; this is an extremely early example of the use of carved decoration for the sima, earlier examples being more usually painted. The guttering was pierced occasionally to allow the rain water to escape through the conventional lion's head spouts.

Of the interior, little has been preserved, and there is much uncertainty as to its form. Above the foundations, the side walls (of poros) stood on a lower course of hard limestone. This course was decorated on the outside with a continuous moulding, a motif foreign to the earlier Doric architecture of the Peloponnese, and adopted from Athenian architecture, which had in turn assimilated it from the Ionic architecture of east Greece. The position of the cella walls is reasonably well established by the remains of the foundations, and the indications on the surface of the natural rock, where foundations have been rubbed away. At the front, at any rate, there are no difficulties; the temple possessed a conventional, fairly deep porch, with two columns aligned to coincide with the space between the second and third columns along the side of the external colonnade. At the rear, the interpretation is less certain. A slight depression cut in the natural rock and shown in the drawing of the temple in its actual surviving state published by the original excavators suggests that the main room of the inner building, in which the cult statue stood was closed to the west by a wall corresponding in its position to the eastern wall with its great door. These walls are thus both opposite the space between the fourth and fifth columns from the end. Such a plan is unusual. In the fourth century temples the position of the rear wall of the cella is more usually nearer the western end of the temple; indeed, the false porch (created in earlier Doric temples by having this wall closer to the centre and extending the side walls towards the end), is often eliminated completely. The fifth century architecture of Athens normally makes the false porch appreciably shorter than the real porch at the eastern end. It might therefore be supposed that the original interpretation of this cutting is incorrect, and that it marks not the position of the rear wall but part of an internal colonnade. Of this colonnade five clearly defined foundation piers survived on the south side of the cella, and the first four corresponding foundations on the north side. Each consists of two blocks placed side by side, and is approximately 1·25m square. A sixth foundation, 1·24m square and similarly comprising two blocks exists to the west of the fifth foundation on the south side. It is on the line of the supposed rear wall, and is closer to the preceding base than is usual. The original publication supposed that it came under an engaged pier which ended the inner colonnade against the cross walls, but this would be unusual, and it looks much more like the normal foundations for a column. The cutting in the rock surface on the other side of the cella could be a similar base, but is larger than necessary. The best solution seems to be a rear wall further to the west than is suggested in the original restoration of the temple, coming opposite the fourth column along the flank; and possibly with the inner colonnade turning in front of it; there is exactly enough room for one central column, spaced at the appropriate distance from each end column of the two internal colonnades.

Sad relic though it is, enough remains of the temple to show us its quality. It was in the forefront of the contemporary architectural design. Its proportions, where these can certainly be recovered, are those of later fifth century Athens, and owe nothing to the earlier architecture of the Peloponnese. There appear to be clear traces of Athenian influence on many of its details, and it is not improbable that craftsmen experienced in Athenian architecture worked on it. It suffered from the absence in the Argolid of white marble, which meant that those parts which for reasons of expense had to be constructed of local stone could not achieve the full quality of the Athenian buildings; but where possible, parts were constructed in imported stone, and its marble roof rivalled that of the temple of Zeus at Olympia itself, and closer at hand, the temple of Poseidon, in the Corinthian sanctuary of Isthmia. Add to this the superb carvings of the metope panels and the figures of the pediment and the temple emerges as one of the foremost buildings of its time.

With the construction of the temple, the rebuilding of the sanctuary ceased. The older ancillary buildings remained, kept in repair but not replaced. Whether there was ever a plan to replace structures like the west building cannot be known; but the position of the west support wall to the terrace of the new temple shows that at the middle of the fifth century the continued existence of that building was presumed. These ancillary structures hardly possessed the venerable character of the temple and there might well be less weighty religious reasons to ensure their preservation. Presumably, as long as they were satisfactory from a functional point of view the Argives saw no good reason to spend money replacing them. Though the fourth century saw the construction in the adjacent territory of Epidauros of a magnificent new sanctuary of Asklepios, and the gradual provision there of a full array of ancillary buildings on which

Argive architects and craftsmen were employed, the sanctuary of Hera remained architecturally quiescent. Other sanctuaries developed the model already established in the Argolid; not even the favour Argos found with Philip of Macedon was able to endow the sanctuary of Hera with new buildings. The importance of the Heraion belongs essentially to its early days and to the fifth century.

Only one structure of later times is of any importance. G. Roux recognized,[24] in the Byzantine church at Merbaka, constructed largely of blocks taken from the Heraion, and also in the sanctuary itself, several moulded and decorated blocks that he interpreted as coming from an altar. This consisted of a profile base, a frieze of triglyphs and metopes, and a crowning moulding. A similar triglyph altar has been identified in Argos itself, in a series of dismantled blocks in the square building of the agora, and probably coming from the sanctuary of Apollo Lykeios. Elsewhere, altars of this type have been found in places connected with Corinth, at Corinth itself, at Perachora and in the Corinthian colonies of Corcyra and Syracuse. They thus emerge as a distinct local type (though this may partly be due to the chances of discovery, and they do appear to exist in other areas as well). The example at the Heraion is late, perhaps the latest in the series. The forms of the mouldings and the triglyphs, and the use of ⌐ shaped clamps to connect the blocks securely indicate a Hellenistic date, in the third century B.C. Before the blocks of this altar had been identified subsidiary excavations in the Heraion itself had revealed a substantial foundation in front of the east end of the new temple, in the usual position of the altar, and of the long narrow proportions usually adopted for altars of the triglyph type. The identification of these remains as the foundation of an altar has been denied, on account of their excessive lengths and, indeed, if an altar were restored on them it would measure about seventeen metres in length and less than two and a half metres in width; but such exaggerated proportions are not unknown elsewhere in Hellenistic times, and it was always the rule that triglyph altars should be long and narrow.

Fragments only of the altar of Apollo Lykeios have so far been found and no trace of the foundations on which they stood. Like the altar of the Heraion, it comprised a moulded base—a vertical plinth section topped by a rounded torus moulding—the triglyph section, and the cornice above the frieze—two vertical sections, the upper projecting further than the lower, and separated by a hawk's beak.

This altar had triglyphs with a slightly rounded and undercut top to the grooves, and should belong to the late fifth or fourth century B.C.

Another monumental altar was built in the sanctuary of Apollo Pythaieus on the Aspis, probably in the fourth century B.C. The core of the altar is a section of natural rock, which is clearly visible;

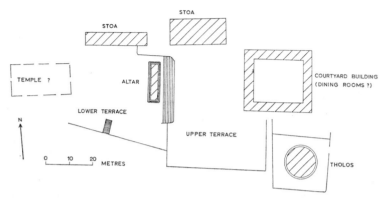

Figure 10   Plan of the sanctuary of Apollo Pythaieus at Argos

but originally this was concealed by a masonry structure. This altar appears not to have been of the triglyph type. Like the triglyph altars, it was long and narrow, but it had a higher base with three steps, where the triglyph altars have only a low base. Its exact form is uncertain, but Roux suggests it was similar to the altar in the sanctuary of Apollo Maleatis at Epidauros; that had a moulded plinth, similar to that of the triglyph altar, but the cornice moulding consisted of a half round ovolo. The middle section is missing, but if it consisted of a smooth slab rather than triglyphs, the contrast between this and the triglyph altar is basically that between Doric and Ionic architecture. It is curious (to say the least) that in the fourth century the sanctuary of Apollo in the newer Dorian part of the city should have an altar that is in Doric form, while the sanctuary of Apollo in the area that was once the pre-Dorian city should have an Ionic altar. The distinction seems hardly to be the result of an accidental coincidence.

The sanctuary on the Aspis is even less well preserved than the Heraion.[25] The religious buildings (or buildings which appear to have been religious in character) were constructed on three terraces, rising from west to east, but little more than the rock cuttings and base foundations have been preserved. The temple has completely disappeared but was possibly situated on the lowest, eastern terrace, facing the altar already described. To the north of this was a small portico, with a single colonnade (the façade being completed at its eastern end as a wall). At the eastern end of this terrace, behind the altar, is a series of rock cut steps, perhaps standing in place of a vertical terrace wall, which would have overpowered the altar, but also providing communication with the next terrace to the west. This terrace still bears the remains of one building, a rectangular hall to the northern side. Its walls, a footing of limestone slabs probably with a mud-brick superstructure (replaced in Roman times by baked bricks) extended along the back and side and made a partial return across the front. Inside, it was divided in two by a line of supports holding up the roof. Its purpose is uncertain; the use of limestone suggests a date in the fifth century B.C. at the earliest. Traces of other buildings on this terrace are completely unintelligible.

The uppermost terrace was smaller, and almost completely occupied by a single courtyard building, entered from the south. Of the building itself, little is preserved apart from the deep square cistern that lay under the court. This contained four rows each of five square pillars which once supported a flat stone roof; on top of this roof was the floor of the peristyle, of pebbles set in plaster, fallen fragments of which were discovered in the excavation. Not enough survives of the superstructure to allow a reconstruction of the rooms that surrounded the court; as a result, both its functions and the date of construction are matters of some doubt. Cisterns of this type are not found before the end of the fourth century B.C., previous cisterns being simpler bottle-shaped cuttings in the rock.

Roux argues that the building is itself a sanctuary of Asklepios. He compares it with similar courtyard buildings in sanctuaries of Asklepios at Delos, Corinth and Troizen; he also remarks that in one of the presumed rooms on the east side of the building was a well, fed by a conduit that led from the central cistern. He supposes that this had a religious purpose, and compares the sacred wells or fountains in the Asklepieia at Corinth, Athens and nearby Epidauros. This is rather doubtful. In all these other sanctuaries the courtyard building is part of larger architectural complexes, which invariably include a recognizable temple of conventional type. The purpose of the courtyard building, even in proved sanctuaries of Asklepios, seems to be for the holding of cult banquets and is distinct from the 'abaton' where the sick passed the night in the hope that while they were asleep they would receive a healing visit from the god himself. Rooms for cult banquets are found in sanctuaries other than those sacred to Asklepios; the Argive Heraion has already furnished us with an early example in the west building. Despite the discovery in the cistern of a statuette of Asklepios, it seems best to regard the building on the Aspis as an integral part of the sanctuary to which it is naturally attached, that of Apollo. This seems the simplest explanation of Pausanias' failure to recognize a separate sanctuary here—the separate sanctuary did not exist. The cult of Asklepios did not gain widespread popularity in Greece until the fourth century B.C., and though certain sanctuaries are undoubtedly older (Corinth, Athens) they were particularly developed in that century, Epidauros being the outstanding example of the deliberate creation of a major sanctuary during that century. Apart from the specialized abaton rooms the forms of building used in these sanctuaries derive from the established forms used in the sanctuaries of more conventional gods. The cult banquet had played an important part in these, since the sacrifices of animals and distribution of the meat to the worshippers is a crucial part of conventional Greek religion. In the case of Epidauros, Argos seems almost an inevitable influence and it is known that Argive architects worked there.

Outside the upper terrace on the Aspis, on a slightly lower level to the south-east is a separate terrace that once supported a circular building, similar in plan to the so-called Tholoi at Delphi and Epidauros; perhaps the sanctuary of Athena Oxyderkous, unless this too is better regarded as part of the general Apollo complex.

It is difficult to derive much of significance from these remains, which appear mostly to be of a comparatively late development carried out in the sanctuary in the course of the fourth century B.C. Nevertheless, the traces of buildings that do survive are sufficient to link this sanctuary with others in the Argolid and its environs, at Epidauros and the Corinthia. The sanctuary—like that of Hera herself—is remarkable for the number of ancillary buildings of quite substantial construction that it contained. The cult of Apollo also required porticoes and, it would seem, a separate building for the cult banquets. We may perhaps detect here the influence of the major sanctuary on the other side of the Argolid, an influence which quite obviously extended beyond the Argolid.

The role of Argos in the development of Doric architecture in the seventh century B.C. should not be underrated. The invention (or adoption) of terracotta as a building material, for tiles and decorative metopes is largely attributed to Corinth; one of the tile forms employed by Greek architects takes its name from that city, and tiles recognizably manufactured at Corinth have been found in remoter parts of Greece. Yet Argos was a particularly flourishing state in the seventh century, the age that is crucial for the development of architectural forms in mainland Greece, and it would be surprising, to say the least, if she did not play her part in it. The evidence of the Argive Heraion, in particular, suggests that she did.

Sculpture

In the Museum at Argos is a collection of stone sculptures, mostly from the area of the ancient city. They are the work of anonymous artists of the Roman period and once adorned such buildings as the baths by the theatre. It is, perhaps, unfortunate that this final phase of Argive sculpture is by far the most frequent to survive, for, although the statues are at least competent, they are no more inspiring, or aesthetically valuable, than the majority of the uninteresting, derivative and repetitious statues of the Roman Empire. In themselves, they give no indication of the former importance of the Argive school.

These late statues are carved in white marble, imported to the Argolid from other parts of Greece, since there is no comparable stone within its borders. Broken marble statues may be fed to the lime-kilns, and so destroyed, but marble is slightly less vulnerable than the material in which the most important works of the Argive school were undoubtedly created which was bronze. Bronze has a high value and is easily melted down for scrap; the destruction of the best Argive works had been thorough in the extreme. Of the other materials used, precious metals are obviously liable to be melted down, like bronze, for their intrinsic value. Wood, frequently used for the original cult statues in the temples, to judge from the references made to them by Pausanias, does not normally survive in the climatic conditions of Greece, and there are no examples from the Argolid; ivory also perishes, or is destroyed by fire (though examples of ivory carving have survived from the Bronze

Age); terracotta, cheap, valueless as scrap, and comparatively indestructible, is used chiefly for the small, almost mass-produced offerings deposited by the humbler worshippers at the shrines of the gods.

In the classical period, sculpture served a religious purpose. It was dedicated to the gods, either in the sanctuaries or in the shrines or other sacred places such as the agora. Argive sculpture, statues made by sculptors of Argive origin, was to be found in other parts of Greece, such as the sanctuaries of Delphi and Olympia; and it is clear that the reputation of Argive sculptors stood so high that they were often asked to produce statues for other cities. Subsequently, the works of the most famous Argive sculptors such as Polykleitos were highly prized by the Romans, and taken from their original place of dedication, to meet an eventual fate no less destructive than that which they would have encountered had they remained in Greece. Roman appreciation of these works of art (as with others of the great classical masters) had one advantage, that it led to their being copied (often by inferior craftsmen, and normally in marble rather than in the original bronze); and sufficient copies have survived to enable us to form some idea of the originals, even if we cannot appreciate their more subtle qualities.

Sculpture in the Argolid begins in the Bronze Age. Sculpture in stone certainly existed, though it is difficult to assess its quality from the surviving examples. The lions which give their name to the chief gate of the citadel at Mycenae suggest work of a much higher quality than the comparatively primitive reliefs on the marker stones of the shaft graves there; but the best stone carving of the late Bronze Age occurs not in figurative art, but in the decorative patterns of the relief work on such structures as the treasury of Atreus. The terracotta statues found recently at Mycenae, where they had been walled up in a shrine at the approach of the danger that eventually destroyed the palace community, are significant for the history of religion rather than art.[26] The Bronze Age had already determined the materials that were available for sculpture— local limestone, more exotic imported stones (though these are the coloured and patterned stones from Lakonia, used for the façade to the treasury of Atreus, rather than the white marble of classical sculpture), terracotta, bronze, ivory (for miniatures and decorative carving for furniture) as well as wood. All this was the concern of the palace communities and those who ruled them, and hardly survived their downfall, except for the crudest and simplest of the terracotta figurines, and possibly—for there is no evidence apart from the hoary and doubtless fictitious antiquity assigned to certain cult statues by Pausanias—wooden figures.

Certainly these wooden figures were recognizably old-fashioned to Pausanias, and though the same was doubtless said of the earliest stone statues, in comparison with the naturalistic appearance of classical and post-classical art, which would have been regarded as the normal form in Pausanias' time, the inference is that he saw in them something older than the earliest stone sculpture. The wooden images were essentially the representations of gods and goddesses that stood inside the temples. Pausanias reports them from the Argolid in the temple of Zeus on the Larisa; one of Hera, originally taken from Tiryns, in the Argive Heraion; in the temple of Ares and Aphrodite by the Deiras gate; in the temple of Athena at Lessa on the borders with Epidauros 'like the one on the Larisa at Argos' (which is perhaps not the wooden image of Zeus which Pausanias had mentioned there, but another of Athena, in her temple). That at Tiryns, at least, ought to be older than the initial absorption of the town into the state of Argos, and may therefore have been carved before the end of the eighth century B.C. Its form and appearance is more likely to have resembled the stylized representation of human figures in Geometric art, or the early, Geometric terracotta figurines than the later representations, which were influenced by external factors, the art of the Levant in particular. Such work would indeed have appeared strange to Pausanias, and if so, it is easy to understand why he attributed it to the remote antiquity of the heroic age. However, while it is reasonable to suppose that these wooden statues were being carved before, say, 700 B.C., it is impossible to say how long before that date they were made.

The earliest surviving examples of sculpture from the Argolid reflect the inward-looking Geometric styles. These consist of miniatures, mostly in bronze, but with cheaper versions in terracotta.[27] These were made as offerings to be deposited by worshippers at the sanctuaries, and have been found at the Argive Heraion, some subsequently removed from the vicinity of the old temple, or washed down into the lower terraces, but others buried in the fill behind the early support wall for the upper terrace on which the old temple stood, so proving their early date. Amongst the bronzes is a series of stylized horses, with slender bodies, flat manes, and extended tails, similar to the horses that appear on the late geometric vases, and presumably made about the same time, towards the end of the eighth century B.C. Such gifts continued to be made to the goddess over a considerable period of time, and their design becomes increasingly naturalistic. Such work reflects the trends in more important aspects of sculpture; they are not in themselves original and creative.

In the course of the seventh century B.C., a new style developed for terracotta figurines. This is found principally in the Dorian centres of Crete (where it may have originated), Corinth, Sparta and the island of Rhodes, and presumably reflects the taste of the ruling ascendancies of those regions.[28] The style, which is conventionally called 'Daedalic' (after Daedalus, who in Greek legend was the first sculptor) was in all probability derived from the Levant regions of Syria and Phoenicia; its adoption in Greece reflects the way in which luxury goods of eastern origin were now imported into Greece for the benefit of the wealthier members of the community. Argos does not seem to have been associated with this development. This may be due to the chances of archaeology, that these figurines have not been found in the Argolid; but, alternatively, political and economic reasons (the establishment of Pheidon's tyranny, the existence of closer relations with Athens, the overwhelming supremacy of Corinthian coroplasts, analogous to that of the Corinthian potters in the seventh century) can be adduced, none of which can be proved on the basis of the inadequate evidence that survives.

By the end of the seventh century B.C. the Greeks had re-opened direct contact with Egypt.[29] From various cities Greeks settled in the Nile valley, as traders and soldiers. A new influence appeared in Greek art, just as it appeared in the architecture. Sculptors now began to work in stone, to produce life-size or greater than life-size statues, in a pose that reflects the conventional Egyptian stance, one leg stiffly forward. These statues were put up in many parts of the Greek world, dedicated in sanctuaries, or placed on tombs to commemorate the dead. The creation of such a statue was a more important undertaking than the production of miniature bronzes and terracottas, and the artists responsible for them were highly skilled men, far more important than the anonymous craftsmen who produced the slighter work. They were proud of their skills, and signed their work, usually on the base on which the statue stood. The name of the artist was almost as important as that of the man or city responsible for the dedication. Among the earliest of these stone statues are two at the sanctuary of Apollo at Delphi, dating perhaps to the early years of the sixth century B.C., representing thickset, massive, naked young men.[30] The inscription on the base, added at a substantially later date, proclaims that they represent Kleobis and Biton, the young men who died as a result of their exertions in dragging the ox-cart in which their mother the priestess rode from Argos to the Heraion. This inscription seems to have been added by the authorities at Delphi, who wanted to make clear what these uncouth statues represented, and it is possible that they were wrong; but there is no doubt about an earlier inscription on the same base, written in what appears to be the Argive dialect, which gives the name of the sculptor, or rather, gave, for the first letters of the name are now missing: '. . . medes [Polymedes or some such name] the Argive made me'.

[Poly]medes is one of the first Greek sculptors, and certainly the first Argive sculptor, known. He worked at a time when artists skilled in the production of large stone statues were unusual and probably much in demand. It is perhaps misleading to think of him as a member of an early Argive 'school' of sculpture. It is unlikely that these statues were made at Argos and transported by land and sea and land again up the rough road to Delphi. The dangers of damage would have been too great, and it is more likely that the artist worked at Delphi itself. Where he learned his art, where, apart from Delphi, he practised, who, if anyone, was his pupil are all questions which cannot be answered. During the sixth century B.C. sculpture in stone became more general, and the number of artists undoubtedly increased; but there was still a considerable mobility among them, and they were ready to move from city to city, as opportunity for the employment of their art was offered to them. Stone statues were made in the Argolid and dedicated, for example, in the sanctuary of Hera, but of these only the scantiest fragments survive, and they tell us no more about this art other than the bare fact that it existed.

By the end of the sixth century B.C. bronze was being used for full-scale statues, not merely for small figurines. The earlier technique was to build up a statue from bronze plates, moulded or hammered to shape, and fixed on to a wooden framework (a technique which continued in later times for statues made of gold and ivory), but this gave way to making the statue entirely from hollow castings, with the head and limbs, perhaps, cast separately from the rest of the body, and attached to it. Such a technique was costly, but at Argos, where there was no good local stone, which for statues had to be imported in the same way as bronze, and where there seems to have been a ready supply of bronze available, it is not surprising that renown in the field of sculpture seems to derive mostly from artists working in bronze.

The earliest of these was Ageladas. None of his work survives, but it was sufficiently important for his name to be recorded and handed down by authors writing on the history of art (or perhaps religion), until it eventually passed into the encyclopaedic compilation known as the *Natural History* made by Pliny the Elder in the first century A.D.[31] Statues by him are also recorded at Olympia by Pausanias, and the bases on which they stood have survived. From this we can calculate his approximate date, and the character (but not, of course, the appearance) of the statues he made. The statues were those set up by wealthy individuals, or their families, to commemorate victories in the Olympic games. They included statues of Anochos of Tarentum, who was victor in the stadion race in 520 B.C., and Timasitheos, all-in wrestler, who won in 512 B.C. Though it is always possible that the statue was dedicated some time after the event and victory it commemorates, this would have spoiled the immediacy, and, perhaps, the effect of the dedication; and the existence of two statues commemorating victories only eight years apart suggests that Ageladas was in fact working at that time, that is, the last quarter of the sixth century B.C. The type of statue must have been that of the young nude male, the 'kouros', of which many examples are known from different parts of the Greek world. Ageladas must have achieved his reputation for the technical skill with which his bronze statues were made, and the refinement of his art, executed within what was still a strictly conventional framework. This framework, the statue of the nude male in a more-or-less conventional pose, continues to dominate Argive sculpture in the fifth century B.C. It is wrong to speak of an Argive 'taste' for statues of the athlete type, but in sculpture, as in other respects, it is possible to detect at Argos a strong streak of conservatism, that made the Argives less ready than their contemporaries at Athens to receive or initiate innovations, whether in art, or other aspects of human society. It is all the more surprising that Ageladas was supposed to have taught his art to the Athenian sculptor Myron,[32] who more than any other man we know strove to shatter the archaic conventions; but if this means anything more than the succession of Myron to Ageladas in the list of important sculptors known to authors like Pliny (and, chronologically speaking, this is reasonable) it need imply only that Myron learnt the technique of bronze casting from the Argive.

Even so, it is clear that Ageladas' reputation extended far beyond Argos. Not only were his statues set up at Olympia (and to honour men who were not Argives, but came from even further away, from southern Italy) but they were commissioned from him by Greeks from a widely diverse area. According to Pausanias he made a statue of Zeus Ithomatas which was dedicated by the Messenians on Mount Ithome.[33] Other cult statues are attributed to Ageladas —another Zeus, for example, and a Herakles—so the creation of such a statue does not go outside the usual repertoire of the sculptor; but it may be significant that an Argive should be commissioned to carry out this work. It has been suspected on historical grounds that there was a Messenian rising against their Spartan overlords in the 490s, which would fall within the period that Ageladas flourished as a sculptor. If the statue was commissioned by the Messenians when they were free (and it is difficult to imagine that they could do so while they were subjects of Sparta) the only alternative occasion for the commission was during the better attested rebellion after the Spartan earthquake of 464 B.C.; but this would give Ageladas a working life of as much as fifty-five or even sixty years (from before 520 to say 460 B.C.), and as it is unreasonable to suppose that a young unknown was commissioned by Anochos of Tarentum, an earlier date for the Zeus is distinctly preferable.

Ageladas was not the only Argive sculptor working in the early part of the fifth century B.C. Like him, the others that we know about are little, if anything, more than names; men such as Hypathadoros and Aristogeiton who made the sculpture dedicated at Delphi in commemoration of the battle of Oinoe. Even if they are only names, their very existence is proof that the art of sculpture flourished in Argos in the fifth century, and achieved a considerable reputation.

It was surely from among this group of sculptors that the greatest of them, and, indeed, one of the greatest names in the whole history of Greek art, arose. This was Polykleitos. Pliny says that he came from Sikyon, but, if that is true, it refers to little more than the accident of his birth.[34] As a sculptor he was trained and worked at Argos; Plato, who was born in his lifetime, calls him an Argive and, as an artist, an Argive he undoubtedly was.[35] Pliny also tells us that he was a pupil of Ageladas, which is just about possible if Ageladas continued to work to the end of the 460s, for although Pliny believed that Polykleitos 'flourished' at the time of the ninetieth Olympiad—420 B.C.—this must derive from the fact that at that time he was responsible for making the new gold and ivory statue of Hera in the rebuilt Argive Heraion. It seems that the Hera was in fact one of his last works, and his earliest statues may belong rather to the 460s. Even if he was not a pupil of the aged Ageladas himself (an idea perhaps invented by the late historians who wanted to see an almost dynastic succession of the 'great' sculptors, and who also believed that the Athenians Myron and Pheidias were Ageladas' pupils), Polykleitos learnt his art in the city where Ageladas had been predominant in the art of sculpture; and that he followed in the footsteps of the older man is likely enough.

Again, no original statues by Polykleitos survive, but his standing as one of the greatest Greek sculptors was such that his works were copied frequently in Roman times, so that we have at least a reasonable idea of their design and appearance (though most of the copies are in marble rather than the original bronze). Like Ageladas, he made statues of athletes which were dedicated in the sanctuary of Olympia; Pausanias mentions statues of Kyniskos of Mantinea, Pythokles of Elis, and Xenokles the Mainalian which were by Polykleitos. The statues themselves have long since disappeared, but the bases on which they stood remained.[36] The letter form of the inscriptions on them indicates that they were put up about the middle of the fifth century B.C. It is possible that the marble statue in the British Museum, the 'Westmacott athlete' is a Roman copy of the statue of Kyniskos, for the pose corresponds to the position of the feet indicated by the cuttings to receive them in the base of the original. The pose is relaxed from the stiff upright rigidity of the earlier kouros statues; can this have been learned by Polykleitos from his predecessors, or is it his own innovation? The line of the body forms a graceful curve, the hips turned slightly to the left, the right leg back, with the heel raised, the weight of the body placed on the left leg, while the head is inclined to the right, and the gaze directed downwards.

The most famous of Polykleitos' statues was called the 'Spearbearer' (the Doryphoros).[37] This, presumably, was the nickname given to a statue which was almost certainly a dedication in honour of a particular individual, whom it was supposed to represent. Who it was, and where it was set up, is quite unknown. Another nickname given to it was the 'Kanon'—the model statue—because, as Pliny puts it 'other artists derived the outline of their art from it, as though from a law'. This does not necessarily mean that they studied the original statue. Polykleitos wrote a treatise on sculpture, long since lost, in which, presumably, he commented on his art, and used this statue (and particularly the proportions employed in it) as an example. The Doryphoros can be identified in several copies, again mostly in marble, though the original was undoubtedly in bronze. Again the statue depicts his spear over his left shoulder; the impression that the statue has 'frozen' someone on the move is noticeable, and is a marked contrast to the unmoved pose of the sixth century statues. This time the right foot is forward, taking the weight of the body, whilst the left foot is back, with the ankle raised; the young man is about to move it forward as he takes another pace. The body again has a curve, slighter than that of the Westmacott athlete, representing its natural line, and the swing of the hips in walking. The head turns slightly to the left. The same pose recurs in the other of Polykleitos' statues of which several undoubted copies exist, the 'young man binding his hair' (Diadoumenos),[38] though here the figure is at rest; the pose is adapted to give the impression of the young man balancing himself as he raises his arms to wrap the binding round his hair.

During the fifth century Greek sculptors had deliberately moved away from the stiff, formal poses of the sixth century kouros. Myron the Athenian is famous for the complicated poses he developed in his statues, best typified by his 'Diskobolos' or discus thrower. Polykleitos, equally, turned away from earlier rigidity, and it is by no means impossible that it was this quality, shared with Myron, that led Pliny's sources to regard both men as the pupils of Ageladas; if so, the innovation may have originated in the work of the older Argive sculptor. Polykleitos' achievement was to introduce the relaxed pose in a completely natural way, and certainly the Doryphoros established a pose which quickly became a convention, perhaps even in Polykleitos' own time, and certainly in the succeding century. Its popularity in Roman times is attested by innumerable statues of the emperors in the Polykleitan pose and even (most unsuitably, in most cases) Polykleitan nudity. However difficult it is

to form any real knowledge, in the absence of originals, of Polykleitos' achievement there can be no doubt that he was a sculptor
of the very highest rank. Here, at last, the Argive contribution to
Greek civilization is clearly and indisputably of the greatest significance.

The only original sculpture of the fifth century to survive from
Argos comes from the Argive Heraion. Polykleitos was involved
with the sculpture of the rebuilt temple, and was responsible for the
cult statue which, following the example of Pheidias' Athena in the
Parthenon at Athens and Zeus at Olympia, was constructed from
plates of gold and ivory. Nothing of this survives. Pausanias says
that it was of colossal size. It represented the goddess seated on a
throne, wearing a crown with the Graces and the Seasons wrought on
it in relief. In one hand she carried a pomegranate, in the other a
sceptre. When the Heraion was excavated a considerable number
of marble fragments were discovered that had come from the external
decoration of the fifth century temple, from the statue groups in the
pediments at either end, and from the relief metope panels of the
entablature. When first revealed, these were hailed enthusiastically
as Polykleitan work, if not from the hand of the master himself,
at least carved by his pupils, and under his supervision.[39] Later, a
reaction set in, and other sculptors were proposed as the men
responsible for this work; it was argued, for example, that the
proportions of the heads that survive are different from those of the
heads of the Polykleitan copies, and that this is of particular significance for an artist as deeply concerned with proportions as
Polykleitos undoubtedly was.

The sculpture of the Heraion is described briefly by Pausanias:
'over the columns, some sculptures represented the birth of Zeus
and the battle of gods and giants, others the Trojan war and the
capture of Troy'. It appears that he is describing decoration applied
at either end of the temple; at the east end, mentioned first, naturally, because it was the front of the temple, the 'birth of Zeus' in
the more important, and larger, pediment scene, with the 'battle
of gods and giants' on the metope panels; and at the western end
the 'capture of Troy' in the pediment, and 'scenes from the Trojan
war' on the metopes. The American excavators thought that from
the number of fragments that they had discovered there must also
have been decorated metopes along the sides of the temple, but it
has been demonstrated that in fact the surviving fragments come

from only a comparatively small number of panels, no more than would be needed for the ends alone.

One metope panel, though in pieces, survives more or less complete. The scene on it is conventional enough; an Amazon, one of the race of warrior women who came to help the Trojans, flees, and is pursued by one of Agamemnon's Greeks. Such scenes became almost commonplace as relief decoration on temples; they represent, perhaps, the victory of Greeks over the forces of barbarism, but in this temple they recall the days when Greece was ruled from the Argolid. There are other, more fragmentary metopes and isolated pieces that once depicted comparable scenes; the Trojan war scenes in the west metopes in particular were the combats of Greeks and Amazons. The pediment sculptures were even more liable to damage, and have survived only as small, broken pieces, enough to show that the sculptures remained on the temple until its destruction, after which, one supposes, most of them were consigned to the lime-kiln. There are fragments of prone and kneeling figures that must have fitted the ends of the pediments; a representation of cult-images, that may depict the shrines of Athena and Aphrodite at Troy, to which Kassandra and Helen fled as the Greeks captured the citadel (and so, like the majority of the metope fragments, coming originally from the west end). It is quite impossible to recover even the outline of the original design, though the quality of the work can be appreciated, particularly in the soft and lovely female head which Sir Charles Walston thought represented Hera, and used to adorn the cover of the first volume on the Heraion. Even if the identification is dubious, the beauty remains.

It is probably unrealistic to regard this as Argive sculpture, though its relevance to Argos is obvious. The decoration of temples was an international craft, with artists recruited from various places; so that it is not unlikely that artists working at the Heraion in the 420s had been employed at Athens in the 430s. Different artists, almost different styles, can be detected in the Athenian architectural sculpture, and though the sculptures of the Heraion, more limited in scale, and probably achieved in a much briefer period of time, may well have been more homogeneous, it is dangerous to be dogmatic about their origins on the evidence of what are, after all, disjointed fragments. They are clearly in place in the general development of mainland Greek architectural sculpture in stone; even if their contribution to that art is not specifically Argive, they at least show that Argos (like Athens, but, one imagines, unlike Sparta) was involved in that development.

Thereafter the role of Argos is less certain. Argive artists were recruited for the work at Epidauros, which dominated the region in the fourth century. In addition, about the time that Philip of Macedon consolidated the state and territory of Argos, they would have been involved with the new temple of Zeus at Nemea. There was a younger Polykleitos, son, or perhaps rather grandson, of the great sculptor, but he is better known as an architect (for example, of the theatre at Epidauros) than as a sculptor.[40] Other Argive sculptors, of lesser importance, undoubtedly existed, producing the routine but essential statues of the Hellenistic age. Some of them are names on the bases, but of their work nothing survives but the reports of statues set up or overthrown at Argos: statues of the third century tyrants, the monument commemorating the death of Pyrrhus, statues of Macedonian kings and the generals of the Achaean league. The line of descent is direct; to the statues of the Roman emperors, and the classicizing works that decorated the Roman baths in Argos town.

Abbreviations

AJA	*American Journal of Archaeology* 1897–
AM	*Athenische Mitteilungen* 1876–
ATL	*Athenian Tribute Lists*
BCH	*Bulletin de Correspondance Hellénique* 1877–
BSA	*Annual of the British School at Athens* 1895–
*CAH*²	*Cambridge Ancient History* (second edition)
CQ	*Classical Quarterly* 1907–
Hesp.	*Hesperia* 1932–
IG	*Inscriptiones Graecae*
JHS	*Journal of Hellenic Studies* 1880–
LAAA	*Liverpool Annals of Archaeology and Anthropology* 1908–
SEG	*Supplementum Epigraphicum Graecum* 1923–
*SIG*³	Dittenberger, *Sylloge Inscriptionum Graecarum* (third edition) Leipzig 1915–24

Notes

Introduction

1 At Mycenae there is a very obvious contrast between the colossal blocks used in the Late Bronze Age, and the smaller blocks used to repair the walls in Hellenistic times.
2 E.g. *Iliad*, II, 108, and Strabo's comments (VIII, 5, 5).
3 Which nevertheless claimed that it was descended from the same family as Philip and Alexander. The genealogy of the older royal family is given in Diodorus, VII, frag. 15. The connection with Argos was invented because the family name was the 'Argeadai'.

Chapter 1 The Argolid

1 Much of this chapter results from observations made in the Argolid itself. The most useful (and easily obtainable) map of the present-day Argolid is that published by the Greek Statistics Office, 1:200,000, sheet 2.
2 These are the modern 'official' names of the mountains, some of which are artificial revivals of the ancient names.
3 It was believed in antiquity that this was the outlet of an underground river flowing from Lake Stymphalos; but the water is collected from the rain that falls on the mountains and an even wider area of inland Arcadia. There are other springs, further to the south, that emerge from beneath the sea.
4 Strabo, VIII, 6, 8.
5 See my publication of the waterworks at Perachora, in neighbouring Corinthia: *BSA*, 64 (1969), pp. 195 f.
6 E. J. A. Kenny, *LAAA*, 22 (1935), p. 189.
7 C. Waldstein, *The Argive Heraeum*, p. 17.
8 E.g. *Iliad*, II, 287.
9 It is noticeable that even in parts of the Argolid unsuited to the commercial growing of citrus fruit, such as the higher ground overlooking the plain between Mycenae and the Heraion, orange and lemon trees may be found in private gardens. In antiquity, when peasant families cultivated crops primarily for their own consumption, the growing of 'unsuitable' plants may well have been more common.
10 Berbati (Prosymna) and Limnai.

11 Pausanias, IV, 14, 3.
12 Pausanias, II, 38, 4.

Chapter 2 The towns

1 Plutarch, *Cleomenes*, 17, 21; *Pyrrhus*, 32. The names of the two hills are interesting: *Larisa* is presumably ancient, and not in origin Greek. The shape of the *Aspis* is that of the round shield, adopted in Classical Greece towards the end of the eighth century. Though, of course, there is no evidence that the name was used before that date, one would expect a part of Argos which was inhabited in the Late Bronze Age and continued in occupation at the end of the Bronze Age to possess a name which had survived from that time; in which case the 'aspis' is not the round bronze shield of the Classical hoplite, but the round shield used by some of the Late Bronze Age warriors, and depicted on Late Bronze Age vases.
2 There are photographs of this in *BCH*, 89 (1965), p. 897. See also W. Vollgraff, *BCH*, 31 (1907), pp. 157 f.
3 Frazer, note on Pausanias, II, 24, 1 'because the place also is called Diras', quoting Leake, *Morea*, 2, pp. 399–401.
4 Livy, XXXIV, 25.
5 Pausanias, II, 18, 4 and following.
6 The total population of Argos in classical times is uncertain. Argos regularly put into the field an army of 6,000 men of military age and certain property qualifications. In addition there was the non-military population, men over and under age, men of inferior social status and women. The total population can hardly have been less than 50,000.
7 *BCH*, 80 (1956), pp. 376 f.
8 *IG*, IV, p. 558, and see p. 213.
9 See p. 217.
10 Thucydides, V, 47, 11.
11 *BCH*, 77 (1953), pp. 243 f.; *BCH*, 78 (1954), pp. 158 f. For the older excavations, W. Vollgraff, *BCH*, 31 (1907), p. 169.
12 If the square hall can be identified as the Prytaneion, it was destroyed in 315 B.C. (Diodorus, XIX, 63; see p. 150).
13 See p. 246.
14 Pausanias, II, 24; and see p. 247.
15 Gomme, Andrewes & Dover, *Historical Commentary on Thucydides*, vol. IV, p. 71, on Thucydides, V, 53, 1. The chief sanctuary of Apollo Pythaieus was at Asine: for the cult there see W. S. Barrett, *Hermes*, 82 (1954), pp. 421–44.
16 W. Vollgraff, *BCH*, 31 (1907), pp. 159 f.
17 Excavated by the late S. Charitonides.
18 S. Charitonides, 'Recherches dans le quartier est d'Argos', *BCH*, 78 (1954), pp. 410–42.
19 Surely the 'Road of Argeia', beside which the women who died in the defence of Argos in 494 B.C. were buried (Plutarch, *De mul. virt.*, 4).
20 See pp. 152 f.

21 *BCH*, 31 (1907), p. 178.
22 Lucian, *Apologia*, 11.
23 It should be noted that there was extensive Middle Bronze Age settlement in the area round what was to become the Classical agora.
24 *BCH*, 31 (1907), p. 181.
25 See my publication of this in *BSA*, 64 (1969), pp. 201 f.
26 Heraion: C. Waldstein, *The Argive Heraeum*, p. 17; Corinth: H. S. Robinson, 'A Sanctuary and Cemetery in Western Corinth', *Hesp.*, 38 (1969), p.1.
27 Book II, 15 f.
28 These are reported in the 'Chronique des Fouilles' in *BCH* (particularly, for the recent excavations, from 1953 onwards).
29 E.g. against Mycenae in the 460s, and at the first battle of Mantinea; see below, p. 124. The alliance may be older than an attack on Kleonai by Corinth 'probably not long before Kimon's time (Plutarch, *Kimon*, 17, 2, and Gomme, Andrewes & Dover, *Historical Commentary on Thucydides*, vol. IV, on Thucydides, V, 67, 2). Kleonai retained independence of action in the fourth century B.C.; she acted as arbitrator between the Administration of the Sanctuary at Olympia and the Arcadians in the restitution of money stolen by the Arcadians between 365 and 363. (*IG*, IV, 616.)
30 A. Boëthius, *BSA*, 25 (1921–3), pp. 408 f.
31 C. Waldstein, *The Argive Heraeum* (for the American excavations). J. L. Caskey, and P. Amandry, *Hesp.*, 21 (1952), pp. 165 f. and pp. 222 f.
32 *IG*, IV, 496. See also L. H. Jeffery, *BSA*, 50 (1955), p. 69.
33 Modern Kephalari.
34 Called Hellenikon. For a discussion of this structure, see L. E. Lord, 'Watchtowers and Fortresses of the Argolid', *AJA*, 43 (1939), pp. 78 f.
35 Frazer (on Pausanias, II, 24, 7) suggests that the wheel was 'this part of the road' so named 'because of its many windings'. Perhaps the wheel was a circular enclosure, or a tower of circular plan, now completely lost. Compare the late-Hellenistic or Roman tower at Roukouni Korfi in Crete (*Archaeological Reports* 1960–1, 24, fig. 25).
36 Strabo, VIII, 6, 10.
37 *BCH*, 87 (1963), p. 746 (Protonotariou-Deïlaki).
38 Katsingri: L. E. Lord, *AJA*, 43 (1939), loc. cit.
39 Frödin & Persson, *Asine*, p. 437.
40 For the cult of Apollo Pythaieus, see W. S. Barrett, *Hermes*, 82 (1954), pp. 421 f.
41 Recently excavated by the American School: reports in *Hesp.* for 1954 to 1959.
42 Pausanias, VIII, 3, 3; 54, 4; X, 9, 12.
43 Otherwise Anthene: Thucydides, V, 41, and Harpocration.
44 Thucydides, IV, 57, 1.

Chapter 3 The creation of Dorian Argos

1 A. J. B. Wace, 'Chamber tombs at Mycenae', *Archaeologia*, 82.

2 The fullest treatment of the problem: V. R. d'A. Desborough, *The Last Mycenaeans and their Successors.* Writing was, of course, known in Late Bronze Age Greece, but inventories are all that have survived.

3 Compare, from historical times, the development of the kingdom of Epirus out of the amalgamation of several tribes living in the same area in emulation of Macedon, and under the influence of Classical Greece. (See N. G. L. Hammond, *Epirus*.).

4 Settlement in Cyprus: *CAH*², II, chapter xxxvi; in Ionia, ibid., chapter xxxviii.

5 Desborough, op. cit.

6 Pausanias, II, 38, 1; Diodorus, VII, frag. 9.

7 E.g. *IG*, IV, 517, dated to 460/450: Πυρ*F*αλίων: Δυμάνς
A]λκαμένης: hυλλεύς
A]μφίκριτος: Πανφύλ-
λ]ας

8 For the list as known, see M. Wörrle, *Untersuchungen zur Verfassungsgeschichte von Argos*, 17, note 32.

Chapter 4 The return of the Herakleidai and the lot of Temenos

1 Thucydides, I, 12.

2 Apollodorus, II, 167 f.

3 Diodorus, IV, 57 f.

4 Herodotus, IX, 26.

5 Diodorus, VII, frag. 9. But the Bacchiadai are a clan or phratry group, with what is more likely to be a 'divine' name.

6 P. Courbin, 'Un fragment de cratère proto-argien', *BCH*, 79 (1955), pp. 1 f., and often illustrated elsewhere, e.g. J. Boardman, *Greek Art*, fig. 44.

Chapter 5 The Dorian settlement

1 The archaeological evidence is given by R. Hope-Simpson, *A Gazetteer and Atlas of the Mycenaean world* and in V. R. d'A. Desborough, *The Last Mycenaeans and their Successors.*

2 *BCH*, 83 (1959), pp. 762 f.

3 It is not likely that the Dorians would have allowed the previous inhabitants to continue in occupation of a fortified site overlooking their own unfortified settlement.

4 Desborough, *Protogeometric Pottery*, p. 211; and *The Last Mycenaeans and their Successors*, p. 264.

Chapter 6 Argos in the ninth and eighth centuries

1 The kings of Argos are listed by Diodorus (VII, frag. 17) on the authority of Theopompus.

2 Traces of potters' workshops, *BCH*, 83 (1959), p. 768.

3 For the Gymnetes see Pollux, 3, 83, and D. Lotze, Μεταξὺ
Ἐλευθέρων καὶ Δούλων

4 E.g. King Eratos who led the Argives against Asine. Pausanias, II, 36, 4.
5 See p. 200.
6 See p. 227.
7 See J. N. Coldstream, *Greek Geometric Pottery*.
8 *BCH*, 81 (1957), pp. 322 f.
9 V. Karageorghis, *BCH*, 87 (1963), pp. 277, 292 f.
10 Though the possibility of direct contact with Cyprus cannot be ruled out.
11 E.g. the colonies in Sicily, for which Thucydides seems to have known accurate foundation dates: Thucydides, VI, 3; but see also the remarks on this in Gomme, Andrewes & Dover, *Historical Commentary on Thucydides*, vol. IV.
12 Strabo, VIII, 6, 20.
13 Pausanias, II, 36, 4.
14 Frödin & Persson, *Asine*, p. 437.
15 See p. 79.
16 Strabo, VIII, 6, 11.
17 The original Asinaians having migrated to Asine in Messenia. Pausanias, IV, 14, 3.

Chapter 7 Pheidon of Argos

1 Pausanias, II, 24, 7.
2 Dionysius of Halikarnassos, III, 1, 2; the second year of the twenty-seventh Olympiad.
3 Other authors put this battle even earlier: see G. Huxley, *Early Sparta*, p. 31.
4 Herodotus, VI, 127; Aristotle, *Politics*, 1310, b26; Diodorus, VII, frag. 17.
5 Herodotus, loc. cit.; Aristotle, *Politics*, 1265, b12.
6 Pausanias, VI, 22, 2.
7 G. Huxley, 'Argos et les derniers Tèménides', *BCH*, 82 (1958), pp. 588 f.
8 Ibid., p. 589.
9 Herodotus, V, 67–8.

Chapter 8 Argos from the end of the seventh century to the Persian wars

1 Herodotus, I, 82.
2 Herodotus, I, 66.
3 R. M. Dawkins, *The Sanctuary of Artemis Orthia*, shows the decline in quality and in quantity of the dedicatory offerings made there during the fifth century B.C.
4 Herodotus, I, 61.
5 Perilaos; see H. Berve, *Die Tyrannis bei den Griechen*, p. 35. There was a statue at Argos which represented Perilaos killing Othryadas (Pausanias, II, 20, 7). Othryadas, according to the Spartans, was the Spartan who survived the battle of the three hundred champions (Herodotus, I, 82).
6 Diodorus, VII, frag. 11 (Eusebius).

7 Herodotus, V, 72. This should not be overstressed; it has the sound of a witty reply made on the spur of the moment when he was refused access, as a Dorian, to the temple of Athena.

8 Argos may have been involved; the Argive sculptor Ageladas made a statue of Zeus for the Messenians. It would seem that they were independent when they commissioned the work, and Ageladas must have been alive at the same time as Kleomenes; but this need not represent official support for the Messenians from Argos (Greek sculptors worked rather on a free-lance basis) and it is just possible that Ageladas was still alive at the time of the Messenian rising in the 460s. If the story of Kleomenes' involvement in such a rebellion is a malicious slander, and if in fact the Messenians had Argive support, we might suppose that it was the resultant fear that led to the severe treatment meted out by Kleomenes to Argos.

9 The dating of this campaign to 494 depends on Herodotus, VI, 19 and 77, which links it with the fall of Miletus to the Persians. An alternative date is at the beginning of Kleomenes' reign, which started in about 520; if the campaign belongs to that time it is surprising that Argos had not recovered enough to play a more prominent part in the Persian wars of 480–479.

10 Pausanias, II, 20, 8.

11 They would not be expected to fight as hoplites, but to hurl missiles from the roofs of their houses. It has been suggested (Frazer, on Pausanias, II, 20, 8) that this story results from a confused explanation of a religious ritual in Argos, of the dual cult of Ares and Aphrodite, in which the women pretended to be warriors. Telesilla's poetry seems from the little we know of it to have been concerned with religious matters.

12 Hence also the story that he was involved in a rising of the Messenian helots.

13 6,000: Herodotus, VII, 148. Another version, referred to scornfully by Plutarch, *De mul. virt.*, 4, put it at 7,777. A lower total: G. Forrest, 'Themistocles and Argos', *CQ*, NS 10 (1960), p. 221.

14 Aristotle, *Politics*, 1303, a6.

15 *Politics*, 1272, a1.

16 They were known as Gymnetes (naked ones): Pollux, 3, 83.

17 Plutarch, *De mul. virt.*, 4.

18 R. F. Willetts, 'The Servile Interregnum at Argos', *Hermes*, 87 (1959), pp. 495 f.

19 See p. 181.

Chapter 9 479–461

1 The general sources of information for this and the succeeding chapters are Thucydides, I, 89–118 and Diodorus, XI–XII.

2 For Themistokles' doings after the Persian wars the chief authorities are Thucydides, I and Plutarch, *Themistokles*.

3 G. Forrest, 'Themistokles and Argos', loc. cit.

4 Were these agents thugs who were to assassinate Themistokles, or envoys sent to request his extradiction, or at least his expulsion from Argos?
5 Diodorus, XI, 54. Thucydides' account is a digression, without any indication of chronology.
6 Diodorus, XI, 65.
7 D. W. Reece, 'The date of the fall of Ithome', *JHS*, 82 (1962), p. 111.
8 Herodotus, IX, 35. Presumably this reference was overlooked by the fourth century historians.

Chapter 10 461–451

1 Thucydides, I, 102.
2 It was also an excuse that served to disguise Sparta's desperate shortage of hoplites.
3 K. J. Dover, 'The political aspect of Aeschylus' *Eumenides*', *JHS*, 77 (1957), p. 230.
4 Pausanias, X, 10, 3; I, 15, 1. L. H. Jeffery, 'The Battle of Oinoe in the Stoa Poikile', *BSA*, 60 (1965), pp. 41 f.
5 Kleonai was attacked by Corinth at this time. Plutarch, *Kimon*, 17, 2.
6 E. Will, *Korinthiaka*, pp. 609 f.
7 See pp. 130 f.

Chapter 11 451–404

1 The chief source for this chapter is, of course, Thucydides.
2 Herodotus, VII, 151.
3 Xenophon, *Hellenica*, II, 2, 7.

Chapter 12 404–370

1 The chief sources for this chapter are Xenophon, *Hellenica*, II–VI and Diodorus, XIV–XV.
2 This may have been apparent to intelligent Spartans before the battle of Aigospotamoi made the complete defeat of Athens possible. Hence the desire of Sparta to achieve a settlement that would restore the shared leadership of the Greek world by Sparta and Athens, even as late as 405 B.C.
3 H. W. Parke, *Greek Mercenary Soldiers*, pp. 20 f.
4 E. Will, op. cit.
5 Compare the joint assembly of the Boiotian federation (the Oxyrhynchus historian, XI, 4).
6 Text, and the most recent commentary, in Meiggs & Lewis, *A selection of Greek historical inscriptions*, no. 42. Presumably another copy was set up at Knossos.
7 A. J. Graham, *Colony and Mother-city in Ancient Greece*, p. 235.

8 E.g. lines 6 and following of the Tylissos fragment; 'Neither party shall make any new treaty, save with the assent of the assembly, and the Argives shall cast the third part of the votes'. (The 'assembly' probably means a joint assembly of the three cities; see Graham and Meiggs & Lewis.)

9 This seems a possible reason for stipulating that 'the Argives shall cast the third part of the votes'. Alternatively, the assembly may have been limited in size, with the Argives forming one third of the total membership, the other two thirds being divided at will between Knossos and Tylissos.

10 Kleonai acts as an ally of Argos, rather than an integral part of the Argive state, in the war against Mycenae (Strabo, VIII, 6, 19) and at the first battle of Mantinea (Thucydides, V, 67).

11 Xenophon, *Hellenica*, IV, 5, 5.

12 Phoibidas, who seized the citadel of Thebes, was not in command of a Spartan force, but accompanying his brother on an expedition against Olynthos (though perhaps a plan to take the citadel of Thebes was the reason why he had gone with his brother in the first place). The authorities at Sparta, but not king Agesilaos, were angered by his action (Xenophon, *Hellenica*, V, 2, 32). Sphodrias was 'bribed by the Thebans' (an unlikely story) to attack Piraeus (Xenophon, *Hellenica*, V, 4, 20). The Spartans wanted to punish him also.

Chapter 13 370–336

1 Until the battle of Mantinea Xenophon's *Hellenica* is one of the chief sources for this chapter. The other, which also continues after the conclusion of the *Hellenica*, is Diodorus, XV–XVII.

2 For the fourth century blockhouses in this area, see L. E. Lord, *AJA*, 43 (1939), pp. 78 f.

3 Isocrates, *Philippos*, 51–2.

4 Unless this refers to a different period of unrest, otherwise unknown.

5 [Demosthenes], LII, *Against Kallippos*, 5.

6 Diodorus, XVI, 39.

7 Demosthenes, XIX, 260–1. For pro-Macedonians in Argos, see Demosthenes, XVIII, 295; Hypereides, III, 31; Polybius, XVIII, 14, 1.

8 Polybius, IX, 28, 7, and see Walbank's note in *A Historical Commentary on Polybius* on IX, 33, 12. Also Polybius, XVIII, 14, 7.

9 Charneux, *BCH*, 82 (1957), pp. 1 f.

10 Polybius, IV, 36, 5.

11 *SIG*³, 407 (dated to 275 B.C. by Dittenberger, a date accepted by Walbank, *A Historical Commentary on Polybius* (IX, 33, 12). Charneux, loc. cit., is less certain).

Chapter 14 Argos in Hellenistic times

1 Diodorus continues as the chief source of information about Argive history until his text breaks off in 301 B.C. Thereafter Argive history, like all other aspects of Hellenistic history, depends on incidental information contained in Plutarch's biographies, and on other chance evidence, such as that afforded by inscriptions until, towards the end of the third century, Polybius takes up the story. Fortunately, Plutarch's life of Pyrrhus gives a vivid account of that king's attack on Argos. His lives of Aratos, and of the Spartan kings Agis and Kleomenes are also relevant to Argive affairs.

2 Perhaps these were the states that had not suffered in the rebellion of Agis, so this again may indicate that Argos held aloof from that war.

3 'Prytaneion' is the Greek word used for this building by Diodorus. See p. 29 and note.

4 He owed it to his success in defeating the Gallic tribes which had entered Greece, devastating and plundering.

5 In which case it is just possible that the tyranny started a generation earlier, with Aristippos' father; but on the whole it is more likely that it was Aristippos who was Demetrius' man from the beginning.

6 Note the co-operation of the Spartan and Macedonian kings on behalf of Argos, despite the traditional hostility between Argos and Sparta. This, of course, results from their common enmity with Pyrrhus, but it affords a useful precedent for Philip V's collaboration with Nabis of Sparta against the common enemy, Rome. See pp. 166 f.

7 During this century Mycenae and Asine revive as urban centres.

8 *IG*, II², 774.

9 Presumably the traditional royal bodyguard of the Spartan kings, the hippeis (Thucydides, V, 72, 4).

10 In fairness it can be argued that Aristomachos had not received the position of authority in the league that he might have expected; and the hostility to Aratos was very deep-rooted.

Chapter 15 The intervention of Rome

1 Here again the treatment of Greece as a mere adjunct to Macedon is noticeable.

2 The sources for this chapter are again Polybius and, where he fails, Livy.

3 Livy, XXXIV, 32, 16.

4 Livy, XXVII, 29, 9.

5 For discussion of the causes of the Second Macedonian War, see E. Badian, *Foreign Clientelae*, pp. 62 f.

6 By Wilhelm (*Wiener Anzeiger*, 1921, pp. 70 f.). 'Apia' seems to have been an 'old' name for the Peloponnese (cf. Homer, *Iliad*, I, 270, with the scholiast's explanation, and Aeschylus, *Supplices*, 260). The choice of name for Aristippos' daughter may indicate a claim to supremacy over the Peloponnese.

7 *IG*, IV², 621.
8 Which were not so crucially important to Rome as to Macedon.
9 *SEG*, III, 312.

Chapter 17 Military organization

1 Tyrtaeus, 1. This poem was discovered on a papyrus found in Egypt, and is in a fragmentary state.
2 Aeneas Tacticus, 11, 7 f.
3 It was intended to prevent the wealthier citizens (the oligarchs) from gathering in a separate unit.
4 Thucydides, V, 67.
5 In addition there were separately mustered contingents from Kleonai and Orneai, states not fully integrated into the Argive political system.
6 First published by W. Vollgraff, *Mnemosyne*, 44 (1916), p. 65.
7 It was then exceptional for the citizens to fight, as they did at the time of Pyrrhus' attack on the city, and when they helped Philokles, Philip V's general, against the pro-Roman Achaean garrison. The citizens refused to fight to remove the tyrants.
8 E.g. ἑκατοστύς at Samos and Kos (Wörrle, *Untersuchungen*, p. 27).
9 A. M. Snodgrass, 'The hoplite reform and history', *JHS*, 85 (1965), pp. 110 f.
10 The 'Panoply Grave': P. Courbin, *BCH*, 81 (1957), pp. 322 f.
11 Frequently illustrated in books on Greek art and vase painting, e.g. J. Boardman, *Greek Art*, fig. 38; P. E. Arias & M. Hirmer, *A history of Greek vase painting*, plate IV.
12 For the early use of advanced tactics by the Argive army, see A. Andrewes, *The Greek Tyrants*, p. 39.
13 G. Huxley, *Early Sparta*, p. 23, based on Aristotle, fr. 532 (Rose).
14 Note Thucydides' remarks (V, 70) on the use of flute-players by the Spartans to keep the army in step; but flute-players are depicted on the Chigi vase.
15 Aigina: Herodotus, VI, 92; Tanagra: Thucydides, I, 107, 5; Mantinea: Thucydides, V, 67, and Diodorus, XII, 75. After Mantinea: Thucydides, V, 81.
16 The events of 370 B.C. suggest that the political élite then was also a military one.
17 Diodorus, XII, 75 confirms that this unit was supported by the state but also says that it was recruited from the wealthiest section of Argive society. This statement probably results from a conflation made by Diodorus' source (presumably Ephorus) of the select band of Mantinea, and the thousand pro-Spartan oligarchs. Thucydides' careful account is preferable.
18 B. D. Meritt, *Hesp.*, 14, pp. 134 f.; 21, p. 351. Meiggs & Lewis no. 35.
19 Thucydides, I, 107, 5.
20 Thucydides says that losses on both sides were heavy, but does not differentiate between Argive and Athenian losses.

21 F. M. Heichelheim, 'Das auswärtige Bevolkerung in Ptolemäerreich', *Klio Beiheft*, 18 (1925), p. 51.

Chapter 18 Political development to the fifth century

1 The fullest and most recent discussion of Argive constitutional history is M. Wörrle, *Untersuchungen zur Verfassungsgeschichte von Argos*.
2 Note that the Corinthian tyrant Kypselos made the reputation which led to his emergence as champion of the people as polemarch (war-commander), though this also involved the administration of legal matters; Nicolas of Damascus, frag. 57 (Jacoby).
3 The Aigialeis: Herodotus, V, 68.
4 The Scheliadai: *SIG*³, 162.
5 E.g. *IG*, IV, 517. *SEG*, XIII, 239.
6 For the Damiorgoi, see Wörrle, op. cit., pp. 61 f.
7 H. Berve, *Die Tyrannis bei den Griechen*, p. 35.

Chapter 19 The Argive democracy

1 And possibly elsewhere in the Peloponnese, in the 460s (the activity associated with Themistokles), and in the 420s (before the battle of Mantinea).
2 E.g. the priestly office of the 'Hiaromnamones': *IG*, IV, 517.
3 Except, presumably, after Sepeia.
4 The name of the priestess of Hera (who, of course, held office for life) is never used to indicate the date, despite Hellanicus' work *The Priestesses of Hera*, which did use them as the basis of a chronological system.
5 *IG*, IV, 554.
6 Diodorus, XIX, 63.
7 Thucydides, V, 47, 9.
8 Vollgraff in *Mnemosyne*, 44 (1916), p. 221.
9 Livy, XXXII, 25, 2.
10 *SEG*, XI, 336; XI, 314; *IG*, IV, 506.
11 *IG*, IV, 497; *SEG*, III, 312.
12 *IG*, IV, 554.

Chapter 20 Religious cults of the Argolid

1 Xenophon, *Hellenica*, IV, 7, 2.
2 Pausanias, II, 15–38. Where no reference is given to the evidence for a particular cult it will be found in this section of Pausanias. Much information about the cults is given in Frazer's commentary.
3 Hiaromnamones: *IG*, IV, 517; Agonothetes (at Mycenae): *SEG*, III, 312.

4 Herodotus, I, 31, 2. He does not say that their mother was *the* priestess of Hera. Plutarch, *Consol. ad Apollon.*, 14 says she was 'priestess of Hera'.

5 For the excavations of the sanctuary see C. Waldstein, *The Argive Heraeum*, and p. 230.

6 Witness the importance of Hera as the protecting deity of the Greeks under Agamemnon of Mycenae in the Trojan war.

7 *SEG*, XIII, 236.

8 Thucydides, V, 47, 11.

9 See W. Vollgraff, *Le Sanctuaire d'Apollon Pythéen à Argos* and G. Roux, *L'Architecture de l'Argolide*, pp. 65–82.

10 Thucydides, V, 53. See the comments on this by W. S. Barrett, *Hermes*, 82 (1954), p. 421 f., and Gomme, Andrewes & Dover, *Historical Commentary on Thucydides*, vol. IV.

11 See W. Vollgraff, op. cit.

12 *IG*, IV, 492.

13 *Archaeological Reports* 1968–9, pp. 11–12.

14 W. Vollgraff, *BCH*, 82 (1958), pp. 556 f.

15 *BCH*, 93 (1969), p. 986.

16 *BCH*, 90 (1966), p. 782; 91 (1967), p. 653.

17 *SEG*, XI, 298.

18 Plutarch, *De mul. virt.*, 4.

19 Lucian, *Amores*, 30.

20 *SEG*, XI, 327.

21 Frazer, note on Pausanias, II, 24, 5.

22 Pausanias, I, 14, 2.

23 *IG*, IV, 558.

24 See also *IG*, IV, 666.

25 S. Charitonides, 'Recherches dans le quartier est d'Argos', *BCH*, 78 (1954), pp. 410 f.

26 R. F. Willetts, *Cretan Cults and Festivals*, pp. 172 f.

27 Meiggs & Lewis, no. 42; W. Vollgraff, *Le Decret d'Argos relatif à un pacte entre Knossos et Tylissos.*

28 See W. Vollgraff, *BCH*, 82 (1958), pp. 516 f.

29 *BCH*, 78 (1954), pp. 414 f.

30 *BCH*, 82 (1958), pp. 556 f.

31 Pausanias, II, 16, 6. Wace & Stubbings, *A Companion to Homer*, p. 397.

32 Cf. Herodotus, VI, 78.

33 Frazer, commentary on Pausanias, II, 18, 1.

34 *SEG*, XI, 329.

Chapter 21 The arts in the Argolid

1 F. Jacoby, *Die Fragmente der griechischen Historiker*, no. 310, and commentary.

2 But [——]medes who made the statues of Kleobis and Biton at Delphi signs his name as 'Argeios', i.e. Argive, and was presumably a citizen. This may indicate either that artists and craftsmen were not restricted to

the lowest ranks of society at this time (c. 600) or that by that time the citizen ranks had been extended (by Pheidon presumably) to include people of humbler rank than the Dorian landlords.

3 H. W. Catling, E. E. Richards & A. E. Blin-Stoyle, *BSA*, 58 (1963), pp. 94 f.

4 See the discussion of this evidence in V. R. d'A. Desborough, *The Last Mycenaeans and their Successors*, pp. 80 f.

5 C.-G. Styrenius, *Submycenaean Studies*.

6 *BCH*, 83 (1959), p. 768.

7 P. Courbin, *La Céramique géométrique de l'Argolide*. See also J. N. Coldstream, *Greek Geometric Pottery*, chapter 4.

8 Although most of the pottery is found in graves, the vessels used are strictly utilitarian in character, not especially designed as grave goods.

9 Courbin, op. cit., p. 553.

10 Illustrated in J. Boardman, *Greek Art*, Fig. 44.

11 C. Waldstein, *The Argive Heraeum* (the full report of the American excavations); P. Amandry, *Hesp.*, 21 (1952), pp. 222 f. (report of later excavations, and re-appraisal of earlier work); B. Bergquist *The Archaic Greek Temenos*, pp. 19 f.

12 H. Payne, *Perachora*, I, pp. 34 f.

13 R. Martin, *Manuel d'architecture grecque*, I, pp. 65 f., and especially p. 70 for Corinth.

14 B. Bergquist, op. cit., pp. 19 f.

15 Compare the temple of Apollo at Corinth, of about 540 B.C.

16 Samos: E. Buschor, *AM*, 55 (1930) Abb. 5 (p. 15). Orchomenos: *BCH*, 38 (1914), p. 82.

17 See p. 254.

18 Cf. a similar building in the sanctuary of Hera at Samos, the 'south' building: *AM*, LV (1930), pp. 59 f.

19 Again, the development at the Samian Heraion, also at a distance from its town, is similar.

20 See my article 'Two buildings in sanctuaries of Asklepios', *JHS*, 89 (1969), pp. 106 f.

21 The old mud-brick temple of Hera at Olympia was carefully preserved, the wooden columns being gradually replaced by stone ones.

22 V. Leonardos, *Praktika*, 1896. There the steps face the temple, and the door in its south side. There is a rough bank, which could have served the same purpose, by the side of the temple of Apollo at Bassai (by the long east side, which again has a door), and a similar arrangement at the temple of Athena Alea, at Tegea.

23 That is, of the architrave (the stone beam placed directly over the columns) and the frieze above, divided into triglyphs, perhaps representing decorated beam ends, with metope panels between. One complete metope panel survives; it preserves the height of the frieze, which was 1·065m. Usually the spacing of the columns can be calculated from the combined width of triglyph and metope, but the surviving metope seems to be one of the abnormally wide ones from the end of the façade.

24 G. Roux, *L'Architecture de l'Argolide*, pp. 62 f.

25 W. Vollgraff, *Le Sanctuaire d'Apollon Pythéen*, and G. Roux, op. cit., pp. 65 f.
26 See p. 207.
27 C. Waldstein, *The Argive Heraeum*, II, pp. 3 f. (terracotta) and pp. 191 f. (bronze).
28 R. J. H. Jenkins, *Daedalica*.
29 J. Boardman, *The Greeks Overseas*, chapter 4.
30 The statues are frequently illustrated, e.g. R. Lullies & M. Hirmer, *Greek Sculpture*, plate 14. For the inscription M. N. Tod, *Greek Historical Inscriptions* (2nd edition), no. 3.
31 Pliny, *N.H.*, XXXIV, 49. Pausanias, VI, 8, 6; 10, 6; 14, 11. The form of the name is that given by Pausanias.
32 Pliny, *N.H.*, XXXIV, 57.
33 Pausanias, IV, 33, 2.
34 Pliny, *N.H.*, XXXIV, 55.
35 Plato, *Protagoras*, 311c.
36 Pausanias, VI, 4, 11. For the base, C. Picard, *Manuel d'archéologie grecque: La sculpture*, II, p. 272 (fig. 120).
37 A Roman copy from Pompeii: G. M. A. Richter, *Sculpture and sculptors of the Greeks*, fig. 645.
38 Copy of the Diadoumenos from Delos: ibid., fig. 650.
39 C. Waldstein, *The Argive Heraeum*, I, pp. 162 f. In contrast, F. Eichler, *Oesterreichische Jahreshefte*, 19–20 (1919), pp. 15 f.
40 Pausanias, II, 27, 5.

Select bibliography

The important *ancient sources* are mentioned in the notes.

I *Topography*

BOËTHIUS, A. 'Hellenistic Mycenae', *BSA*, 25 (1921–3), p. 408.
—'Zur Topographie des Dorischen Argos', *Strena Philologia Upsaliensis*, 1922.
FRAZER, J. G. *Pausanias's Description of Greece*, London, 1898.
LEHMANN, H. 'Argeia', *Die Antike*, 1938, p. 143.
LORD, L. E. 'Watchtowers and Fortresses of the Argolid', *AJA*, 43 (1939), p. 78.
—'Blockhouses in the Argolis', *Hesperia*, 10 (1941), p. 93.
MATTON, R. *Mycènes et l'Argolide antique*, Athens, 1966.

II *History*

BERVE, H. *Die Tyrannis bei den Griechen*, Munich, 1967.
CHARNEUX, P. 'Inscriptions d'Argos', *BCH*, 82 (1958), p. 1.
DESBOROUGH, V. R. d'A. *The Last Mycenaeans and their Successors*, Oxford, 1964.
DOVER, K. J. 'The political aspect of Aeschylus' *Eumenides*', *JHS*, 77 (1957), p. 230.
FORREST, G. 'Themistocles and Argos', *CQ*, NS 10 (1960), p. 221.
GRAHAM, A. J. *Colony and Mother-city in Ancient Greece*, Manchester, 1964.
GRIFFITH, G. T. 'The Union of Corinth and Argos', *Historia*, I, p. 236.
HUXLEY, G. 'Argos et les derniers Tèménides', *BCH*, 82 (1958), p. 588.
—*Early Sparta*, London, 1962.
JEFFREY, L. H. 'The Battle of Oinoe in the Stoa Poikile', *BSA*, 60 (1965), p. 41.
LOTZE, D. Μεταξὺ Ἐλευθέρων καὶ Δούλων, Berlin, 1959.
MEIGGS, R. and LEWIS, D. M. *A selection of Greek historical inscriptions*, Oxford, 1969.
MERITT, B. D. WADE-GERY, H. T. and MCGREGOR, M. F. 'The thirty years truce between Argos and Sparta', *ATL*, III, p. 304.

Select bibliography

MITSOS, M. Πολιτική 'Ιστορία τοῦ 'Αργοῦς, Athens, 1945.

—'Αργολική προσωπογραφία, Athens.

SEYMOUR, P. A. 'The Servile Interregnum at Argos', *JHS*, 42 (1922), p. 24.

VOLLGRAFF, W. 'Novae Inscriptiones Argivae' in *Mnemosyne*, 43 and 44.

WILL, E. *Korinthiaka*, Paris, 1955.

WILLETTS, R. F. 'The Servile Interregnum at Argos', *Hermes*, 87 (1959), p. 495.

WÖRRLE, M. *Untersuchungen zur Verfassungsgeschichte von Argos*, Munich, 1964.

III *Art and archaeology*

Excavations at Argos. For the older excavations, see especially W. Vollgraff, *BCH*, 31 (1907), p. 157. The recent excavations are recorded in the 'Chronique des Fouilles' in *BCH* from 1953 onwards.

AMANDRY, P. 'Observations sur les monuments de l'Heraion d'Argos', *Hesperia*, 21 (1952), p. 222.

BEYEN, H. G. and VOLLGRAFF, W. *Argos et Sicyone*, The Hague, 1947.

BLEGEN, C. W. *Prosymna*, Cambridge, 1937.

BOVON, A. *Lampes d'Argos*, Paris, 1966.

CASKEY, J. L. and AMANDRY, P. 'Investigations at the Heraion of Argos, 1949', *Hesperia*, (1952), p. 213.

COLDSTREAM, J. N. *Greek Geometric Pottery*, London, 1968.

COURBIN, P. *La Céramique géométrique de l'Argolide*, Paris, 1966.

—'Un fragment de cratère proto-argien', *BCH*, 79 (1955), p. 1.

—'Une tombe d'Argos', *BCH*, 81 (1957), p. 322.

DESBOROUGH, V. R. d'A. *Protogeometric pottery*, Oxford, 1952.

EICHLER, F. 'Die Skulpturen des Heraions bei Argos', *Oesterreichische Jahreshefte*, 19–20 (1919), p. 15.

FRÖDIN, O. and PERSSON, A. *Asine*, Stockholm, 1938.

JENKINS, R. J. H. 'Archaic Argive terracotta figurines to 525 B.C.', *BSA*, 32 (1931), p. 23.

RICHTER, G. M. A. *Sculpture and sculptors of the Greeks*, New Haven, 1950.

ROUX, G. *L'Architecture de l'Argolide*, Paris, 1961.

STYRENIUS, C.-G. *Submycenaean Studies*, Lund, 1967.

VOLLGRAFF, W. *Le Sanctuaire d'Apollon Pythéen à Argos*, Paris, 1956.

WALDSTEIN, C. *The Argive Heraeum*, Boston, 1902.

Index

Achaea, Roman province, 172
Achaean league, 151, 152, 156–62, 164–72
  passim
  approaches Aristomachos II, 158
Achaeans, Homeric, 59, 93, 224
Adonis, 217
Adrastos, Argive hero at Sikyon, 84
Adriatic Sea, 164
Aegean Sea, 54, 92, 114
Aemilius Paullus, L., 172
Aeneas Tacticus, 193
Aeschines, 144
Aeschylus, 103
Aetion, father of Kypselos, 84
Agamemnon, 1, 59, 88, 113, 170–1, 214, 260
  cult at Mycenae, 281
Ageladas, sculptor, 255–7, 258
Agesilaos, king of Sparta, 137
Agesipolis, Spartan king, 138, 140
Agis II, king of Sparta, 121–2, 124, 140, 176, 198
  punished by Spartans, 123
Agis III, king of Sparta, 148
Agis IV, king of Sparta, 159
Agonothetes, 201
Agora at Argos, 21, 23, 64, 154, 168, 205, 217, 219, 220
Agricultural labourers (gymnetes), 68, 98–99
Agriculture, 11f., 72, 73, (Hysiai) 37, (Kleonai) 30, (Mycenae) 32, (Thyreatis) 46, (Berbati) 34
Aigina and Aiginetans, 46, 93, 99–100, 124, 165, 181, 182, 184, 197
  fleet, 93
Ainesidemos, 166
Aiolos, 210
Aischylos, Argive, 156
Aitolia and Aitolians, 148, 161–2, 164, 171
Akhladokampos (Hysiai), 13, 37
Akte, 8, 40, 42, 205
Alcyonian lake, 213
Alexander the Great, 2, 147–8, 171, 186

Alexander, son of Krateros, 155
Alexander, son of Polyperchon, 149–50
Alexander of Sikyon, 176, 197
Aliaia, assembly at Argos, 107, 118, 133, 166, 167, 190, 192–3, 197, 199
Alkamenes, king of Sparta, 76
Alkibiades, 121, 198
Alkiphron, Spartan proxenos at Argos, 198
'All the Gods', temple at Orneai, 217
Alliances:
  Achaean–Macedonian, 160, 161, 163
  Aitolian league–Rome, 164
  anti-Spartan, (in Peloponnese) 106, 107, (in Corinthian war) 129, (at second Mantinea) 142
  Argive, (with Arcadia) 83, 90, 91, (with Athens) 91, 111, 118–23, 195, 205, (with Knossos and Tylissos) 134–6, 185, 196, 216, (with Philip) 144
  Athenian, 102, 111, 112, 114, 127, ('50 years', with Sparta) 117
  Greek–Macedonian, 147–8
  Megalopolis–Argos, Sikyon, Messenia, Thebes, 144
  Philip V–Hannibal, 164
  Spartan, 91, 101, 108, 117
Amazon, on Heraion metope, 260
Ampelidas, Argive, 118
Amphiaraos, sanctuary at Argos, 219
Amyklai, 180
'Anakes' (Dioskouroi), 213
Anatolia, 7
Ancestral constitution, 126, 161
Anigraia, 45
Anochos, 255, 256
Antigonid dynasty, 152, 186
Antigonos (Gonatas), 151–3, 154, 158
Antigonos Doson, king of Macedon, 160–1
Antigonos (Monophthalmos), 149–51
Antiochos III, 171
Antipater, 148–9
Apega, wife of Nabis, see Apia
Aphrodite, sanctuaries of: (Argos) 20, 21, 208–9, 252, (Temenion) 44

279

Index

Aphrodite Nikephoros, statue at Argos, 208

Aphrodite Ourania, 208

Apia (Apega), 167, 169–70

Apollodorus, 58, 216

Apollo Lykeios, temple and sanctuary at Argos, 20, 23, 64, 196, 204–5, 208, 210, 246–7

Apollo Maleatis, sanctuary at Epidauros, 247

Apollo Pythaieus, sanctuaries of: (Argos) 23, 205–7, 247–9, (Asine) 43, 205–6, (Hermione) 205

Apollonides, 150, 195

Arachnaion, Mt, 42, 215, 216

Aratos of Sikyon, 156–61

Arbitration, 157

Arcadia, 8, 37, 45, 97, 114, 119, 129, 142, 145, 149, 185, 215

Arcadians, 80, 83, 84, 106, 107, 121, 144, 184, 186
  alliance with Argos, 83, 90, 91, 102

Archaic art in Greece, 87

Archelaoi (non-Dorian tribe at Sikyon), 84, 189

Archidamian war, 117

Architecture, 230–50

Archon at Athens, 197

Areopagus, council at Athens, 196, 217

Ares and Aphrodite, 208

Areus, king of Sparta, 153

Argeia, 130

Arginousai, 98

Argos (sacred grove and hero), 93, 94, 219

Aristeas, 152–3

Aristippos I, 152, 154–5, 157, 161

Aristippos II, 157

Aristocracy: (Argos) 71, 75, 84, 187–91, (Corinth) 74, 84, (Athens) 103, (Sparta) 103

Aristodemos (Heraklid), 60

Aristogeiton, sculptor, 256

Aristokrates, king of Orchomenos?, 83, 84

Aristomachos I, son of Aristippos, 155–7

Aristomachos II, brother of Aristippos II, 157–60

Aristomachus (Heraklid), 60

Aristotle, 81, 97–9, 188

Armour, 71, 178, 179, 180

Army and military system of Argos, 83, 86, 93, 96, 100, 121, 125, 131, 134, 135, 144, 175–87, 199

Artaxerxes I, king of Persia, 104

Artaxerxes III, king of Persia, 144

Artemis, temples and sanctuaries of: (Argos) 23, 210, (Ephesus) 239, (Mt Artemision) 211, (Orneai), 211

Artemis Orthia, 210–11

Artemis Peitho, 210

Artemis Pheraia, 210

Artemis, Pyronian, 212

Artemision, Mt, 8, 83, 211

Artists at Argos, 221–61 *passim*

Artynai, 195, 198

Asia Minor, 129

Asinaia, 13, 42, 75

Asine, 13, 41, 42–3, 75, 76, 77, 79, 98, 219, 226
  sanctuary of Apollo Pythaieus, 43, 205–206
  Argive citizens at, 42

Asklepios, sanctuaries of: (Argos) 23, 211, 219, 248, (Athens) 211, 248, (Corinth) 211, 248, (Delos) 248, (Epidauros) 211, 238, 245, 248, (Troizen) 238, 248

Aspis (second citadel at Argos), 16, 23, 64, 65, 66, 153, 168, 205, 224

Assyrians, 71

Astros, 47

Athena, priest of, at Tiryns, 41
  sanctuaries of: (Aspis) 23, (Larisa) 24, (Lessa) 42, 207, (Mycenae) 207

Athena Oxyderkous, 23, 207, 249

Athena Polias, 24, 206–7, 252

Athena Saitis, 207–8, 218

Athena of the Trumpet, 206

Athene (town in Thyreatis), 46

Athens, 12, 52, 65, 91, 98, 101, 129, 149, 151, 194, 195
  Acropolis, 205; temples of Athena, 239, Parthenon, 242
  democracy at, 192
  democratic, ally of Argos, 86, 192
  Herakleidai and, 59
  Kleomenes in, 92–3
  oligarchs in, 2
  pottery, 66
  relations with Argos after Peloponnesian war, 126–41
  rivalry with Sparta, 101–2
  fifth-century building programme, 242, 244, 245; temple of Hephaistos, 242

Athenians, 96
  attack Aigina, 99
  authors, 222
  contingent of 600 in Argolid, in 416, 125
  contingent in Peloponnese (Mantinea), 123
  fight Alexander son of Krateros, 155
  fleet, 101, 124, 184
  hoplites, 89
  losses at Mantinea, 124
  military system, 177, 182

Atreus, 59

Atreus, treasury of, at Mycenae, 232

Attalos I, king of Pergamon, 165, 167

Attalos (sculptor), 23

Attika, 91, 113

Aurelius Orestes, L., 172

Ayios Adrianos, 42

Bacchiadai, 61, 74, 75, 84, 85, 188
Bachriami, Mt, 8
Barbarians, 51–5
Baton, 219
Berbati, 13, 34
Biton, 202, 235, 238, 254
Boiotia and Boiotians, 10, 111, 113–14,
    117, 120, 122, 132, 139, 219
Boiotian league, 117, 132–3, 139
Bola, council at Argos, 194–5
Boule at Athens, 194
Bouleuterion (?) at Argos, 22, 195
Bronze Age: in Argolid, 1, 2, 7, 15, 44, 51–
    52, 62, 64, 93; arts in, 223
  Argos town in, 17, 23, 24; in middle
    Bronze Age, 18, 64
  Asine, 42, 206
  Dendra, 41
  Midea, 41
  Mycenae, 31, 207
  Prosymna, 235
  Tiryns, 41
  Late Bronze Age communities, 77
  architectural influence, in building
    models, 231–2; on Argive Heraion,
    235, 241
  continuity, 203
  continuity of cults, 200; anakes, 213;
    at the Heraion, 34, 205; of Hera, 203;
    at Mycenae, 207
  roads, 30
  sculpture, 251
Building models, Heraion, 231–2
  Perachora, 231–2
Burial practices, 55
Byzantine church at Merbakas, 40

Calendar, Argive, 202
Carthage, 172
Cassander, 149–51
Catalogue of ships (*Iliad*), 113
Cavalry at Argos, 71, 181
  Pyrrhus, 153
  Achaean, 159
Cemeteries: Tiryns, (Geometric) 41
  Dendra, (Bronze Age) 41
  Argos, (Classical) 24, (early) 66, 67,
    (near agora) 24, 64, (near Deiras
    ridge) 23, 64, (panoply grave) 71, 77,
    178, (eighth century) 70
Chabrias, 142
Chaironeia, battle of, 145
Chalcedon, 216
Chalcis, 72
'Champions', battle of, 88–9, 120, 184
Charadros, river, now Xerias, 8, 35, 38,
    208
Chares, river, 157
Charmenes, soothsayer, 156
Cheilon, 162

Chigi vase, 179
Christian basilica at Argos, 23
Citizenship, 175
Citizenship at Argos, membership of tribe
    qualification for, 56
Classical scholarship and Argos, 222
'Clytemnestra, tomb of', 32
Colonies, 74
Commission of Twelve, 118–19
Confiscation of property, 194
Corcyra, 216
  triglyph altar, 246
Corinth and Corinthians, 1, 7, 29–30,
    39, 56, 60, 71, 72, 74, 85, 113–14, 117,
    118–19, 122, 127, 129, 150, 151,
    154, 155, 156, 162, 165, 166, 172,
    185–6, 188
  architecture, 232, (triglyph altar) 246
  assembly, voting rights at, 133, 136
  sculpture, 253
  citadel (Acrocorinth), 29, 132, 137, 155,
    156, 160, 161, 166, 167, 171
  Dorians at, 56
  gulf, 29, 31
  Pheidon and, 81, 82, 84
  pro-Spartans at, 128, 130, 131, 136, 139
Corinth, Isthmus of, 7, 51, 59
  sanctuary of Poseidon, 131
Craftsmen, 66, 67–8
Crete and Cretans, 7, 54, 65, 69, 78, 98,
    137, 212–13, 214, 216
  archers, 153
  colonized from Argos, 135
  sculpture, 253
  Cretan Dionysus, 208, 212
Cyclopes, 1
Cyprus, Late Bronze Age refugees in, 55
  contacts with Argos, 72
  fire dogs, 72
  Hellenistic, 151

Daedalic sculpture, 253
Damokles, 168
Danaos, 10, 20, 23, 45
Deiphontes, 219
Deiradotes, *see* Apollo Pythaieus
Deiras gate, 24, 26, 38, 208
Deiras ridge, cemetery near, 23, 224
  stadium near, 24
  sanctuary of Apollo Pythaieus, 205–6
  sanctuary of Dionysus, 212
Delos, 214
Delphi, 112, 145, 146, 206, 235
  Argive sculpture at, 251, 254, 256
Demeter, sanctuaries of: (Argos) 212,
    (Athens) 212, (Lerna) 212, (Mysia)
    34, 212
Demetrius (the besieger, son of Anti-
    gonos), 151
Demetrius of Phaleron, 149

Index

Demiourgoi (damiorgoi): (Argos) 189, 198, (Elis) 195–6, 198, (Mantinea) 195, 198, (Mycenae) 198
Democracy at Argos, 19, 113, 139, 182, 185, 189, 191, 192–221 *passim*
Democracy at Corinth, 128, 130, 131, 134, 137, 138, 192
Demosthenes, 143, 144–5
Dendra, 41
Despoina, sanctuary at Lycosoura, 241
Deukalion, 216
'Diadoumenos' statue, 258
Diaios, 172
Dialect, 254
Diamperes gate, 25, 26, 153
Diodorus, 58, 59, 82, 104, 114, 116, 118, 132, 133, 139, 144, 149
Dionysius of Halikarnassos, 80
Dionysus, 212–13
Dionysus, craftsmen of (actors' guild at Argos), 19, 213
Dioskouroi, 213
Dipaia, 102, 105, 107, 108, 117
'Diskobolos' statue, 258
Doriadai, 57
Dorians, 53, 58–62, 75
  Argive influence over, 135–6
  and Nabis, 170
Dorian settlements: (Argos) 65, 67, 187, (Crete) 65, 69, 135, (Lakonia) 65
Dorian tribes, 54, 86, 182
  basis of military organization at Argos and Sparta, 175, 176, 179
  political significance of, 55, 188, 193
  at Sikyon, 84
Dorian war chant, 125
'Doric Argive' foot, 22, 243
Doric order: at the Heraion, 237, 238, 241, 242, 243
  Athenian, 241, 242, 244
  in Peloponnese, 244
  role of Argos in, 250
'Doryphoros' statue, 257–8
Dryads at Mycenae, 217
Dryopes, 206
Dymanes, 54, 86

Earthquakes: at Sparta, 102–9, 110, 181, 256; at Kleonai in 414, 125
East Greeks, 92, 102, 129, 138
Echemos, king of Tegea, 59
Egypt and Egyptians, 7, 10, 52, 114, 144, 150, 161, 186, 207–8
  architecture, 235
  Persian conquest, 92
  sculpture, 253
Egyptian gods, 218
'Eighty', the, 195–6
Eileithuian gate, 24, 26, 213, 218
Eileithuia sanctuary at Argos, 25, 213–14

Ekklesia (assembly at Athens), 193
Elephants, 25, 153–4
  'Nikon', 154
Elis, 83, 117, 119–20, 121, 123, 145, 195, 199
Enomotia, 176
Enyalios, 209–10
Epaminondas, 145
Ephors, 162
Ephorus, historian, 105, 132, 216
Epic poetry, 55, 58; oral transmission, 61
Epidauros, 8, 40, 84, 121, 142, 148, 149, 205–6, 211, 238, 245, 261
Epirus, 151
Epitelides, the, 20, 217
Erasinos, river, 10, 34, 93, 96, 213, 214, 220
Eretria, 72
Erinyes, 217
Euboia, 116
Eupolemos, architect of new temple of Hera, 242
Eurotas, 74, 78
Eurybates, Argive commander, 197
Eurybotos (Eurybates, Athenian), 79–80
Eurypontids (Spartan royal family), 167
Eurysthenes, 60
Eurystheus, king of Tiryns, 59
Eusebius, 80
Eva, 46

Farms and farming, 43
Federal leagues and federalism, 132, 135
Financial organization: (Argive) 118, (Athenian) 127, (Spartan) 127, 129, (Persian) 129
Fire dogs, 72
Flaminius, 166–9, 171
Fleet: Achaean, 171
  Aiginetan, 93
  Argos, lack of, 184
  Athenian, 93, 101, 114, 124, 193
  Greek, 101
  Persian, 92, 114–15
  Polykrates', 92
  Spartan, 127, (Nabis') 171
Flowery Hera, sanctuary at Argos, 23
Fortifications: Argos, 17, 24, 94, 157; long walls, 124; Argive, overlooking Phleious, 142
  Asine, 43
  Athens (long walls), 124
  near Ayios Adrianos, 42
  Corinth (long walls), 131, 134, 137
  Hellenikon blockhouse, 35
  Hysiai, 37
  Isthmus, 51
  Kleonai, 29
  Midea, 41
  Mycenae, 32
  Nauplia, 45

282

Fortune, temple of, at Argos, 23
'Freedom of Greece', 149, 150, 151, 155, 161, 167

Garrisons: Achaean, in Argos, 166
  Argive, in Corinth, 185
  Macedonian, in Argos, 150; in Corinth, 152, 154, 155, 165
  of Philip V, 166
  Spartan, of Nabis, in Argos, 167, 168, 169
Gauls, 153
Generals: of Argos, 123, 175
  of Athens, 197
  of Macedon, 149, 150
  Roman, 199
  board of five, 178, 197–9
Genesion, 45, 215
Geometric pottery, 57
  Late Geometric (Argos) 70, 71, 72, 73, (Athens) 71, (Corinth) 71
Geraneia, Mt, 137
Gerousia at Sparta, 196
Glympeis, city of Kynouria, 162
Gorge of the Charadros, 10, 38, 198
Grave of Hyrnetho, 219
Grave of Linos, 219
Grave of Pelasgos, 210, 216
Graves, early, 224
Gulf of Argos, 7, 143
Gymnetes, 68
Gymnon, 40
Gytheion, 168, 171

Hades, 34
Hannibal, 164
Harbours in the Argolid, *see* Nauplia; Temenion
Hegisistratos, son of Peisistratos, 92
Hekate, 214
Helen, 214, 260
Helenos, son of Pyrrhus, 154
Helios, 214
Hellanicus, 202–3
Helos, 76, 78, 79
Helots, 74, 90, 94, 98, 106, 170, 179, 181
  rising, 91, 93, 104, 118
Hephaistion, 221
Hera Akraia, sanctuary at Argos, 23, 204
Hera Argeia, 203–4
Hera: cult at Nauplia, 204, 215
  sanctuary at Mycenae, 204
  temple at Tiryns, 41, 204, 252
Heraies, 57
Heraion, 2, 3, 33–4, 65, 94, 95, 152, 203–4, 230–46
  altar, 233, 246
  buildings:
    early temple, 230, 232–4, 236, 238, 239

later temple, 237, 239, 242–5
  courtyard (west) building, 230, 237, 238
  earliest building, 231
  east building, 237
  north-east building, 237, 238
  north stoa, 237, 238
  north-west building, 237
  south portico, 237, 240, 241
  stoas, 230, 237
  fire at, 239, 241
  precinct wall, 236
  road to, from Argos, 25
  sculpture, 257, 259–60
  terrace walls, terraces, 232, 236, 239, 241
    stepped, 240
  terracotta model, 231–2
  wooden columns, 233
  wooden statue from Tiryns in, 252
Heraion of Samos, 234
Herakleidai, 56, 58–63, 66, 93, 95, 118
Herakles, 44, 62, 187, 219, 256
Hermes, 214
Hermione, 8, 205
Herodotus, 1, 58–9, 76, 78, 88, 89, 96, 105, 195, 196, 197
  on Pheidon, 81
  on Kleomenes, 93
  on consequences of Sepeia, 97–8, 182, 190
Heroes, 57, 218–20
Hiaromnamones: of Argos, 201, 209
  of Perseus, at Mycenae, 209, 220
Hippias, son of Peisistratos, 92
History of Argos, recording of, 105
Homer, 1, 10, 58, 61, 113
  blinding of Polyphemus, on Argive vase, 61
Hoplites, 33, 94, 97, 110, 129, 144, 175–86
  Argive, 178–9
  Athenian, 89, 111, 118
  and lochos-pentekostys system, 179
  Spartan, 90, 101
Hoplite armour, 178–80
Horai (seasons), 217
Houses, 27
Hylleis, 54, 86, 182
Hyllos, 59
Hypathodoros, sculptor, 256
Hypermnestra, 20, 209
Hyrnathioi, non-Dorian tribe at Argos, 86, 183, 189, 190, 193, 219
Hyrnetho, 219
Hysiai, battle of, 36, 79–85, 87, 179, 180, 184, 236
Hysiai, town, 37–8, 45, 102, 115
  destroyed by Spartans, 124

Ialysos, 59

Index

Iliad, 113
Inachos, river, 8, 38, 214, 220
  valley, 13, 38, 39, 122
Ionia and Ionians, 55, 57, 183, 213
  rebellion, 95
Ionic order, in East Greece, 244
  altar, 247
Iphikrates, 132, 137
Ipsus, battle of, 151
Irrigation of the Argive plain, 10f.
Isis, 218
Isocrates, 143, 144
Isthmian games, 131, 132, 136, 137
Italy, Greeks of, 152
  Hannibal's invasion of, 164
Ithome, 105, 110–11, 256

Joint-artynoi, 198

Kameiros, 59
Kanathos, sacred spring at Nauplia, 204
'Kanon', *see* 'Doryphoros'
Kassandra, 260
Kastor and Polydeukes, 213, 216
Kato Belesi, 38, 40
Kenchreiai (Argolid), 34–7
Kenchreiai (harbour of Corinth), 157, 160
Kephalarion (springs of the Erasinos), 10
Kephalobryson, 40
Kephisos, river, 220
Keüx, king of Trachis, 59
Kimon, 103, 111, 115, 118
Kings of Argos, 67, 68, 69, 187–8, 196
  Pheidon, 81
  elected religious officials, 69, 197
Kings of Sparta, 68, 76, 87, 92, 152, 167
  as generals, 197
  dual kingship, 61
  restriction of authority, 123
King's Peace, 138
Kiveri, 13, 35, 45
Kleander, prophet, 97
Kleinias, father of Aratos, 156
Kleisthenes, tyrant of Sikyon, 84
Kleobis and Biton, 202, 235, 238
  statues of, 254
Kleomenes I, king of Sparta, 87, 92–5,
  100, 190, 219
Kleomenes III, king of Sparta, 159–62
Kleonai, 14, 29–30, 39, 40, 43, 108, 113,
  124, 125, 133, 136–7, 157, 168, 189,
  196
Kleonymos, 152
Klytaimnestra, 214
Knossos, treaty with Argos, 134–6, 185,
  196, 216
Koile (the Hollow), district of Argos, 26
'Kontoporeia' the, 13
Kos, 216
Krathis, Mt, 212

Kresphontes, 60
'Kriterion' (Judgment place) at Argos, 20,
  217, 218, 220
Kroisos, king of Lydia, 88
Ktenias, Mt, 8
Kybele, 217–18
Kylarabis, gymnasium of, at Argos, 25, 26,
  168
Kylarabis gate, 25, 26, 53, 212
Kyniskos of Mantinea, 257
Kynoskephalai battle, 167
Kynouria, 14, 114–15, 116, 120, 146, 185,
  193, 221
Kyphanta, city of Kynouria, 162
Kypselos, tyrant of Corinth, 82, 84, 89,
  188
Kythera, 14, 76, 88

Lakonia, 14, 43, 46, 54, 65, 80, 112, 142,
  146, 168, 170, 171, 251
Laloukas, 40
Lamia, Lamians and Lamian war, 149
Landowners, 32, 99, 193
  in Roman times, 28
  at Athens, 110
  at Corinth, 113, 131
  at Sparta, 181
'Lapiths' (non-Dorian people of Pelopon-
  nese), 84
Larisa, the (citadel of Argos), 8, 15, 65,
  153, 168
  sanctuary of Athena, 24, 206
  sanctuary of Zeus, 24, 207
Latona (Leto), sanctuary at Argos, 23, 214
Lechaion, 131, 134
Leontion, 40
Lerna, 35, 43, 45, 160, 207, 212
Lessa, 42, 207
  wooden statue at, 252
Leto (Latona), 23, 214
Leukai, city of Kynouria, 162
Leuktra, 139, 140, 142
Levant communities, 52, 253
Libya, 143
Lichas (Argive), 118
Light armed troops, 153
Likymnios, 59
Lindos, 59
Linos, 219
Lion gate (Mycenae), 43, 218
Livy, 164, 166, 168, 169, 197
Lochos (brigade), 176–9, 181, 183, 184,
  185, 197
Lokris, 172
  conference at, 166
Long walls:
  Argos, 124
  Athens, 124
  Corinth, 131, 134, 137
Longopotamos, river, 29

284

Lucian, 25, 210
Lycia, 205
Lydia, 88, 92
Lydiades, tyrant of Megalopolis, 158–9
Lykon, 143
Lykone, Mt, 210
Lykourgos, king of Sparta, 162–3, 164
Lyrkea, 17, 38–40
Lyrkeion, Mt, 8
Lysander, 127–8
Lysippos, 215

Macedon and Macedonians, 1, 92, 144, 147–71 *passim*, 172, 186, 218
Machanidas, regent of Sparta, 164–6
Malea, Cape, 88
Mantinea, 8, 17, 38, 39, 40, 83, 102, 107, 119, 120, 121, 123, 124, 125, 129, 130, 139–40, 142, 144, 157, 195, 199, 208
first battle (418), 39, 123, 126, 129, 176–178, 181, 182, 183, 184, 185, 192, 197, 216
second battle (362), 143, 145
Marathon, Herakleidai at, 59
battle of, 92, 99
Marcus Aurelius, 25
Marriage of Dorian Argive women, after Sepeia, 97–9
Massacres: in Argos, 2, 140, 143, 193
at Corinth, 131
at Elis, 145
Megalopolis, 144, 145, 149, 158, 162
Megalovouni, Mt, 8
Megara and Megarid, 74, 117, 122, 216
Megavouni, Mt, 8
Melantas, 'king' of Argos, 196
Melissa, wife of Periander, 84
Meltas, grandson of Pheidon, 84
Menelaos, brother of Agamemnon, 170
Merbakas (Ayia Trias), 40, 246
Mercenary soldiers, 129, 144, 153, 168, 176, 186
Messenia, 60, 74, 76, 78, 79, 80, 81, 83, 84, 85, 89, 104–6, 108, 110–12, 114, 127, 142, 144, 145, 148, 188, 256
2nd Messenian war, 175, 177, 236
Midea, 41, 51, 75, 77
Miletus and Milesians, 94
Moklai, 57
Mountains, boundaries of Argolid, 8
Movement of populations, 52–6
Mummius, L., 172
Museum, 65, 250
Mycenae, 1, 28, 31–3, 51, 53, 64, 67, 97–8, 100, 113, 122, 152, 157, 209, 212, 224
cult of Athena, 203
destroyed by Argos 468?, 31, 102, 104, 107, 108, 115, 191, 239
in Hellenistic times, 32, 198, 213

Lion gate, 251
Nabis and, 170–1
road to, 24, 25
temple of Athena at, 31, 207
Theatre at, 213
treasury of Atreus, 232, 251
Myloi, 13
Myron, 255, 256, 257, 258
Mysia, 34, 212

Nabis, king of Sparta, 32, 165–71, 186, 202
Naukydes, 214
Naupaktos, 60, 114
Nauplia, 7, 13, 26, 28, 40, 41, 44–5, 75, 77, 93, 152, 204, 215
Naupliadai, 57, 77
Neith, 207–8
Nemea, 122
agriculture, 12
district, 30–1, 43
river, battle at, 129, 130, 131, 137
road to, 24, 121–2
sanctuary of Zeus, 31, 133
temple, 261
Nemean games, 12, 14, 137, 160, 169, at Argos, 24, 161, 165, 215
Nemean gate, 24, 26
Nemean Zeus, sanctuary at Argos, 23, 215
Nemesis, temple at Rhamnous, 242, 243
Neris, 46
Nikandros, king of Sparta, 76
Nikias, Peace of, 128
Non-Dorians at Argos, 68, 86, 176, 183, 189, 190, 193, 219

Odeion, at Argos, 19, 20
Oinoe, 38, 112
sculpture at Delphi commemorating battle of, 256
Oligarchy and Oligarchs, 187–92
at Argos in 387, 140
at Athens, 125, 141
established by Antipater, 149
established at Sikyon and Argos in 418, 124
need for support, 138
put to death at Argos, 139
Spartan support for, 126–8, 139, 141
Olisseidai, 57
Olympia, sanctuary of Zeus, 183, 245
Argive sculpture, 251, 256
and Pheidon, 81–3
Olympic games, 71, 81, 120, 255
as chronological system, 73, 79, 82
Orchomenos (Arcadia), 83, 123, 151, 172
archaic temple, 234
Orchomenos (Boiotia), 10, 132
Orneai, 38–40, 124, 125, 144, 217
Oropos, 219

Index

Ostracism, of Kimon, 11, 115
  of Themistokles, 103, 110
Othryadas (Spartan survivor of battle of
  the Champions), 88–9
Overseas contacts, Argos and East
  Mediterranean, 72, 228
  and Cyprus, 72
Oxyrhynchus historian, 132, 133

Palamedes, 215
Pamphyloi, 54, 86
Pan, 213, 214
Panoply grave, 71, 77, 178
Pantaleon, king of Pisa, 83
Paravounaki, Mt, 37
Parnassus, Mt, 206, 216
Parnon, Mt, 14, 46–7, 79, 80, 161, 162,
  165, 214
Parthenios, Mt, 8
Pasion, 143
Pausanias (author), 76, 221
  cults in Argolid, 200f.
  dedication at Olympia after Tanagra,
    183
  on Argos and Argolid, 15, 18f., 28f.,
    64
  on sculpture at the Heraios, 259
  Heraklids, 60f.
  Hysiai, 79
  Perilaos, 189
  Pheidon, 81, 83
  Telesilla, 94
Pausanias, regent of Sparta, 106
Peace Treaties:
  of Corinth, 145
  after Mantinea, 124
  after Tegea and Dipaia, 112
  (Argos–Sparta 451), 112, 114, 116
  (Athens–Sparta '30 years peace'), 116
  (Athens–Sparta 421), 117
  of 217, 164
Peisistratos, tyrant of Athens, 91, 189
Pelasgos, 212, 216
Pellene and Pellenians, 122
Peloponnese, 2, 7, 53, 55, 56, 58, 59, 60,
  62, 63, 75, 78, 79, 81, 82, 83, 84, 89,
  91, 101, 102, 103, 106, 108, 114, 115,
  124, 139, 142, 144, 145, 147, 148, 150,
  156, 160, 161, 162, 165, 170, 185, 236,
  241
Peloponnesian war, Argos in, 116–25,
  126–7
Pelops, king of Sparta, 164, 169
Pentekostys, 176, 177, 178, 179, 185, 197
Perachora, 165, 231–2
  waterworks, 27
  triglyph altar, 246
Peraia, 137
Periander, son of Kypselos, 84
Perikles, 103

Perilaos (Perillos), tyrant of Argos, 92, 189
Perioikoi, 97–9
  Spartan, 101, 181
Persai (Aeschylus), 103–4
Perseia, fountain at Mycenae, 204
Persephone, 34
Perseus, king of Macedon, 172
Perseus, sanctuary of, at Mycenae, 220
Persia and Persians, 33, 96, 129, 137
  financial support, 138, 144
  invasion of Greece, 87, 92, 95, 97, 99,
    100, 110, 182, 191, 196
  king of, 1, 138, 186
  negotiations with Argos (449), 116
Phalanx, 178, 179
Pharmacas, Mt, 8
Pheidias, sculptor, 257
  statue of Athena in Parthenon, 259
  statue of Zeus at Olympia, 259
Pheidon, king of Argos, 81–4, 86, 89, 180,
  184, 188–90, 196, 253
Pheidon of Corinth, 81
Pheraia, Artemis, 210
Philip II, King of Macedon, 2, 144–6,
  147–9, 246–61
Philip V, king of Macedon, 161–3, 164–8
'Philippos' of Isocrates, 143
Philokles, general of Philip V, 165, 166
Philosophers, lack of, at Argos, 221
Phigaleia, 97
Phleious, 12, 31, 40, 121–2, 124, 125, 129,
  138, 139–40, 142, 158
  Dorians at, 56, 60, 62–3
Phoroneus, 220
Phratry, at Argos, 56–7, 176, 197
Piracy and Pirates, 77, 78, 143, 145
Piraeus, 7, 124, 140
Pisa, 83
Plataia, 33, 105
Plato, 257
Pliny the Elder, 255, 256, 257, 258
Plutarch, *Life of Aratus*, 156, 157, 158
  Life of Pyrrhus, 25, 152–4
  'corrects' Herodotus on consequences
    of Sepeia, 98
Polemarchoi, at Mantinea, 195
Polichnai, city of Kynouria, 162
Political organization of Argos, 187–91
Polybius, 146, 167, 169
'Polykleitan' pose, 258
Polykleitos, 3, 216, 256–9
Polykleitos the younger, 214, 261
Polykrates, tyrant of Samos, 92
[Poly]medes, sculptor, 254
Polyperchon, 149–50
Polyphemos, blinding of, on Argive vase,
  61, 230
Pontinus, Mt, 207
Population of Argos and Argolid, 18, 64,
  91

Poseidon, contest with Hera, 204, 220
Poseidon, sanctuaries of: (Argos) 215, (Genesion) 45, 215, (isthmus) 131, (Nauplia) 45, 215, (Temenion), 44, 215
Poseidon, temple of, at Isthmia, 245
at Sounion, 242
Potniai, 217
Potters and pottery:
Argos, at end of Bronze Age, 55, 66, 223
Protogeometric, 65, 224
Geometric, 61, 224, 225, 226–9
late Geometric, 70, 71, 72, 73
post-Geometric, 91; Polyphemus vase, 230
decline of, 86
figure decoration, 229
Asine, 226
Athens, 66, 224
late Geometric, 71, 229
post-Geometric, 91
influence on Argolid, 227
Corinth, late Geometric, 71, 228, 229
Protocorinthian, 71
Mycenae, 224
Tiryns, 224
'Praetors' at Argos, 166, 197
Prasiai, city of Kynouria, 162
Praxiteles, 214
President of council at Argos, 194
Priene, 206
Priestesses of Hera, 202–3
Prokles, the Heraklid, 60
Prokles, tyrant of Epidauros, 84
Pro-Spartans at Argos, 39, 107, 122, 124–125, 141, 216
Prosymna, 13, 34, 235
Protogeometric town at Argos, 205
Proxenoi, 198
Prytaneion at Argos, 195
Prytaneis at Athens, 195
Ptolemy I, son of Lagos, 150
Ptolemy II, 151
Ptolemies (dynasty), 186, 218
Pylos, 62
Pyramid (Hellenikon), 35–6
Pyrrhus, king of Epirus, 25, 26, 27, 94, 151–4, 209, 212, 218, 261
Pythagoras, Spartan commander in Argos, 168, 169
Pythokles of Elis, 257

Ransom, 94
Religious observances, 69, 93, 94, 96, 124, 137
Sparta and Olympic truce, 121
sacred procession, at the Heraion, 238
sacred meals, in West building of the Heraion, 238
Rhegnidas, grandson of Temenos, 60

Rhodes and Rhodians, 54, 59, 151, 196
sculpture, 253
Rivers, 8
Roads, Late Bronze Age, 30, 33
Rome and Romans:
Argolid in Roman times, 28
Argos in Roman times, 2, 15
Asine, 42
Kenchreiai, 36
Nauplia, 45
Pyrrhus' wars against, 153
relations with Greeks, 164–72 *passim*
reliefs and inscriptions in church at Merbakas, 40
Roman baths at Argos, 18, 21, 28, 250, 261
Roman confederacy, 164
Roman Empire, barbarian attacks, 51–2
Roman sculpture, 250

St Constantine, church of, at Argos, 25
St George (modern Nemea), 40
Sais (Egypt), 207–8
Salamis, battle of, 103
Santorini, eruption of volcano, 204
Saminthos, 122
Samos, 92
Sarantapsycho, 47
Sarapis, 218
Sardis, 88
Saronic gulf, 29
Schinochori, 39
Sculpture, 3, 250–61
archaic, 87
Secretary of council at Argos, 194
Select brigade (lochos), 176, 181–6, 197, 216
Sellasia, battle of, 161, 162
Semnai, 217
Sepeia, battle of, 33, 87, 93–100, 102, 108, 117, 180, 181, 182, 184, 189, 190, 206, 209, 210, 219
Shrines of Athena and Aphrodite, at Troy (on Heraion sculpture), 260
Sicily, Greeks of, 152
Argives in, 185
Sigeion, 92
Sikyon, 22, 84, 122, 131, 134, 144, 148, 150, 151, 156, 188, 236, 256
non-Dorians at, 189
Skopas, 214
Skytalismos, 140, 143, 193
Slaves, 18, 97–9, 169; *see also* Gymnetes
armed by Telesilla, 94, 180
kill Aristomachos, 156
Smireidai, 57
Social organization: at Argos, 56, 67, 222
aristocratic, 71
Dorian, 67
Social revolution, at Sparta, 159, 169
Nabis, at Argos, 169

Index

Sokrates of Argos, 221
'Southern' gate ?, 26
Sparta and Spartans, 1, 26, 46, 54, 60, 74,
    84, 86, 87–96, 101–46 *passim*, 148,
    152, 159, 161, 162, 164–71, 175–86,
    196, 236, 239
    allies, 123, 127–30
    army, 68, 88–90, 92, 93, 101, 110, 112,
        127, 159, 162, 175–86 *passim*
    regiment destroyed by Iphikrates,
        132, 137
    royal bodyguard of 300 hippeis, 88,
        160
    austerity, 90
    cult of Dioskouroi, 213
    fleet, 127
    garrisons at Sikyon, 131, 134
    kings, 68, 76, 87, 92, 152, 167
        as generals, 197
        dual kingship, 61
        restriction of authority, 123
    magistrates (ephors), 162
    manpower resources, 177
    military organization compared to
        Argive, 175–82
    proxenos at Argos, 198
    relations with Argos, 2, 33, 36, 39, 45,
        46, 58, 75–8, 79–81, 83, 85–9, 91, 93–
        96, 101–46, 166–71
    relations with Athens, 101–9, 110–15,
        116–20, 125
    sanctuary of Artemis Orthia, 210
    sculpture, 253
    social system, 184
    women, 94
Sphyredai, 57
Stadium at Argos, 24
Statues of:
    Aphrodite Nikephoros at Argos, 208
    Aristippos' dynasty at Argos, 161
    Athena on the Larisa, 207
    cult statue of Hera from Tiryns, 204
    Hekate by Skopas, Polykleitos the
        younger, Naukydes, 214
    Hermes at Argos, 214
    Hygieia at Argos, 211
    Kleobis and Biton at Delphi, 234, 254
    Leto at Argos, 214
    Nemean Zeus at Argos by Lysippos,
        215
    Philip II, 145
    Zeus on the Larisa, 207
    Zeus Meilichios at Argos by Polykleitos,
        216
Statues by Ageladas:
    Anochos of Tarentum, 255
    Timasitheos, 255
    Zeus Ithomatas, 256
Statues by Polykleitos:
    Diadoumenos, 258

Doryphoros, 257–8
Hera, at the Heraion (gold and ivory),
    257, 259
Kyniskos of Mantinea (? Westmacott
    athlete), 257
Pythokles of Elis, 257
Xenokles the Mainalian, 257
Statues, Roman copies, 222, 231
'Stepped theatral areas', 241
Stoa in agora (Argos), 21
Stoa Poikile (Athens), 112
Strabo, 15, 44, 77
Street-plan of Argos, 27
Stymphalos, 215
Sulpicius, 165
Survivor communities (at end of Bronze
    Age), 64, 65, 66
    at Mycenae, 64, 67
    at Tiryns, 64, 67
Syracuse, Argives at (in 413), 125, 185
    triglyph altar, 246

Tanagra, battle of, 105, 111, 113–14, 176,
    181, 182, 183, 184
    town, 216
Tanaos, river, 45, 46
Taÿgetos, Mt, 74
Tegea, 8, 34, 46, 59, 80, 83, 90, 102, 119,
    121, 123, 129, 145, 161, 162, 184
    battle of, 102, 105, 107, 117
Taras, 213
Teisamenos of Elis, seer, 105
Telesilla, Argive poetess, 94, 206, 209,
    210, 221–2
Temenidai, 62, 82
Temenion, 26, 44, 60, 62, 215, 220
Temenos, 44, 60, 62, 188, 219, 220
    dynasty of, 44, 67, 81, 84, 95, 187, 189
Temenos, 'The Lot of Temenos', 67, 82,
    83, 146
Tenea, 29
Teos, 213
Terracotta tiles, 232, 236, 250
Theatres: (Argos) 18, 65, 208, 209,
    (Athens) 19, (Epidauros) 19,
    (Mycenae) 32
Thebes and Thebans, 52, 126, 128, 129,
    132, 139, 140, 142, 143, 145, 148
Themistokles, 102–4, 110, 111
Theoroi at Mantinea, 195
Thermopylai, 33, 88
Thesmophylakes, at Elis, 196
'Third power group', 117
Tholos (circular building): (Argos) 207,
    249, (Delphi) 207, 249; Epidauros,
    249
Thrace, 92
Thrasylos, Argive general, 198, 199
Thucydides, 1, 39, 46, 58, 102, 105, 112,
    114, 116, 117, 122, 126, 176, 181, 182,

288

185, 195, 198, 205, 206, 216, 239
'Thyestes, tomb of', 34
Thyreatis and Thyrea, 14, 45–7, 76, 79,
    80, 81, 88–91, 93, 102, 108, 115, 116,
    120, 125, 146, 185, 189, 193, 221
Timasitheos, 255
Timokrates of Rhodes, Persian agent, 129
Timokrates, commander of Nabis' garri-
    son in Argos, 167–9
Timomachos, 180
Tiryns, 1, 28, 41–2, 51, 53, 64, 67, 75, 77,
    93, 97–8, 100, 102, 104, 115, 191, 224,
    239
Tisamenos, king of Mycenae, 60
Tlepolemos (Heraklid, at Argos), 59
Topography, 7f.
Town-excavations at Argos, 17, 20, 25, 65,
    66
Trade:
    Bronze Age, 1, 53
    Classical, 72, 74
    modern, 1
Tretos pass, 29, 30, 31
Treasurer (tamias) at Argos, 196, 198
Tribes:
    at Argos, 175–6, 188–9, 193, 196
    at Sikyon, 84
    Dorian, 54, 86, 182
    German, 54
    reorganized, at Corinth, 85
Tribal regiments at Athens, 182, 185
Triglyph altars, 246
Trikorythos, 59
Tripolis, 18, 35
Triremes, 125, 184
Troizen, 8, 148
    non-Dorians at, 189
Trojan war, 58, 62, 230
    on Heraion sculpture, 259–60
Truce, negotiated with Agis by pro-
    Spartan individuals, 122
Tsiristra, 40
Turbe, 213
Turkey, Greek settlers on west coast of, 55
Tyche (Fortune), 23, 215
Tylissos, treaty with Argos, 134–6, 185,
    196, 216
Tyrannies, 85

Tyrants: at Argos (Pheidon), 81, 180, 188
    at Megalopolis, 158
    at Sikyon, 156
    Kleisthenes, 84
    Kypselos, 82, 84, 188
    Peisistratos, 91, 189
    Peisistratid (Hippias), 92
    Perilaos (Perillos), at Argos, 92, 189
    Polykrates of Samos, 92
    Spartan antipathy to tyrants, 92
Tyrants, Hellenistic, at Argos, 176
    Aristippos I, 152–5, 157
    Aristomachos, 155–7
    Aristippos II, 157
    Aristomachos II, 157–60
Tyros, 146
Tyrtaios, 176, 177, 178

Union of Corinth and Argos, 130–9

Warrior caste, 65, 67
Warships, fire dogs in form of, 72
Waterworks and water supplies: (Argive
    Heraion) 11, 28, (Argos) 10, 27, 65,
    153, (Corinthia) 28, (Perachora) 27
Westmacott athlete, 257, 258

Xabrio, river, 35
Xenokles, the Mainalian, 257
Xenophon, 125, 185
    on union of Argos and Corinth, 130–
    133, 136
Xerias, river, formerly Charadros, 8, 35
Xerias, river at plain of Kiveri, 35, 36
Xiropigadi, 45

Zarax (Hieraka), 146, 162, 171
Zeus, 215
    birth of, on Heraion sculpture, 259
    sanctuary on the Larisa, 24, 207, 216,
    252
    sanctuary at Olympia, 183, 245
    statue, by Pheidias, 259
Zeus Ithomatas, statue by Ageladas, 256
Zeus Machaneus, 216
Zeus Phyxios, 216
Zeus the saviour, sanctuary at Argos, 23,
    216